Inclusive Schooling
National and International Perspectives

◆ ✺ ◆

The RUTGERS INVITATIONAL SYMPOSIUM
ON EDUCATION Series

O'Donnell/King, Eds. • *Cognitive Perspectives on Peer Learning*

Vitello/Mithaug, Eds. • *Inclusive Schooling: National and International Perspectives*

Inclusive Schooling
National and International
Perspectives

Edited by

Stanley J. Vitello
Rutgers University

Dennis E. Mithaug
Teachers College, Columbia University

LEA LAWRENCE ERLBAUM ASSOCIATES, PUBLISHERS
1998   Mahwah, New Jersey   London

Copyright © 1998 by Lawrence Erlbaum Associates, Inc.
All rights reserved. No part of this book may be reproduced in
any form, by photostat, microfilm, retrieval system, or any other
means, without prior written permission of the publisher.

Lawrence Erlbaum Associates, Inc., Publishers
10 Industrial Avenue
Mahwah, NJ 07430

Cover design by Kathryn Houghtaling Lacey

Library of Congress Cataloging-in-Publication Data

Inclusive schooling : national and international perspectives /
edited by Stanley J. Vitello, Dennis E. Mithaug.
        p. cm.
Includes bibliographical references and indexes.
ISBN 0–8058–3039-1 (cloth: : alk. paper)
    1. Inclusive education--United States.   2. Hansicapped stu-
dents--Education--United States.   3. Inclusive education--
Cross-cultural   studies.   4.   Handicapped
students--Education--Cross-cultural studies. I. Vitello, Stanley J.
II. Mithaug, Dennis E.
    LC1201.I54   1998
    371.9'046--dc21   98–20206
                                             CIP

Books published by Lawrence Erlbaum Associates are printed on
acid-free paper, and their bindings are chosen for strength and dura-
bility.

The final camera copy for this work was prepared by the author, and
therefore the publisher takes no responsibility for consistency or
correctness of typographical style.

Printed in the United States of America
10 9 8 7 6 5 4 3 2 1

Contents

Acknowledgments

We acknowledge the excellent writings of the contributors to this text. Throughout the project they completed their work in a timely and professional manner. Special thanks to Dr. Louise Cherry Wilkinson, Dean of the Rutgers University Graduate School of Education, for her steadfast support in the preparation of this book.

We are grateful to Naomi Silverman, senior editor at Lawrence Erlbaum Associates, who gave us the opportunity to publish the papers delivered at the 11th annual Rutgers Invitational Symposium on Education. Sara Scudder, our production editior, did a wonderful job in making the material literally correct.

We also express our appreciation to Kathleen Gryzeski for the superb job she did in typing the book.

The text is a joint effort with an equal contribution by both editors.

—*Stanley J. Vitello, PhD, JD*
—*Dennis E. Mithaug, PhD*

Series Foreword

Louise Cherry Wilkinson
Dean and Professor of Education Psychology
Rutgers Graduate School of Education
June 22, 1998

The profession of education was shaken nearly two decades ago when national attention focused critically on education and on educators. Both critics and friends have raised some basic questions about our profession, including whether educational professionals have met the challenges that the students and the schools present, and even more fundamentally, if they are *able* to meet those challenges in the future. Beginning with the highly publicized *A Nation at Risk*, seemingly endless and often contradictory criticisms, analyses, and recommendations have appeared from virtually every segment of contemporary American society.

In this explosion of concern and ideas for education reform, we saw a need for a general and national forum, in which the problems of education could be examined in light of research from a range of relevant disciplines. Too often, in the academy, analyses of complex issues and problems occur solely within a single discipline. Aspects of a problem that are unfamiliar to members of the discipline are ignored largely, and the resulting analysis is limited in scope and unsatisfactory. Furthermore, when educational issues are investigated only by members of one discipline, there is seldom an attempt to examine related issues from other fields, or to apply methods developed in other fields that might enhance understanding.

The national debate on educational reform has suffered from this myopia, with problems and issues identified, and analyses and solutions proposed, only within the narrow confines of a single disciplinary boundary. In the past, national discussions have been ill informed or uniformed by current research, in part, because there are two few mechanisms for interdisciplinary analyses of significant issues.

The series of symposia, the *Rutgers Invitational Symposia Education,* addresses this gap. Each symposium focuses on timely issues and problems in education by taking a critical and interdisciplinary perspective. The symposia papers are published in separate volumes, with eleven thus far. Each volume focuses on a particular problem, such as the critical contributions of early childhood education to learning, how to assess literacy skills, the structure of effective schools, the role of cognitive psychology on how to teach mathematics, and optimizing peer tutoring in schools. The series presents a cumulative corpus of high quality educational research on topics of interest to practitioners and policy makers. Each volume provides an interdisciplinary forum though which scholars disseminate their original research and extend their work to potential applications for practice, including guides for teaching, learning, assessment, intervention, and policy formulation. These contributions increase the potential for significant analysis and positive impact on the problems impact on the problems that challenge educators.

This volume is based on original papers presented by the authors at a conference in fall 1997, in New Brunswick, New Jersey, at the Rutgers Graduate School of Education. The topic could not be more timely. At the national level, the implementation of legislation supporting inclusion and the rights of all children to benefit from comprehensive schooling is paramount. This collection of original research papers places the U.S. perspective on schooling of disabled children within an international framework. It is work great pleasure that we contribute this volume to the series, *The Rutgers Invitational Symposia on Education*.

Preface

The purpose of inclusion policy is to prevent the marginalization of people who experience unfavorable circumstances in life. It is an approach to the education of students with disabilities that is based on what all members of a free society deserve in order to become fully participating members—a fair chance to find a place in their own communities. This book is a kind of status report on what inclusive education has achieved and what it may achieve in the future for children and youth with disabilities. It describes the philosophical, legal, and practical terrain covered by inclusion policy in general and inclusive schooling in particular. The book provides new information on how various inclusion policies have been implemented in different schools and school districts, and in different countries.

Chapters 1 and 2 describe the philosophical and legal bases for inclusion policy in the United States, how and why this foundation has shifted in recent years. In chapter 1, Mithaug argues that the present inclusion proposal to reform general education is derived from the four great equal opportunity experiments conducted in the 1960s and 1970s—school desegregation, affirmative action, welfare, and special education. Consequently, it is justified via similar reasoning that disabled students deserve the same chance to engage mainstream opportunities as their nondisabled peers. This reasoning leads Mithaug to conclude that the effectiveness and significance of this newest version of inclusion depends on the extent to which the policy equalizes access to the means all persons need to succeed in adult life, the extent to which this equalized access also equalizes engagements in self-determined pursuits in adult life, and the extent to which these self-determined pursuits equalize respect for community participation after school.

Chapter 2, Vitello analyzes recent court decisions about inclusionary practices in general education. In the early 1990s, the plaintiffs challenging special education placements recommended by local schools were parents of elementary school-age students with severe disabilities who wanted their children to receive the social benefits available only in general education. Vitello points out that more recent cases have involved students with disabilities who are older and who are disruptive, and that in these cases the courts have sided with the school district in recommending more restrictive placements (e.g., special classes). Vitello suggests that this shift toward more restrictive placements has perhaps promoted another trend toward class action lawsuits against state departments of education for failing to develop personnel development programs that prepare general education teachers to work with students with disabilities in general education settings.

Chapters 3 through 7 describe the conditions and circumstances affecting the implementation of inclusionary policies and practices in various schools and districts throughout the country. In chapter 3, Ferguson describes how collaboration among action researchers at the university level, professional development agents at the state level, and school administrators and teachers at the local level have improved inclusionary practice at three rural school districts in Oregon. The three strategies implemented by these groups included the development of a comprehensive information system for school improvement, the improvement of access to professional development programs, and the provision of support services for inclusionary practice delivered by individual and collective action researchers. In chapter 4, McLaughlin, Henderson, and Rhim report results of their interviews with principals, district-level administrators, program coordinators, teachers, and parents from five urban school districts involved in school reform. They found that the effort among special educators to create more inclusive classrooms was usually separated from the school reform agenda; and that special educators tended to concentrate their efforts on the placement of students in inclusive settings rather than on altering the nature of the general education curriculum. The authors questioned the relationship between proclamations for full participation of students with disabilities in school reforms and the educational goals and expectations that are important for students with disabilities to achieve before they leave school and are on their own. In chapter 5, Snell reports findings from several studies on teachers' understanding of implementing change, changes in teachers' roles and responsibilities, teachers' means of accommodating differences, teachers' use of peer interactions to promote inclusion, and child-focused problem solving between teachers. She concludes that inclusion requiring extensive support is possible under rather ordinary circumstances, that it can be beneficial to students with and without disabilities, and that it can be viewed favorably by teachers and parents. However, in order for these successes to be obtained, there will have to be changes in teachers' roles and skills, teachers will have to use novel combinations of instructional strategies, staff scheduling will have to be more flexible, and teachers will have to be willing to engage in collaborative teaming.

Chapter 6 by Lipsky and Gartner provides a sweeping view of changes in the inclusion movement past to present and lists the second-generation issues that reflect new concerns about implementing reform. Their analysis of 1,000 school districts involved in inclusive education identifies seven factors associated with successful reform: visionary leadership, collaboration, refocused use of assessment, support for staff and students, funding, effective parental involvement, and use of effective program models and classroom practices. The authors also describe a trend toward early childhood inclusive programs and the policies supporting this movement. They conclude with a discussion of the challenges and future opportunities for inclusive schooling. In chapter 7, Soodak addresses five questions related to the involvement of parents in special education reform, "What do parents value in the education of their children with disabilities?" "How and why do parents differ in their support of, and advocacy for, inclusive education?" "How do parents' perspectives on inclusion change over time?" "What are parents' perspectives on the outcomes of inclusive education?" and "How can parental involvement in inclusive education be fostered so as to benefit students and their families?" Soodak reports the results of two research projects involving 22 parents who were knowledgeable about inclusion and actively involved in promoting it for their children. She found that all parents wanted their children to be accepted by others, to have friends, and to have an opportunity learn. Also, most parents believed these goals were best achieved in general education settings. Soodak concludes by identifying various empowerment strategies necessary to foster the types of parental involvement in inclusive education that would benefit students and their families.

Chapters 8 through 10 describe the status of inclusive schooling in Canada, western Europe, and Scandinavia. In chapter 8, Winzer describes the Canadian system of special education as being influenced by events, philosophies, and pedagogy in the United States. Consequently, attitudes toward special education and students with disabilities are similar to those in the United States. She claims that what makes the Canadian system unique is that general education is so decentralized geographically and politically by province and territory that there is no common set of school laws, acts, policies, regulations, procedures, or legislation that defines special education practice. This is why adoption of the ideology of inclusion has been so inconsistent among general educators. Winzer concludes that although the majority of Canadian teachers embrace the ideal of integration, they question whether they should be held responsible for adopting inclusive practices given their present levels of training and support.

Chapter 9, by Hegarty, describes three recent achievements in the education of students with disabilities in Europe. The first is the degree to which inclusive education has been accepted. Although this was due in part to the Scandinavian concern for normalizing life experiences for people with disabilities and the Italian move to eliminate psychiatric institutions and special schools, other reasons also can be identified. As a result, there is a general acceptance of the notion that students with disabilities should be educated alongside their peers in regular schools whenever possible and appropriate. A second achievement is the emergence of schools with curriculum and pedagogical reforms that serve the educational needs of each student regardless of their learning difficulties. The third achievement is that this trend toward inclusive schooling has occurred in the absence of entitlement legislation guaranteeing equal education access for all students with disabilities. The legislation that has been enacted is permissive rather than prescriptive.

The status of inclusive schooling in the Scandinavian countries is perhaps the most advanced of the western countries, more so even than in the United States where competing political ideologies tend to constrain the full implementation of inclusion reforms. Chapter 10, by Vormeland accounts for this difference by describing how the evolution of values for education in Norway over the past century have paralleled the development of a shared belief "in reverence for life, taking care of the weak, and social and education equality of worth and rights of all persons." Vormeland's historic account of special education legislation during the last 25 years that reflects the current school-for-all policy was made possible by the 1976 repeal of a 1951 special school law that justified separate schools for children with disabilities. He identifies the social, education, and political factors that were necessary for this change. They included the use of regional resource centers (previously the locus for segregated schooling) as promoters of inclusion, the development of extended support systems as agents for inclusion, and the identification of single schools and classrooms as arenas for inclusion. Vormeland also argues the common cultural experiences of Sweden and Denmark predisposed these countries toward values, ideologies, and policies that are consistent with including all children in a common educational experience.

1

The Alternative to Ideological Inclusion

Dennis E. Mithaug
Columbia University

In 1954 when the Warren Court ruled in *Brown v. Board of Education* that a separate education was an unequal education, Americans were introduced to the moral principle that no person should be left out of the mainstream of society's opportunities because of race, poverty level, or disability. In the decades following *Brown*, four innovative social experiments were constructed to reflect the inclusion ideal. They included a busing experiment to desegregate the public schools, an affirmative action experiment to eliminate discrimination in employment, a welfare rights experiment to reduce the harm caused by poverty, and a special education experiment to include disabled children in the mainstream of public schooling.

The events leading to the busing experiment were set in motion in 1964 when Congress enacted Section 402 of the Civil Rights Act that authorized the commissioner of education to conduct a national survey to determine the condition of inequality in U.S. schools. James Coleman directed that survey of 4,000 elementary and secondary schools and found that African-American and Puerto Rican students enrolled in segregated schools performed lower on standardized achievement tests than White and Asian students in nonsegregated schools. He concluded that school integration across socioeconomic lines would increase the achievement of African-American students (Coleman, 1990). This was the basis for the nation's first experiment with inclusion policy: mandatory busing to desegregate the public schools.

During the same period, a second experiment was conducted to reduce the social unrest that began in 1965 when nearly 100,000 African-Americans participated in riots in the Watts section of southern Los Angeles. The riots lasted 6 days and resulted in 34 deaths, more than 1,000 injuries, and 4,000 arrests. The riots that followed Watts motivated business leaders to advocate racial hiring to defuse social unrest (cited in Skrentny, 1996). Alfonso J. Cervantes argued in the *Harvard Business Review* that "If the businessman does not accept his role as leader in the push for the goals of the 'Great Society' . . . we will be increasingly smothered by a growing welfare state ridden with riots

1

and arson and spreading slums largely unchecked by the proliferating programs for the unemployed poor" (Skrentny, 1996, p. 89). Wharton School professor Herbert Northrup agreed, claiming that "The more educated, the more experienced, and more integrated the Negro labor force becomes, the less tension and the fewer problems we'll have in this country. . . . Industry in this country cannot survive with an unintegrated, angry minority" (cited in Skrentny, 1996, p. 90). And President Lyndon Johnson added to this growing belief that including "left-out" people in employment would eliminate social unrest. "You can put these people to work . . . you won't have a revolution because they've been left out. If they're working, they won't be throwing bombs in your homes and plants. Keep them busy and they won't have time to burn your cars" (cited in Skrentny, 1996, p. 91). An affirmative action policy emerged from the ashes of Watts to constitute the nation's second experiment with inclusion.

The third experiment began in the late 1960s and early 1970s when the federal government expanded its commitment to support the poor by easing eligibility requirements for Aid to Families with Dependent Children (AFDC), by giving food stamps to the poor, providing a guaranteed minimum income for the elderly and disabled through Supplemental Social Security, and establishing a national health insurance program for welfare recipients and the elderly under the Medicaid and Medicare programs (Katz, 1989). Advocates for the poor sustained these entitlements in the courts, which resulted in increased benefits to hundreds of thousands of poor women and their children (Katz, 1989). This was the nation's third experiment with inclusion.

The fourth experiment began on the heels of *PARC v. The Commonwealth of Pennsylvania* (1971) and *Mills v. Board of Education* (1972), which established the legal claim that no child should be denied a public education due to mental, behavioral, physical, or emotional disabilities (Scheerenberger, 1983). In 1975, Congress followed this precedent and that established by various state laws mandating public education for disabled children by enacting Public Law 94–142, which guaranteed a free and appropriate public education (FAPE) in the least restrictive environment (LRE) for all children with disabilities. This last of the four great inclusion experiments welcomed the most vulnerable of the country's children into the mainstream of U.S. education opportunity.

The new beliefs supporting these experiments provided a moral and theoretical foundation for arguing that the country's educational, occupational, and social security benefits should be available to all Americans regardless of their circumstances. This altered perhaps forever our concept of what it means to be a person in a democratic society based on the ideals of freedom and equality. No longer was it acceptable for the majority to allow members of a minority to be excluded due to circumstances of race, poverty, or disability. The emerging consensus among policymakers was that any institutional practice that marginalized or excluded individuals or groups on these grounds was wrong and was to be prohibited. The significance of this claim was its justification by the inclusion ideal, which was now on a par with the ideal of equal freedom in the formulation of social policy. After all, what does it mean to promise the right to self-determination for all when some are systematically excluded from experiencing that right?

THE RESULTS

Unfortunately, these experiments did not turn out as hoped. By the 1970s, Coleman's follow-up study on the school desegregation policy revealed negative effects on the White population. He concluded that "In the large cities (among the largest 22 central-city school districts) there is a sizable loss of whites when desegregation takes place." And that, "In addition to the effects of desegregation on white loss, both the absolute proportion of blacks in the central city and their proportion relative to those in the surrounding metropolitan areas have strong effects on loss of whites from the central-city district" (Coleman, 1990, p. 193). Even more problematic for Coleman was his finding that desegregation had marginal effects on the achievement of Black students. "In general, these results can be summarized by saying that achievement benefits of school desegregation for blacks are sometimes found, sometimes not, and where they are found, are generally small, much smaller than would have been predicted from the Coleman report." Finally, Coleman (1990) concluded that "the psychological effects (such as effect on self-esteem) and the attitudinal effects (such as interracial attitudes) of school desegregation are not uniformly in a positive direction, and are sometimes negative" (pp. 200–201).

The special education experiment also produced mixed results. In 1983, Glass evaluated the performance gains of students with disabilities enrolled in regular and special classes and found no significant differences, which suggested that the specialized instruction students received had not produced measurable benefits. Also during that year, a colleague and I conducted a statewide follow-up study of special education students who graduated from Colorado schools and found they were under-employed, underpaid, and overly dependent on parents and family (Mithaug & Horiuchi, 1983). A follow-up interview with their parents indicated that these students were unable and perhaps unwilling to pursue their own ends in life. Most of them lived at home awaiting direction from others about what to expect and what to do (Mithaug, Horiuchi, & McNulty, 1987). Other statewide follow-up studies reported similar findings (Hasazi, Gordon, & Roe, 1985; Wehman, Kregel & Seyfarth, 1985).

By the 1990s, the collateral effects of the special education system were also revealed. A 1993 cover issue of *U.S. News & World Report* was entitled "Separate and Unequal: How Special Education Programs Are Cheating Our Children and Costing Taxpayers Billions Each Year." A year later *The New York Times* ran an article entitled "Special Education Absorbs School Resources," (Dillon, 1994b) which reported that "It costs $6,394 to educate a student in a conventional classroom in New York City, while each special education student costs $19,208." The article noted that the special education system had "grown unchecked for 20 years, starting from an enrollment of 20,000 students in 1974 [one year prior to the passage of PL 94-142] to today's 130, 037, about 13 percent of the city's one million schoolchildren. With its $1.67 billion budget, special education has become a Cadillac in a school system of broken-down Fords" (Dillon, 1994a p.A1, B5). And a subsequent article concluded that the New York City "Board of Education has allowed special education and bilingual programs to develop bloated payrolls, draining money from students in regular classrooms" (Dillon, 1994, p. A1).

The welfare experiment was also evaluated in the 1980s by Murray (1994), who reported on the relation between welfare policy and poverty, unemployment, wages, education, crime, and family well–being. In *Losing Ground: American Social Policy 1950–1980*, Murray concluded that welfare policy had little if any effect on reducing much less eliminating poverty. In fact, declines in poverty were greater between World War II and the 1960s than they were during the 1970s when the policy was in effect. Murray argued that the policy had deleterious effects on the poor: It contributed to the decline in two-parent families among Blacks, increased crime rates among Black males, and increased illegitimate Black births to unmarried women. Mead (1986) drew a similar conclusion in *Beyond Entitlement: The Social Obligations of Citizenship*.

> Starting in the late 1960s, black single mothers and their children went on AFDC in large numbers, making welfare the economic mainstay of ghetto communities around the nation. Black reliance on government thus increased dramatically. In 1969 black families living in poverty still drew 63 percent of their income from their own earnings and 37 percent from other sources, mainly government income programs. By 1976 the proportions had more than reversed, with 65 percent of poor blacks' income now coming from outside sources and only 35 percent from earnings. The proportion of their income coming from welfare doubled from 22 to 44 percent. Black use of other income programs also increased. By 1973 nearly three-fifths of all black families received unearned income from some source, usually from government, and a quarter of them were on welfare. (p. 40)

Affirmative action policy, the last of the four inclusion experiments to be challenged, was promoted by the federal government and adhered to on a voluntary basis in education and industry throughout the 1970s and 1980s. Although some claimed it was successful and should end, that it failed and should end, or that it was partially successful and should continue, many believed it was discriminatory and hence, unfair (Bergmann, 1996). In 1978, Allan Bakke won this argument before the Supreme Court in a claim that the University of California Medical School had unfairly denied him admission in favor of less qualified Black applicants. This judgment was reaffirmed in 1995 when a federal appeals court disallowed a University of Maryland Blacks-only scholarship, when the Supreme Court curtailed a minority set-aside program that had been awarded road-building jobs to minority-owned business on the basis of racial inequality, and then in 1996 when a federal appeals court ruled in *Hopwood v. Texas* that race could not be used as a factor in college admissions (*Newsweek*, 1996). Later that year, California voters approved Proposition 209, which prohibited the state from discriminating against or granting preferential treatment to any person or group in public employment, education, or contracting. In 1997, the U.S. Court of Appeal for the Ninth Circuit in San Francisco upheld Proposition 209 and the Supreme Court refused an emergency request to block California from enforcing it (Greenhouse, 1997).

THE AFTERMATH

By now it should be apparent that the inclusive society as conceived by the policymakers of the 1960s and 1970s is not going to happen. There have been too many policy failures and unexpected negative consequences in the last decade. Consider this sampling. School desegregation policy failed to desegregate the nation's schools and to improve school achievement of Black students, but it did produce White flight from the inner city to the suburbs. Special education failed to improve learning or employment outcomes for students with disabilities but it did produce a separate system of public education that competed successfully with regular education for school dollars. Welfare assistance to poor single mothers failed to eliminate poverty, but it did increase the number of single mothers depending on welfare for long-term support. Affirmative action failed to equalize wages among White and Black men and women, but it did produce a White backlash to eliminate race-based preferences in employment and in higher education admissions.

What happened during these great experiments is that the value of inclusion came into conflict with other values Americans held just as dearly—freedom and equality. When Blacks were forcibly integrated in predominately White schools, for example, many White families acted on their freedom of association and moved to the suburbs. When special education policy provided a new system of services for students with disabilities, it provided separate and unequal educational resources for those students. When welfare benefits were extended to include more poor people under the protective parameters of a national safety net, many recipients of that new protection chose to remain where they were rather than to risk entering the mainstream of competitive employment. Finally, when affirmative action policies were enacted to equalize opportunities for education and employment for Blacks, Whites claimed they were treated unequally and hence unfairly by the practice of *reverse discrimination*.

Clearly, the desire to include left-out members in the mainstream of community life was not the only value influencing support for inclusion policies during the post-1970s era. Because if it were, there would have been nothing to prevent policymakers from constraining the liberty of Whites by prohibiting them from moving to the suburbs. There would have been no reason to claim that spending more on special education students than regular education students was unfair. There would have been no reason to claim that working poor people who struggle to support themselves were morally superior to poor people who lived on welfare. And there would have been no claim of unequal treatment among those

already in the mainstream because they were denied those opportunities promised
to people often excluded from the mainstream.

IDEOLOGICAL INCLUSION

By the 1990s, this troubling debate over the inclusion of left-out groups polarized
along ideological lines that were defined by welfarism, liberalism, conservatism,
and libertarianism. Welfarists and liberals argued that social policy should
maximize the inclusion of left-out people; whereas conservatives and libertarians
argued that social policies should minimize the exclusion of left-out people.
Although all four ideological groups acknowledged that inclusion was a moral
ideal toward which society should evolve, each group proposed a different means
of reaching that end. Proinclusion advocates insisted the ideal be reached by
guaranteeing that all members have opportunities to participate and that all
members be protected from hardship, whereas antiexclusion advocates insisted
the inclusion ideal be reached by demanding that all new members be of good
character and that they be meritorious. Each is considered in turn here.

The proinclusion argument we hear from liberals in today's debates about
helping the needy is that individuals who are left out of the mainstream of
society's social and economic life have been denied opportunities to participate
due to gender, race, or ethnic origin. Because this is unfair, the collective should
take action to prevent the harm caused by this type of discrimination. Good
societies do this routinely because they are based on the belief that every person is
of equal moral worth. Consequently, every person deserves to be protected from
unfair obstacles to living the rewarding life, as Galbraith (1996) explained in *The
Good Society: The Humane Agenda.*

> If put in sufficiently general terms, the essence of the good society can be
> easily stated. It is that every member, regardless of gender, race or ethnic
> origin, should have *access* to a rewarding life. Allowance there must be for
> undoubted differences in aspiration and qualification. Individuals differ in
> physical and mental facility, commitment and purpose, and from these
> differences come differences in achievement and in economic reward. This
> is accepted.
>
> In the good society, however, achievement may not be limited by factors
> that are remediable. There must be economic opportunity for all . . . And in
> preparation for life, the young must have the physical care, the discipline,
> let no one doubt, and especially the education that will allow them to seize
> and exploit that opportunity. No one, from accident of birth or economic
> circumstances, may be denied these things; if they are not available from
> parent or family, society must provide effective forms of care and guidance.
> (p. 23, italics added)

The proinclusion argument we often hear from welfarists claims that the
collective should protect individuals from threats to their well-being over which
they have no control. This too is fully inclusive in that any vulnerable person is

eligible. It is also the reasoning behind the welfare state that "employs mechanisms that conventionally are intended to relieve distress" (Goodin, 1988, p. 14). Beneficiaries of the collective's protection include, for example,

> Widows, orphans, and the congenitally handicapped . . . [who are] "deserving" of state assistance . . . merely in the negative fact that there is nothing there to warrant their present pains . . . . They have done nothing to deserve the suffering that fate has bestowed upon them, and *that* is why public action to relieve their distress is said to be justified. (Goodin, 1988, p. 283)

In this country, the legislative expression of welfare ideology is the Social Security Act of 1935 which, according to Gordon (1994),

> [was] a major achievement in itself and a historic transformation in the role of the federal government. One historian has called the New Deal expansion of the federal government a "third American revolution;" another described its shift in economic philosophy as "a general attack on the doctrines of laissez-faire individualism. . . . No longer were poverty and unemployment to be condoned as the fruits of improvidence." . . . Millions of Americans were protected from impoverishment through its provision, and millions more, while they remain in poverty, were at least kept alive. AFDC in particular rendered critical support to women, support that contributed to safety and self-respect for millions (p. 4).

The Act provided the legal foundation for the federal government assuming responsibility for protecting its citizens from the cruelties of old age, sickness, disability, unemployment, and poverty (Gordon, 1994). Because unfortunate circumstance can threaten the well- being of any person, the government is obligated to protect and to help all who suffer, without exception or exclusion.

The other two inclusion arguments in today's debates over social policy focus on minimizing the harm of exclusion by making explicit those standards that individuals must meet in order to participate fully in mainstream opportunity. The antiexclusion argument we hear from conservatives is that all persons must act responsibly doing their part to take care of themselves, obey the law, and conform to the norms of the community. When they live up to these expectations, they can enter as moral equals. The implication is that if you have been excluded, it is because you have failed to meet the standard. However, if you improve your conduct, you will be readmitted. Mead (1986) said that "the welfare problem emerges as one of authority rather than freedom. The best hope for solving it is . . . to require recipients to function where they already are, as dependents. Even more than income and opportunity, *they need to face the requirements, such as work, that true acceptance in American society requires.* To create those obligations, they must be *less* free in certain senses rather than more" (p. 4, italics added).

The antiexclusion argument put forth by libertarians claims that merit is the best means for deciding who participates in mainstream opportunity. Given that individuals differ in talent and ability, and that fairness demands that opportunities be distributed according to merit, those who are most capable and industrious should have access to the best opportunities. Therefore, getting into the mainstream will require some demonstration of meritorious achievement. As a consequence, there will always be two classes of people: those who win and deserve to be rewarded for their accomplishments, and those who lose and deserve sympathy for their failures. Murray (1994) drew this conclusion in *Losing Ground:* "The most persuasive interpretation [of the economic and social trends of the 1980s] is that the United States has settled into a long-term evolution in which the people who have something going for them—especially high cognitive ability—will do better and better, socially and economically, while those who do not will do worse and worse" (p. xix). This prediction was further developed in *The Bell Curve: Intelligence and Class Structure in American Life* (Herrnstein & Murray, 1994).

A CRITIQUE OF IDEOLOGICAL INCLUSION

These are the main ideological arguments for inclusion, today. Two arguments recommend policies to maximize the inclusion of left-out persons and two recommend policies to minimize the exclusion of left-out persons. Proinclusion advocates insist inclusion be reached by guaranteeing that all members have opportunities to participate (first argument) and that all members be protected from unreasonable hardship (second argument). Antiexclusion advocates insist inclusion be reached by demanding that all members be of good character (first argument) and that they be meritorious in the rewards they receive through inclusion (second argument). The arguments are useful inasmuch as they operationalize the ideals of freedom and equality in a way that promises some version of an inclusive society. They accomplish this, however, by focusing on different conceptions of freedom and equality.

With regard to freedom, the first approach argues from the negative conception of *being free from* obstacles that prevent or constrain one's right to self-determination, whereas the second approach argues from a positive conception of *being free to* fully express that right self-determination. Proinclusion advocates use the negative version of freedom to construct policies that minimize obstacles to self-determination whereas antiexclusion advocates use the positive version of freedom to construct policies that maximize the expression of one's self-determination. For proinclusion advocates, freedom means being free from unfair and unreasonable obstacles, which translates into protective policies that maximize the inclusion of morally equal persons. For antiexclusion advocates, freedom means being free to act on one's own interests, which translates into empowerment policies that minimize the exclusion of morally deserving persons.

With regard to equality, one of the proinclusion arguments and one of the antiexclusion arguments are based on the assumption of equal moral capacity, whereas the other proinclusion and antiexclusion arguments are based on the assumption of unequal natural capacity. The assumption of equal moral capacity allows liberals (proinclusionists) and conservatives (antiexclusionists) to claim that individuals are equally capable of acting morally in the conduct of the self-determined life, although they draw different conclusions from this position. Liberals conclude that because individuals are of equal moral worth they deserve equal opportunities to act freely, whereas conservatives argue that because individuals have equal capacity to act morally they are equally responsible for their actions.

The other proinclusion and antiexclusion arguments are based on the assumption of unequal capacity. Welfarists argue that because people are naturally unequal in their capacity to secure what they need and want in life, some individuals will experience unusually difficult circumstances over which they have no control. Libertarians, in contrast, argue that because individuals are naturally unequal in their capacity, there will always be some who are more successful than others. Both agree that inequalities in ability and talent require individuals to be treated differently in society, although they disagree on the type of unequal treatment individuals deserve. Welfarists claim more protection is necessary for those made helpless by their lack of ability, whereas libertarians claim greater rewards are necessary for the meritorious achievement of those who are talented.

Figure 1.1 shows how these assumptions about freedom and equality interact to produce different versions of ideological inclusion. The left column represents the negative freedom assumption and the right column represents the positive freedom assumption. The first row represents the assumptions of equal moral worth and the second row represents the assumption of unequal natural capacity.

The four cells present the four inclusion arguments constructed from these different assumptions. In Cell 1, the assumptions of negative freedom and equal moral capacity justify the liberal argument that the inclusion ideal requires all individuals to have equal opportunities to act freely. In Cell 2, the assumptions of positive freedom and the equal capacity justify the conservative argument that inclusion should be contingent individuals acting responsibly with their freedom. In Cell 3, the assumptions of negative freedom and the unequal natural capacity justify the welfare argument that the inclusion ideal requires governmental protection for individuals from hardship over which they have no control. And in Cell 4, the assumptions of positive freedom and unequal natural capacity justify the libertarian argument that inclusion should be contingent securing a position in the community through one's own talent and ability.

This analysis clarifies policy disagreements among the four ideologies. Compare, for example, Galbraith's (1996) argument that society should equalize opportunities for excluded groups with Mead's argument that individuals should be responsible for their actions. Galbraith assumed that because all people are morally equal, society is responsible for protecting every person from the types of discrimination that prevent them from pursuing a rewarding life (Cell 1).

Therefore, members of minority groups deserve compensation for these unfair obstacles to their pursuits. Mead, by contrast,

Conditions of Equality	Freedom From Obstacles to Act on One's Circumstances	Freedom To Act on One's Circumstances
Equal Moral Capacity	Cell 1 Liberal Argument Inclusion requires opportunities for individuals to participate in society	Cell 2 Conservative Argument Inclusion is contingent on the responsible conduct of individuals
Unequal Natural Capacity	Cell 3 Welfare Argument Inclusion requires protection of helpless individuals from uncontrollable hardship	Cell 4 Libertarian Argument Inclusion is contingent on the meritorious achievement of individuals

FIG. 1.1. The ideological basis of four policy arguments on -inclusion.

assumed that because all individuals are free to act on their own to get what they need and want in life, they are responsible for the results of those actions (Cell 2). Therefore, if they fail to take care of themselves, it is because they have not acted responsibly. Welfare recipients must prove they are responsible before they receive governmental support.

Now consider policy differences between Goodin's (1988) assumption that there will always be vulnerable people in need of protection (Cell 3) and Murray's (1994) assumption that there will always be people with talent who should be rewarded (Cell 4). Goodin argued that because some individuals suffer from circumstances over which they have no control, society has an obligation to help them deal with their hardship. Therefore, the disabled and poor should be protected from harm. Murray argued that because some people are intrinsically smarter and more capable than others, the former will always secure a greater share of the rewards than the latter. Moreover, in the free society there is little government can do to alter this inexorable division between "haves" and "have nots."

The problem with the four arguments is not that their assumptions are wrong, but that they are usually inaccurate and almost always incomplete. This is because none of them considers the effects of positive freedom and negative freedom on a person's circumstances, nor do any of them account for variations in the individual's moral, acquired, or natural capacity to improve those circumstances. The solutions they offer are only partially and occasionally responsive to the circumstances that prevent left-out individuals and groups from including themselves in the mainstream. Therefore, the four policies can be justified only to the extent that the persons targeted for their help are, in fact, victims of discrimination, irresponsible free riders, hopelessly helpless, or congenitally incompetent.

Unfortunately, people excluded from the mainstream usually do not fit neatly into these diagnostic categories of need. They vary in their moral capacity to choose as they should in the free society, just as they vary in their natural and acquired capacities to produce the outcomes they need and want in life. Consequently, it is unfair and insensitive to enact inclusion policies that label a person of color a victim of discrimination, a person on welfare as a freerider, a disabled person as piteously helpless, or a poor person as a looser in order to justify helping that person enter the mainstream. These labels and the assumptions on which they are based do not address the circumstances that prevent left-out individuals and groups from including themselves in the free society.

Nevertheless, they persist in public debates about inclusion, perhaps because they are consistent with beliefs about what constitutes the good society. Welfare inclusion policy to protect all vulnerable people from hardship, for example, appeals to people who believe the good society is secure for all persons, liberal inclusion policy to rescue minority members from discrimination appeals to people who believe the good society is diverse, conservative inclusion policy to enforce responsibility to community standards appeals to people who believe the good society is a well ordered community, and libertarian inclusion policy to reward individuals for their accomplishments appeals to people who believe the good society is meritocratic. For these advocates, inclusion policy is a means of advancing society toward one of these views of what is best for everyone. Liberals advocate for victims of discrimination because they believe diversity is good for society and because they want to rescue people who have suffered from unfair treatment. Conservatives advocate for individual responsibility because they believe a well-ordered community is good for society and because they want new members to conform to the standards that hold it together. Welfarists advocate for the helpless because they believe security for all people is good for society and because they want to protect the helpless from uncontrollable harm. And libertarians advocate rewarding the talented and productive because they believe in a meritocracy and because they want to encourage the most capable people to contribute to the material progress of society.

In other words, debates over ideological inclusion are not about people who are excluded. They are about different conceptions of the good society. Consequently, every debate is a competition over which conception will prevail. The prize for winning is having sufficient political power to construct policies in accordance with these concepts of a good society. For liberals it is diversity, for conservatives it is order, for welfarists it is security, and for libertarians it is merit. We can see some of the results of these ideological competitions in the recent changes to the four inclusion policies constructed during the 1960s and 1970s. Fig. 1.2 illustrates these changes. Prior to the 1990s, special education, school desegregation, and affirmative action policies were protected by the liberal claim (Cell 1) that society is obligated to equalize opportunities for left-out

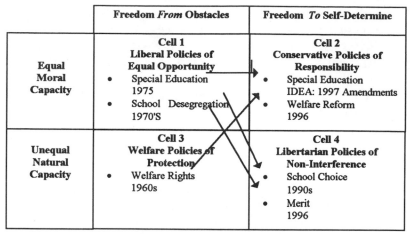

	Freedom *From* Obstacles	Freedom *To* Self-Determine
Equal Moral Capacity	**Cell 1** **Liberal Policies of** **Equal Opportunity** • Special Education 1975 • School Desegregation 1970'S	**Cell 2** **Conservative Policies of** **Responsibility** • Special Education IDEA: 1997 Amendments • Welfare Reform 1996
Unequal Natural Capacity	**Cell 3** **Welfare Policies of** **Protection** • Welfare Rights 1960s	**Cell 4** **Libertarian Policies of** **Non-Interference** • School Choice 1990s • Merit 1996

FIG. 1.2 Ideological shifts in inclusion policy from 1960s to present.

members; and AFDC policy for poor single-parent families was protected by the welfarist claim (in Cell 3) that society has an obligation to protect the vulnerable. These bases were weakened in the 1980s and 1990s by assaults from the right, which argued for greater personal responsibility (Cell 2), and for more choice and rewards based on merit (Cell 4). The arrows in the table show these changes.

Special education policy that was once protected by liberal ideology now has a conservative emphasis as indicated by the arrow in Cell 1 connecting the policy constructed in 1975 with the revised policy constructed in 1997 (Cell 2). The amendments to the Individuals with Disabilities Education Act (IDEA; PL 105-17) authorize treatment of students with disabilities who are law-breakers to be the same as that meted out to nondisabled students who are law-breakers. Under Section 615 of PL 105-17, a disabled student who violates a school rule or code of conduct may be considered for disciplinary action lasting more than 10 days. Moreover, depending on the relation between conduct and disability, the student may be placed in a more restrictive setting for the same period of time mandated for a child without a disability who exhibits similar misbehavior. This action is warranted if a disabled student (a) carries a weapon to school or to a school function, (b) knowingly possesses or takes illegal drugs or sells or solicits the sale of a controlled substance, or (c) engages in conduct likely to result in injury to the student or to others ("The IDEA Amendments," 1997). Any of these circumstances is sufficient to revoke the disabled student's right to the LRE as determined by the individualized educational program.

Support for school desegregation policy has also shifted toward the right. The 1960s argument that schools should desegregate to improve educational opportunities for Black students has been challenged by the right with the argument that parents should be able to choose the schools their children attend. It matters not that this may re-segregate the nation's schools because libertarian ideology holds freedom rather than diversity as the highest good. So although Orfield, a spokesperson for the left, worries that "There is a clear trend. For both Black and Latino students, contact with Whites is going down," Finn, a school reformer from the right, explained that all parents prefer good schools to desegregated schools. "More and more minority parents, when asked what they care about for their kids' schools, no longer say they care about the skin color of the kid in the next seat. They care if their child is going to a safe school that teaches them to read and write" (Cited in Applebome, 1997, p. A10). Indeed, a recent Gallup poll conducted for the Phi Delta Kappa has found that Blacks favor vouchers more than Whites (Brooke, 1997). Also, experiments with school vouchers tend to support Finn's claim about the benefits of parental choice. A Cleveland voucher program, for example, has been popular among minority and nonminority parents and is yielded promising results in math and reading (Lewin, 1997).

Now consider the shift in support for affirmative action policy. After going largely unchallenged for nearly two decades, the policy was struck down by a federal appeals court in a 1996 decision prohibiting the University of Texas Law School's admissions committee from using race as a factor in its admission decisions (Verhovek, 1996). This was followed by an intense competition between the right and left during the 1996 presidential race with Republican candidate Robert Dole stating "Now, we've reached another turning point, this time for equality and opportunity in America. And the California Civil Rights Initiative allows the voters of this state to endorse a great principle, the principle that racial distinctions have no place in our lives or in our laws. That's the way it should be in America . . ." ("*Excerpts from Dole's*," 1996, p. 1). Two months later, President Clinton joined the fray by attacking the California ban on affirmative action (Homes, 1996). But when the Supreme Court refused to hear an appeal by the state of Texas to overturn the federal appeals court ruling against the use of race in university admission decisions, and when another federal appeals court "reaffirmed California's right to do away with racial and sex-based preferences" in state-run programs, it appeared the rightward shift was inexorable (Greenhouse, 1997, p. A22). These recent judicial decisions disallowing the policy are indicated by the arrow from Cell 1 to Cell 3 in Fig. 1.2. The change in welfare rights policy was perhaps the most dramatic of the four. The arrow connecting its positions in Cell 3 and Cell 2 of Fig. 1.2 indicates the shift from welfare as an entitlement to welfare as a contingency for staying in mainstream competitive work. The welfare reform law of 1996 reflected the new view that governmental support should empower the poor to do their part to find jobs and become self-sufficient. In the 1992 presidential campaign, Clinton promised welfare reform would "empower people with the education, training, and child care they need for up to two years so they can break the cycle of dependency." It would "'make work pay' by preparing people for well-paid, high skill jobs that would help them attain self-sufficiency"(Kilborn & Verhovek, 1996, p. A1). House Speaker Newt Gingrich argued similarly, but with the moral tone of a conservative claiming "We committed to reform welfare because what we are doing to the poor in America is destructive and immoral." And Christopher Shays of Connecticut added that, "Today, what we have shown is that we are a caring country. Instead of giving the food, we are going to help people learn to grow the food" (DeParle, 1995, p .2). The new approach to helping the poor constituted a permanent change from the protectionism justified by the welfare ideology in Cell 3 to the expectations for personal responsibility and self-sufficiency that were in line with the conservative ideology in Cell 2.

THE EQUAL OPPORTUNITY ALTERNATIVE

Looking back, it appears that the consensus on inclusion policy that was constructed from the experiences of the 1960s and 1970s has dissolved. In its place are clusters of ideologically driven advocates and their followers who support the four inclusion policies justified by the arguments summarized in Fig. 1.2. Liberals support the proinclusion argument in Cell 1 that there is a collective obligation to include all persons. Therefore, society should equalize opportunities through policies like special education, school desegregation, and affirmative action. Conservatives support the antiexclusion position in Cell 2 that freedom for all imposes responsibilities to conform to the laws and norms of the community. Therefore, welfare cheats should be required to work like the rest of us, and disabled students who misbehave should be punished just as nondisabled students are punished when they misbehave. Welfarists support the proinclusion argument in Cell 3 that there is a collective obligation to protect the vulnerable from unfortunate circumstances over which they have no control. Therefore, the safety net constructed in the 1960s to protect dependent mothers and their children should be maintained. Moreover, the welfare reform law of 1996 should be repealed because it will harm children who are the most vulnerable members of society. Libertarians support the argument in Cell 4 that a person's inclusion in the mainstream of social and economic opportunity should be based on meritorious accomplishment. Therefore, affirmative action policies should be abolished because they distribute opportunities on the basis of race. School desegregation polices should be abolished too, if they are contrary to the preferences of parents who should be free to choose the schools their children attend.

What is troublesome about ideologues who promote these different versions of inclusion policy is that they presume they are always right and their opponents always wrong. This polarizes thinking about social issues and exacerbates apparent contradictions in the different conceptions of liberty, equality, and the good society. It also discourages nonideological thinking about what might constitute a fair and reasonable solution to the problem of excluding many individuals and groups from mainstream opportunity in this country. Carville's (1996) *We're Right, They're Wrong,* which represents the proinclusion ideologies of the left (Cells 1 and 3) and Frum's (1994) *Dead Right,* which represents the antiexclusion ideologies of the right (Cells 2 and 4) illustrate this polarization. They may be useful for marshaling political support during presidential campaigns, but they are not useful when attempting to understand how left-out individuals can become fully participating members of their communities after campaigns are over.

The equal opportunity alternative provides a nonideological solution to the exclusion problem. It views inclusion as an ideal against which policies that maximize freedom and equalize circumstances should be evaluated. Moreover, it incorporates both conceptions of freedom and a full range of capacity conditions that define equality of circumstance—moral capacity, natural capacity, and acquired capacity. This allows policymakers to determine the extent to which an inclusion policy based on a given circumstance of freedom and equality actually helps individuals enter the mainstream on their own terms.

Figure 1.3 illustrates the model. Although similar in structure to Fig. 1.1 and 1.2, the equal opportunity perspective offers a dynamic rather than static description of factors influencing the inclusion of left-out persons. The two types of polices identified at the top of the diagram correspond to negative and positive freedom. Protective policies correspond to the concept of negative freedom (in the left column of Fig. 1.2) and empowering policies correspond to the concept of positive freedom (in right column of Fig. 1.2).

The left side of the diagram lists the three conditions of equality: equality of access to the means necessary to reach one's ends in life, equality of prospects for acting on those means to reach those ends, and equality of respect for securing a valued position in the community that is consistent with one's needs, interests, and abilities. The arrows in the diagram illustrate the causal sequence postulated between policies that protect and empower left-out individuals to be self-determined and the conditions of equality that indicate how their freedom experience compares with other people in the mainstream. Policies that protect one's the right to self-determination, for example, impact the opportunity side of the access condition, whereas policies that empower one's ability to act on that right impact the capacity side of the access condition.

This conceptualization gives new meaning to the concept of equal access. Access is equal among a group of actors when all members have sufficient opportunity and capacity to act on their circumstances to pursue their own ends in life. When policy makes use this perspective, they construct policies that combine opportunity enhancements with capacity building to equalize prospects for self-determined engagement in mainstream opportunity. Consequently, policies of protection and empowerment are effective when they alter the opportunity and capacity relation sufficiently to produce self-determined engagement. They are significant when these self-determined pursuits lead to positions in the community that are consistent with the individual's needs, interests, and abilities. And they are successful (effective and significant), when they produce an equality of access that leads to equality of engagement which, in turn, leads equality of respect.

CONDITIONS OF FREEDOM

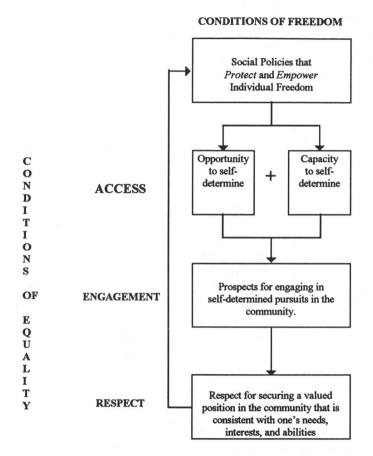

FIG. 1.3. The equal opportunity model for inclusion.

The advantage of viewing the inclusion process this way is that it allows policymakers to discriminate between the effectiveness and the significance of a policy. A policy that improves access but does not alter prospects for engagement in self-determined pursuits is effective but not significant. Only when it also improves prospects for engagement that results in respectable positions in the community is it also significant.

This perspective places the past failures of inclusion policies in a different light. Consider Coleman's (1990) conclusion that school desegregation policy was not significant. He indicated that "the earlier hope that school desegregation would constitute a panacea for black achievement, or contribute substantially to the goal of increasing black achievement, appears to have been misplaced" (1990, p. 201). The policy improved educational opportunities for Black students by giving them a chance to attend racially mixed schools. Its goal was to equalize access by improving educational opportunities. However, because this opportunity enhancement did not increase the academic capacity of Black students, Coleman believed it could not produce a significant increase their community integration after graduation.

The problem with this conclusion is that Coleman assumed academic capacity building was the only means through which the policy could equalize prospects for entering mainstream of White opportunity. He did not consider the possibility that the social capacity building students experienced in desegregated schools could also lead to improved prospects in adult life. A study by Wells and Crain (1995) suggested this may have occurred. They examined these effects in a follow-up study on school desegregation and found that Black students who developed social contacts with White students while enrolled in desegregated schools were predisposed to access similar social networks when they advanced themselves after graduation. They concluded, "There is a strong possibility . . . that when occupational attainment is dependent on knowing the right people and being in the right place at the right time, school desegregation assists black students in gaining access to traditionally 'white' jobs" (p. 552). Based on this finding, it would appear that school desegregation was effective in building the social capacity students needed to engage self-determined pursuits in White communities after graduation, and it was significant because these pursuits resulted their gaining entry into White-dominated occupations.

The purpose of special education policy was similar to that of school desegregation in that it also focused on equalizing access to educational opportunities. Again, the expectation was that educational opportunity would improve students' academic capacity to succeed later in life. Remember that prior to Public Law 94-142, most disabled students were denied public education. The Education for All Handicapped Children Act changed that by guaranteeing access to the public school experience. Now, more than two decades later, no child with a disability can be denied an education due to disability. In this sense, access to the educational means that are necessary for adjustment to adult life has been equalized. Disabled students can enroll in public schools the same as nondisabled students. On this basis, the policy is effective. However, on the question of significance, a different answer is in order because their prospects for self-determined engagement in community life after graduation have not improved. Follow-up studies of special education graduates indicated that they were no more likely to find employment and to participate fully in their communities now than before the policy was enacted. Therefore, the policy was effective but not significant.

Welfare policy differed from school desegregation and special education policy in that it focused on one of the access factors: capacity building. It provided income supports for poor people so they would have the financial capacity to extricate themselves from their difficult circumstances. Although the policy did not eliminate poverty, it protected many from suffering from severe economic hardship (Katz, 1989). The policy also failed the significance test because it did not improve poor people's prospects for engaging mainstream work opportunities on their own. Instead critics argue, the policy encouraged dependence on government support.

Affirmative action also focused on only one of the access factors: opportunity enhancement. It redressed the harm caused by racial discrimination in higher education and employment by providing compensatory consideration for Blacks whose opportunities were unfairly limited. The assumption underlying the policy was not that Blacks lacked capacity to act on their own, but that they were denied a fair chance to engage their capacity to pursue opportunities routinely afforded Whites.

The policy can be judged to be effective to the extent it increased the number of Black applicants seeking entry into higher education and White-only professions, and it can be judged to be significant to the extent this increased engagement led to valued positions in society. The evaluation of progress on both criteria is favorable. Perhaps this is why the policy is so hotly debated. The success of Blacks in finding a place in mainstream opportunity was perceived to have displaced Whites from those highly regarded positions. And this motivated the latter to claim the policy was unfair. So the argument over affirmative action is not so much that it failed the effectiveness or significance tests, but that it failed the fairness test. If the policy had been ineffective or insignificant, there would have been no reason to claim unfairness because Whites would not have been denied opportunities set aside for Blacks.

CONCLUSION

Several conclusions can be drawn from this analysis of inclusion policy. The first is that it is unlikely future policies to include left-out individuals and groups will be based on some end-state concept of the good society, regardless of whether that view be the diverse society, the well-ordered society, the protective society, or the meritocratic society. To be sure, there will be ideologues arguing to distribute new opportunities according to their view of what is good for all of us. But it is unlikely those arguments will prevail given that we continue to hold to the ideal of equal freedom for all people. What renders ideological inclusion arguments moot, I believe, is that the equal freedom ideal translates into the expectation that every person should have a fair (equal) chance to live the self-determined life— the perspective expressed by the equal opportunity model put forth in Fig. 1.1. This means that people excluded from the mainstream also deserve a fair chance to enter the mainstream on their own terms. Therefore, we should construct policies of protection and empowerment that equalize their prospects for these self-determined entries.

This first conclusion suggests a second one, that the success of the self-determined entry will depend on the capacity and opportunity of individuals to engage the mainstream in order to make those circumstances more favorable for their own pursuits. Moreover, policies of protection and empowerment will be effective to the extent they find that combination of capacity building (empowerment policy) and opportunity enhancement (protective policy) that promotes these self-determined engagements. Past inclusion policies failed to consider this relations and, as a consequence, failed to take into account how it affects an individual's prospects of engaging new opportunity.

The debate over education reform illustrates this oversight. Conservatives want higher standards to assure that all students master the skills and knowledge necessary for success later in life (Hirsch, 1996), and liberals want to change schools to improve instruction so all students will learn (Darling-Hammond, 1997). The former is an empowerment policy that focuses on building the capacity of students to demonstrate new skills and acquire new knowledge, and the latter is a protective policy that focuses on preventing children from failing in school due to unfair and inadequate opportunities to learn. Although advocates on both sides are busy arguing why their policy is right and the other wrong, equal opportunity approach recasts the reform question to focus on the capacity building and opportunity enhancements that will increase student engagement in their own learning. After all, if the goal is for students to become self-directed, lifelong learners in pursuit of their own ends in adult life, then they must learn content they can use to engage opportunities for that self-directed learning. When educational reform focuses on these self-determined engagements in schooling, it will prepare all students for those "thinking for a living" futures described by Marshall and Tucker (1992).

The debate on restructuring special education is also divided unnecessarily between academic skill building in special classes (an empowerment policy) and opportunity enhancements through full inclusion in regular classes (a protection policy) (Fuchs & Fuchs, 1994). The empowerment policy is based on the argument that the small class size and individualized instruction made possible by the present system produces greater educational benefits for students than does the full inclusion system proposed by the special education reform movement. The protection policy advocates, by contrast, argue that fully including disabled students in the mainstream provides greater social opportunities than are possible in the special class system. Again, the equal opportunity perspective examines how different combinations of empowerment and protection policy affect students' prospects for self-determined pursuits in the mainstream of adult opportunity. Given that disabled students must also become lifelong thinkers and learners in order to adjust successfully to the circumstances they face after graduation, they too must learn to engage themselves in their own learning so that they can direct their own pursuits after they leave school. It is not simply a matter of building academic skills effectively and efficiently in special class settings or a matter of immersing students fully in the mainstream social environments of schools so they can benefit from being with nondisabled students. Rather, it is a matter of building students' capacity to act in various social circumstances as self-directed, self-determined persons capable of managing their own adjustments in different school and community environments. Given this overriding purpose of inclusion policy, the question addressed by the equal opportunity perspective is What combination of capacity building and opportunity enhancement will engage students in these self-determined learning pursuits? The recent federal initiative to increase students' levels of self-determination in school and beyond is in keeping with this approach to special education reform (Ward, 1996).

Viewing welfare reform from the equal opportunity perspective also redirects attention to the capacity building and opportunity enhancements that encourage engagement in mainstream circumstances. In this case, the capacity-building component focuses on education, work training, child care, and various support services that empower welfare recipients to participate in community work, and the opportunity enhancement component focuses on job search services and modified work expectations that will match worker capacity and motivate this engagement (DeParle, 1997). This approach individualizes expectations for participation so that some individuals can work in subsidized jobs prior to making the transition to full-time work, others can work part time, and others can move directly to full employment. Accordingly, the policy will be successful to the extent these variations in capacity-building and opportunity enhancements motivate individuals to take charge of their lives in order to enter mainstream community work on their own terms.

Affirmative action policy also has new meaning when viewed from the equal opportunity perspective. This is because the principle underlying the concept of equal opportunity is that every person deserves an equal chance to participate in mainstream opportunities on their own terms. The equal opportunity model operationalizes this principle by identifying equal access as the chief means of equalizing these self-determined engagements. Given this, one can argue that affirmative action, with its opportunity enhancements for left-out individuals, is a legitimate means of equalizing access. People with unfavorable prospects for entering the mainstream compared to others already in the mainstream are at an unfair disadvantage for success in life. Consequently, they deserve those opportunity enhancements that will equalize their prospects. This justification for affirmative action is not, of course, race based. It is needs based. Any person with unfavorable prospects deserves favorable consideration for new opportunity. This justification is also in line with the public's view of how it ought to work, and it is consistent with President Clinton's argument for the policy. "If you get down to brass tacks, I think people in both parties of good faith, what they want is a society where everybody who needs it gets a hand up, [so that] everybody's got a fair chance" (Bennet, 1997, p. A25).

Equal opportunity inclusion is the fair alternative to ideological inclusion because it does not require a definition of the "typical" left-out person in order to justify helping people enter the mainstream. People who are excluded do not need to be defined as victims of discrimination in order to be eligible for liberal inclusion, nor do they need to be defined as free riders avoiding responsibility in order to be eligible for conservative inclusion. They are also free from being regarded as hopelessly helpless in need of protection in order to receive welfare's version inclusion, just as they are free from being judged chronically incompetent in order to receive the libertarian version of inclusion. None of these odious eligibility requirements or demeaning labels is necessary for a person to be eligible of equal opportunity inclusion. The only condition that must be present is a less favorable prospect for the self-determined entry into the mainstream than that experienced by those already in the mainstream.

This approach to inclusion is fundamentally fair in the broader sense as well. If the free society holds that every person must enter the mainstream on his or her own in order to earn the respect from others for that achievement, then every person should have equal access to the means necessary for that inclusion. Moreover, if we claim that every person has the same right to self-determination, then we are obligated as a society to provide the means to act on that right. The equal opportunity theory presented here summarizes this argument (Mithaug, 1996):

- All individuals have the right to self-determination.
- All societies have some individuals who lack the capacity to self-determine.
- All societies generate unequal opportunities to self-determine.
- Consequently, some individuals do not experience the right to self-determine because they lack the capacity and opportunity to do so.
- Therefore, all societies should optimize prospects for self-determination among these least advantaged members by increasing their capacity and improving their opportunity to self-determine. (p. 11)

In summary, the equal opportunity alternative to ideological inclusion promises to be an effective, significant, and fair policy for inclusion in that it seeks that combination of capacity-building and opportunity enhancement policies that will equalize access, equalize prospects for self-determination, and equalizes respect in the community. The approach seeks an optimal solution to the exclusion problem in that anything less than what it prescribes will threaten the individual's right to autonomy and experience of self-respect, and anything more will strain the free society's obligation to be fair and compassionate when giving help.

REFERENCES

The Assault of Affirmative Action. (1996, April 10). *Newsweek, 55.*
Bennet, J. (1997, December 17). Clinton urges education aid for minorities. *The New York Times,* pp. A25.
Bergmann, B. R. (1996). *In defense of affirmative action.* New York: Basic Books.
Brooke, J. (1997, December 27). Minorities flock to cause of vouchers for schools. *The New York Times.* pp. A1, A7.
Brown v Board of Education, 347 U.S. 483 (1954).
Carville, J. (1996). *We're right, they're wrong: A handbook for spirited progressives.* New York: Random House.
Coleman, J. S. (1990). *Equality and achievement in education.* Boulder, CO: Westview Press.

Darling-Hammond, L. (1997). *The right to learn: A blueprint for creating schools that work.* San Francisco, CA: Jossey-Bass.

DeParle, J. (1997b, August 24). Getting Opal Caples to work. *The New York Times Magazine* pp. 33–37, 47, 54, 59–61.

DeParle, J. (1995a, December 3). Less is more: Faith and facts in welfare reform. *The New York Times Week in Review* 1, 16.

Dillon, S. (1994a, August 14). Badillo contends that the cost of special education is inflated. *The New York Times* pp. 1, 40 .

Dillon, S. (1994b, April 7). Special education absorbs school resources. *The New York Times* pp. A1, B5.

Excerpts from Dole's address on affirmative action. (1996, October 29). *The New York Times,* pp. A21.

Frum, D. (1994). *Dead right.* New York: Basic Books.

Fuchs, D., & Fuchs, L. (1994). Inclusive schools movement and the radicalization of reform. *Exceptional Children, 60,* 294–309.

Galbraith, J. K. (1996). *The good society: The humane agenda.* Boston, MA: Houghton Mifflin.

Glass, G. V. (1983). Effectiveness of special education. *Policy Studies Review, 21*(1), 65–78.

Goodin, R. E. (1988). *Reasons for welfare: The political theory of the welfare state.* Princeton, NJ: Princeton University Press.

Gordon, L. (1994). *Pitied but not entitled: Single mothers and the history of welfare 1890–1935.* Cambridge, MA: Harvard University Press.

Greenhouse, L. (1997, September 5). Justices allow an anti-bias law to go into effect, *The New York Times* p. A22.

Hasazi, S. B., Gordon, L. R., & Roe, C. A. (1985). Factors associated with employment status of handicapped youth exiting high school from 1979–1983. *Exceptional Children, 51,* 455–469.

Herrnstein, R. J. & Murray, C. (1994). *The bell curve: Intelligence and class structure in American life.* New York: The Free Press.

Hirsch, E. D. (1996). *The schools we need: Why we don't have them.* New York: Doubleday.

Homes, S. A. (1996, December 21). Clinton decides to join a fight on preferences: U.S. will oppose ban passed in California. *The New York Times,* pp. A1, A14.

The IDE Amendments of 1997. (1997, August). *Nichy News Digest.*

Katz, M. B. (1989). *The undeserving poor: From the war on poverty to the war on welfare.* New York: Pantheon Books.

Kilborn P. T., & Verhovek, S. H. (1996, August 2). Clinton's welfare shift ends tortuous journey. *The New York Times,* pp. 1, A18.

Lewin, T. (1997, September 18). School voucher study finds satisfaction. *The New York Times,* pp. A16.

Marshall, R., & Tucker, M. (1992). *Thinking for a living: Education and the wealth of nations.* New York: Basic Books.

Mead, L. M. (1986). *Beyond entitlement: The social obligations of citizenship.* New York: The Free Press.

Mills v Board of Education, 348 F. Supp. 866 (D.D.C. 1972).

Mithaug, D. E. (1996). *Equal opportunity theory.* Thousand Oaks, CA: Sage.

Mithaug, D. E., & Horiuchi, C. N. (1983). *Colorado statewide follow-up survey of special education students.* Denver: Colorado Department of Education.

Mithaug, D. E., Horiuchi, C. N., & McNulty, B. A. (1987). *Parents reports on the transitions of students graduating from Colorado special education programs in 1978 and 1979.* Denver: Colorado Department of Education.

Murray, C. (1994). *Losing ground.* New York: Basic Books.

Parc v Pennsylvania, 334 F Supp. 1257 (E.D. Pa. 1971).

Scheerenberger, R. C. (1983). *A history of mental retardation.* Baltimore, MD: Paul Brookes.

Skrentny, J. D. (1996). *The ironies of affirmative action: Politics, culture, and justice in America.* Chicago, IL: The University of Chicago Press

Supreme Court to consider major court case concerning race in the workplace. (1997, October 6). *The New York Times,* pp. A13.

Separate and Unequal: How Special Education Programs are Cheating our Children and Costing Taxpayers Billions each Year. (1993, December 3). *U.S. News & World Report.*

Verhovek, S. H. (March 23, 1996). For 4 whites who sued university, Race is the common thread. *The New York Times,* pp. A6.

Ward, M. J. (1996). Coming of age in the age of self-determination. In D. J. Sands & M. L. Wehmeyer (Eds.), *Self-determination across the life span: Independence and choice for people with disabilities,* pp. 3–16. Paul Brookes.

Wehman, P. , Kregel, J., & Seyfarth, J. (1985). Transition from school to work for individuals with severe handicaps, A follow-up study. *Journal of the Association for Persons with Severe Handicaps,* pp. 10, 132–136.

Wells, A., & Crain, R. (1995). Perpetuation theory and the long-term effects of school desegregation. *Review of Educational Research, 62,(4),* 552.

2

The Law on Inclusion

Stanley J. Vitello
Rutgers University

The current state of inclusion law can best be described as a " mixed bag." In the early 1990s, a line of cases resulted in students with disabilities being placed in general education classes. More recently, there have been as many cases that have upheld a special education placement. Like much of special education law, it is becoming clear that the interpretation of the least restrictive environment requirement (LRE) is fact specific. That is, the characteristics of the individual student determine the outcome of the case.

EARLY 1990 CASES

Appropriate Social Benefits

The early 1990 cases established several principles underlying the inclusion of students with disabilities in general education classes. The inclusion cases affirmed the holding in *Board of Education v. Rowley* (1982) that a student with a disability is entitled to a free, and appropriate public education (FAPE). An FAPE "provides personalized instruction with sufficient support services to permit the child to benefit educationally from that instruction" (p. 16). The first and most important consideration regarding the education of students with disabilities is ensuring that they will receive an appropriate educational program. The courts have held that the students educational placement is secondary to their receipt of an appropriate educational program. See *Lachman v. Illinois State Board of Educ.* (1988), and *Murphysboro v. Illinois State Board of Educ.* (1994).

The courts have broadened the concept of *educational benefit*. Educational benefits include social as well as academic benefits. Social benefits include opportunities to interact with nondisabled students, modeling their appropriate social and communication skills. Typically, parents of young students with disabilities, oftentimes severe, want their children included in a general education classroom for the social benefits even if the academic benefits are minimal. On the other side, school districts recommend a more restrictive placement in a resource room or special class to ensure academic progress. Invariably, in the earlier cases the courts have held in favor of the parents. Consider the case of *Sacramento City Unif. School District v. Rachel Holland* (1994). An 11 year-old California student with severe mental retardation attended special education classes in her local public school district. Her parents requested full-time placement in a general education class. The school district rejected this request and proposed special education instruction in academic classes and mainstreaming in nonacademic subjects and activities. The parents then enrolled the student in general classes at a private school and requested a hearing before a state hearing officer. The hearing officer found that the district had failed to comply with the Individuals with Disabilities Act's (IDEA) least restrictive educational placement requirement, that the student had benefited from her placement in general classes at the private school and that she was not too disruptive to attend general classes in public school. The hearing officer ruled that the district had overstated the cost of placing the student in general education classes and ordered the district to place her in a general education classroom with support services. The U.S. District Court for the Eastern District of California affirmed the hearing officer's decision; the school district appealed to the U.S. Court of Appeals, Ninth Circuit. On appeal, the district argued that the student was too severely disabled to benefit from full-time general education placement. The parents argued that the student was learning *social* and academic skills in the general education placement. The appellate court had determined that the hearing officer and district court had properly considered the applicable factors in their decisions to include the student in the general education classroom. *Holland* (1994) set forth the four factors that should be considered in the determination whether a student should be placed in a general education classroom. These included (a) the academic benefits of full-time placement in a general education classroom, (b) nonacademic or social benefits, (c) the negative effects of the placement on other students in the general education class and (d) the costs of the placement. In affirming the district court decision the appellate court held "benefits obtained by a child with mental retardation as a result of placement in a regular classroom include development of social and communication skills and generally improved self-esteem" (p.1396). The court of appeals affirmed the district court's judgment in favor of the parents. The social benefit outcome determined the court's decision in favor of inclusion in the following cases: *Greer v. Rome City School Dist. (1991), Oberti v. Bd. of Education of the Borough of Clemeton School Dist. (1993) and Statum v. Birmingham Public School Board of Educ. (1993)*.

General Education Placement Presumption

The court cases uphold the presumption under the IDEA that a student with a disability be placed in the least restrictive environment (LRE) and that placement in the general education class be given first consideration. The school district must make a good faith effort to determine whether a student with a disability can be educated in a general education classroom. There must not only be a discussion of the placement but steps taken to implement the student's instructional program in the general education classroom. If it is determined that the student cannot receive instruction in the general education class then the student is to be mainstreamed to the maximum extent appropriate. Consider the following four cases.

Parents of a child with Down Syndrome attempted to enroll their daughter in a general kindergarten class. The school district refused to allow enrollment without an evaluation. Nevertheless, the parents enrolled their daughter in the general kindergarten class the next year and a due process hearing was initiated. The hearing officer determined that the child should be evaluated. After the child was evaluated, a placement meeting was held and the team recommended a self-contained classroom. The parents rejected this placement and requested their daughter be placed in the general kindergarten class with speech therapy. The school board rejected the parents' proposal. The parents then initiated a suit in a federal district court alleging that the IEP had violated the IDEA by failing to consider placement in the LRE placement—the general education class. The trial court determined that the proposed IEP did not *sufficiently* provide for inclusion. The school district appealed to the U.S. Court of Appeals, Eleventh Circuit. The appellate court noted that the IDEA mandates that a student with a disability be educated in the general education classroom unless such education cannot be achieved satisfactorily with the use of supplemental aids and services. The school district had failed to consider an IEP that would allow the child to remain in the general education kindergarten with supplemental aids and services. Furthermore, the court determined that such a consideration should be made prior to and during the development of the IEP, not afterward. The court held that the school district failed to comply with the LRE mandate of the IDEA and ordered a new IEP (*Greer v. Rome City Sch. Dist.*, 1991).

In another case involving a student with Down syndrome, a New Jersey school district placed the student in a segregated special education class. As a result of a mediated settlement with the student's parents, the school district agreed to half-day placement in a general education classroom and half day in a special education program. The student exhibited behavior problems in the general education program. A second due process hearing resulted in a decision favorable to the school district. Based on a finding by the hearing officer that the student's disruptive behavior prevented him from obtaining any meaningful educational benefit in a general education class, a special education placement was upheld. The student's parents appealed the hearing officer's decision to the U.S. District Court in New Jersey, which reversed the hearing officer's decision. The school board appealed to the U.S. Court of Appeals, Third Circuit. The court of appeals observed that the student could be educated in a general education classroom with appropriate supplementary aids and services. Integrating the student into a general education classroom would enable him to improve his social skills by interacting with nondisabled students. The school district had not taken *meaningful* steps to integrate the student into a general education class and the student's alleged behavior problems may have been exacerbated by the school district's failure to provide appropriate aids and services. The district court's decision was affirmed by the appeals court *(Oberti v.Bd. of Educ. of the Borough of Clementon School Dist.,* 1993).

In a New York school, a student with mental disabilities attended the same kindergarten class for 3 consecutive years. The student was eventually classified mentally retarded and placed in a special education class. In this placement, the student's speech therapy program was continued and mainstreaming was limited to music and gym classes. The parents expressed dissatisfaction with the special education placements. They complained about the lack of any special education services to assist their daughter with integration into general education classrooms. The school district argued that the student's behavior deteriorated in her mainstream classes. An impartial hearing officer determined that the student had been appropriately classified but remanded the matter to the child study team to prepare a new IEP. The hearing officer later affirmed the modified IEP even though mainstreaming was only provided in the art, music and gym classes. The decision was confirmed by the state commissioner of education and the parents appealed to the U.S. District Court for the Northern District of New York. The court determined that the appropriate analysis to apply in inclusion cases was set forth in *Daniel R. v. State Board of Educ.* (1989). According to that case, it must first be determined whether satisfactory instruction of a student with a disability can take place in a general education classroom with the use of supplemental aids and services. Next, it must be determined whether the school has mainstreamed the student to the maximum extent appropriate. The school district bore the burden of showing that its proposed placement complied with the IDEA's presumption in favor of the least restrictive placement. In this case, the student had *not received an opportunity* to show that she could be included because the district had never provided *sufficient* supplemental aids and services. The relevant inquiry was whether the student could achieve IEP goals in a general education classroom with assistance of appropriate aids and services. The case was remanded to the special education committee of the school district with instructions to develop an IEP in compliance with the least restrictive environment requirement *(Mavis v. Sobol.,* 1993).

The parent of a 7 year-old student with severe physical and mental disabilities appealed a hearing officer's decision that affirmed the district's recommendation to place the student in a self-contained program. The student had been placed in a general education kindergarten, with accommodations, during the previous school year but the district's placement team determined that a more restrictive environment was required in the current school year in order to address the student's IEP goals and objectives. The parent maintained that her daughter would continue to benefit from general education placement, if provided with adequate supplementary aids and services. The court first determined that the burden of proof in this case was on the district, as the party seeking to have the student removed from the general education classroom. Based on the factors enunciated in the *Holland* (1994) case, the court concluded that the *district failed to demonstrate* that the student could not be satisfactorily educated in a general education setting. In particular, the district failed to show that the self-contained program would enhance the student's education to any significant degree, that the student's IEP goals and objectives could not be implemented in the general education classroom without supplementary aids and services, that the implementation of these goals and objectives in the general education classroom would have an adverse effect on the other students, or that the costs of the supplementary aids and services necessary to educate the student in the general education classroom would impair the district's ability to educate other students to whom the obligation was owed. Accordingly, the court ordered the district to educate the student in the general education classroom with appropriate supplementary aids and services for the duration of the current school year (*Statum v. Birmingham Public Schools Board of Education*, 1993).

LATER 1990s CASES

More Concern About Academic Benefits and Behavior Problems

Recent cases illustrate that the least restrictive environment can differ for two students who have the same classification. This is seen in two recent district court decisions involving students with autism. The student in the first case was a 10 year-old with severe autism and profound mental retardation. For this student, the court ruled that a self-contained, special education classroom with opportunities for mainstreaming in physical education, recess, lunch, and assemblies constituted the LRE (*Student v. Somerset County Board of Educ.*, 1996). In contrast, the student in the second case was 11 years old and his autism was not accompanied by any mental retardation. The court ruled that the LRE was a general education classroom with a one-to-one aide and a properly adapted curriculum (*Hartmann by Hartmann by Loudoun County Bd. of Educ.*, 1996).

A closer examination of the facts in these cases partially explains the differences in the outcomes of the decisions. Although the student in *Somerset* (1996) had never actually been placed in a general education classroom, the court found sufficient evidence that he would not benefit there based on the student's prior mainstreaming experience in nonacademic activities. In applying the Holland four-factor test, the court found that academically the student's educational goals would be significantly different from the students in the general education class. He required constant supervision, had a short attention span, did not socialize or model his behavior after others, exhibited no sense of danger, and was not toilet trained. Moreover, his behavior, which included a tendency to run away from the classroom and inappropriate laughing and squealing for extended periods of time, would have a disruptive effect on the general education classroom environment.

In contrast, significant consideration that supported the general education placement in *Loudoun County* (1996) included evidence that the child had a fairly high level of mental acuity, interacted with others, and did not pose any significant behavior problems. In a general education classroom in a neighboring district where his parents enrolled him after they became dissatisfied with their district's position on inclusion, he solved arithmetic problems and identified coins and the homes of presidents. Additionally, the court cited several instances of the school district's shortcomings. Although the district did attempt to include the student in the fourth grade, its efforts tapered off in the midst of the school year evidenced by personnel changes and the discontinuation of supplementary consulting services by inclusion experts. Moreover, the student made minimal noise in the classroom but no behavior management plan was developed for the student until late in the school year. If properly managed, the court found that the student would be no more disruptive than his classmates. However this case was reversed by the Fourth Circuit Court of Appeals (1997). In a complete break from earlier inclusion cases emphasizing the social benefits of inclusion the appellate court held "Any such benefits, cannot outweigh his failure to progress academically in the regular classroom. The mainstreaming provision represents recognitive of the value of having disabled children interact with non-handicapped students. The fact that the provision only creates a presumptive, however, reflects a congressional judgment that receipt of such social benefits is ultimately a good subordinate to the requirement that disabled children receive educational benefits." (p.166). The circuit court found that the district court erred when it failed to give due weight to previous administrative proceedings and testimony.

Two cases involving the placement of 14 year-olds with profound mental retardation resulted in similar outcomes. In *Kari H. v. Franklin Special Sch. Dist.* (1995), the LRE for a 14 year-old with Cri du Chay syndrome, a form of severe mental retardation characterized by persistent catlike sounds, was a placement in a comprehensive developmental special education classroom with mainstreaming in nonacademic areas. Any gains the student might obtain in a fully inclusive general education placement were deemed marginal. The student had a far better chance to learn in a setting where all the students and the teacher could communicate with her in sign language. In addition, her habits of handclapping, making loud noises, and walking around the classroom were considered disruptive to the general education classroom.

Similarly, in *Hudson by Hudson v. Bloomfield Hills Public Sch.* (1995), the LRE for a 14 year-old student classified as trainable mentally retarded was a special education classroom with partial mainstreaming delivered in a district's middle school program. Testimony revealed that during the time this student spent in a general seventh-grade classroom, she worked in isolation and was completely reliant on her personal aide who provided her with her own first- or second-grade level instructional program. The court ruled that no amount of supplementary aids and services would meet the student's needs in the general education setting. Also, the student's educational objectives included development of independent living skills as well as social skills, and extensive evidence from prior inclusive placements demonstrated that the student could not make any progress toward those objectives in the general education class. Together, these two cases stand for the proposition that, as students with severe disabilities enter the junior and senior high-school years, the academic benefits available in a placement outweigh the social benefits that were given more weight when the student was younger and resulted in a general education classroom placement.

The LRE for a 13 year-old student with moderate to severe mental disabilities, hydrocephalus, communication disorder, a seizure disorder, cerebral palsy, and visual deficits was a special education classroom, not the general education classroom his parents requested *D.F. v. Western Sch. Corp.* (1996). According to the court, the student would not benefit academically from a general education placement and would not be able to meet his IEP goals in a general education classroom. Through the years, the district had provided the student with a number of opportunities for mainstreaming including lunch, music, art and gym. The district considered the potentially negative effects of an inclusive placement and relied on the student's performance in these more limited mainstream settings. The student did not imitate the behavior of the more advanced students with disabilities nor did the interactions with nondisabled children produce any significant positive modeling. Also, the student repeatedly engaged in self-stimulating behavior and did not actively interact with other students.

In its 1992 Policy Guidance on the Education of Deaf Students, the Department of Education (1992) stated that the unique needs of this group may require a placement other than a general education classroom. In *Poolaw v. Bishop* (1995), this suggestion was put to the test. A residential placement constituted the least restrictive placement for the deaf student who was almost 13 years old and could barely read or write. Evidence documented that the student had a proven track record of failure in inclusive settings over a period of several years in other school districts. Describing the student's communication as primitive, the court became convinced that the student required intensive instruction in American Sign Language (ASL), an educational program which was only available at the residential school. The Ninth Circuit Court shared valuable guidance on the parameters of the IDEA's LRE requirements for all types of disabilities when it stated:

> In some cases, such as where the child's handicap is particularly severe, it will be impossible to provide any meaningful education to a student in an integrated environment. In these situations, general education classroom placement would be inappropriate and educators may recommend placing the student in a special education environment. (p. 400)

Learning Disabilities Cases

The LRE for students with learning disabilities, a subject on which relatively little guidance existed before, was the focus of several recent decisions. In all five cases, parents sought reimbursement for private schools specializing in learning disabilities, premising their cases on a least restrictive placement argument. Three of the courts found that the public school setting complied with the LRE, although the profile of acceptable educational programs in those cases ranged from placement in a special education classroom on a full-time basis to regular education with special education components such as resource room instruction and other services (*S. D. by J. D. v. Independent Sch. Dist. No.283, 1996; Evans v. Board of Educ. of Rhinebeck Cent. Sch . Dist.,* 1996; *Mather v. Hartford Sch. Dist.,* 1996).

The remaining two cases arrived at the opposite result, finding that the LRE was met in a private school. *The Ft. Zumwalt Sch. Dist. v. Missouri State Bd. of Educ.,* (1996) case exhibits what is probably the most unusual interpretation of the LRE placement requirement yet, and one that runs starkly counter to the generally accepted thought on the issue. In awarding parents 2 years' reimbursement at a private school for learning disabilities, the court reasoned that the facility provided the completely segregated environment that the student required. According to the court, the district's mainstreaming program, which combined resource room components with general education, was inappropriate for the elementary school student, as the student's "self-esteem and behavior were aggravated by his associations with students from whom he felt different and that consequently, his academic progress was hindered" (p. 224). To date, the basic premise underlying inclusion has been that self-esteem has the greatest chance to flourish when students with disabilities receive optimal opportunities for interaction with nondisabled students. Similarly, a court found that a program of inclusion with a study hall in the resource room was too complex and fast-paced for a ninth-grade student with a serious learning disability. The parents earned an award of more than $80,000 to cover 3 years of expenses at a residential placement where they unilaterally placed the child *(Briere by Brown v. Fair Haven Grade Sch. Dist.,* 1996).

But more recently, *in Jonathan G. v. Lower Merion School District* (1997) the court ruled in favor of the school district. In this case the parents were opposed to their LD son's seventh-grade placement in a general education class because " he was very anxious to measure up to his peers, he often made comments indicating that he thought he was dumb because special accommodations were made for him in the classroom, and that he spent inordinate amounts of time completing his homework assignments and studying for tests" (p. 16). The district court found that he was benefiting from instruction in the general education class and that accommodations could be made to address his parents' concerns (e.g., counseling).

On the continuum of placements, private placements are more restrictive than public placements. However, *Ft. Zumwalt* (1996) and *Briere* (1996) illustrate a fundamental concept of special education law where the FAPE and LRE requirements conflict, FAPE overrides LRE. In both cases, the districts' placements were deemed educationally inappropriate. Likely, the results in these cases have more to do with FAPE than LRE, and the courts' findings that the students did not receive any educational benefit in the public placements seem to be the pivotal factor in their outcomes.

The Ninth Circuit further observed that the IDEA'S preference for mainstreaming is not an "absolute commandment."

Just as the courts have recognized that serious disabilities may warrant a special education placement, they have likewise held that the mild to moderate disabilities can be accommodated in the general education classroom. Where the parents of a high school student with attention deficit hyperactivity disorder sought tuition reimbursement for a unilateral placement at a private school for students with learning disabilities on the basis of an LRE argument, their request was flatly rejected. The court ruled that the student's disability was not so severe as to require a segregated placement and the student could be adequately served in the public school system (*Monticello Sch. Dist. No. 25 v. Illinois State Board of Educ.*, (1995).

The negative effects that a student with a disability can have on the general education environment are given serious weight in the courts. This consideration becomes particularly relevant when a student's disabilities manifest themselves in violent or disruptive behavior. When the student's misbehavior poses a threat to the general welfare of the classroom environment, it can provide the basis for removal. This scenario was played out in a case in which a 15 year-old repeatedly engaged in violent outbursts, the use of profanity, vandalization of school property and harassment of other students in a learning disabled (LD) classroom. The student had problems following school rules and showed an inability to maintain appropriate relationships with peers and teachers. The assignment of a one-to-one aide in the student's LD classroom did not improve the student's behavior. Given his maladaptive behavior, the court agreed that the student was more properly classified as seriously emotionally disturbed and recommended placement in another school district that offered an emotional support program *Dallas Sch. Dist. v. Richard C.*, 1996).

CASES ON SYSTEMIC REFORM

A major barrier to the inclusion of students with disabilities in general education classes is the lack of preparation among general education teachers. School districts have been slow to provide inservice training experiences that would enable general educators to meet the instructional needs of students with disabilities. Consequently, lacking training, general educators are often reluctant to have students with disabilities placed in their classes.

A class action suit, *Gaskin v. Commonwealth of Pennsylvania*, (1995) now before a federal court for the Eastern District of Pennsylvania addresses this problem. The plaintiffs, students with various disabilities and their parents, argue that the Pennsylvania Department of Education (PDE) is in violation of the IDEA for failure to (a) provide a comprehensive plan of personnel development, (b) to adopt promising educational practices and materials, (c) provide each student with a disability an appropriate educational program that is reasonably calculated to confer real educational benefits, and (d) educate students with disabilities to the maximum extent appropriate with students who do not have disabilities.

The plaintiffs further argued that the PDE has failed to assure that local school districts provide "the whole range" of supplementary aids and services for students with disabilities in general classes and personnel are not trained to provide those services adequately. Consequently, students with disabilities remain in segregated settings and those that are integrated are denied specially designed instruction, modification of the regular curriculum, and other supplementary aids and services they need to receive an appropriate education.

The 1990 reauthorization of the IDEA required the PDE to assure that each local educational agency develop and implement a plan for comprehensive personnel development. Such plans must ensure that all personnel receive the training necessary to fulfill the purposes of the IDEA, including the integration of students with disabilities in general education classes. This requirement is even more strongly stated in the 1997 reauthorization. The plaintiffs argued that the PDE has failed to discharge its duty under the IDEA to assure that each local education agency in Pennsylvania develops and implements a plan for comprehensive personnel development.

The plaintiffs are seeking injunctive relief in the form of an order to PDE to assure that school district personnel are adequately trained to educate students with disabilities in general education classes and to assure that students with disabilities have access, to the maximum extent possible, to supplementary aids and services in general classrooms.

Similar court cases pending in Los *Angeles (Chanda Smith v. Los Angeles United Sch. Dist.,* (1991) and Boston are challenging the state educational system's failure to provide staff development activities to further the inclusion of students with disabilities in general education settings as required by federal law. The 1997 reauthorization of the IDEA emphasizes this requirement when it states that state plans must show,

> how the State will address the identified needs of in-service and pre-service preparation to ensure that all personnel who work with children with disabilities (including both professional and paraprofessional personnel who provide special education, general education, related services, or early intervention services), have skills and knowledge necessary to meet the needs of children with disabilities. . . (P.L.105–17, 111 Stat. 127).

SUMMARY

A number of inclusion cases decided in the early 1990s resulted in the placement of students with disabilities in general education classes. Typically, the plaintiffs in these cases were elementary school-age students with severe disabilities. And their parents who brought these cases were more concerned with their children receiving the social benefits of general education placement than the academic benefits of the district's proposed special education placement. More recent cases involving students with disabilities who are disruptive and older have resulted in placements that are more restrictive (e.g., special classes). In addition, several class action lawsuits have been brought against state departments of education for their failure to develop comprehensive programs of personnel development to prepare professionals to work with students with disabilities in inclusive settings.

REFERENCES

Board of Education of the Hendrick Hudson Central School District v. Rowley, 458 U. S. 176 (1982).
Brier by Brown v. Fair Haven Grade Sch. Dist. 25 IDELR 805 (C. D. Ill. 1996).
Chanda Smith v. Los Angeles United Sch. Dist., 93-7044 (Cir. 1991).
D. F. v. Western Sch. Corp. 23 IDELR 1121 (S. D. Ind. 1996); 921 F. Supp.
Dallas Sch. Dist. v. Richard C., 24 IDELR 241 (Pa. Commw. Ct. 1996).
Daniel R. v. State Board of Educ., 874 F. 2d 1036 (5th Cir. 1989).
Department of Education, 1992 Policy Guidance on the Education of Deaf Students, 19 IDELR 463.
Evans v. Board of Educ. of Rhinebeck Cent. Sch. Dist. 24 IDELR 338 (S.D. N. Y. 1996).
Ft. Zumwalt Sch. Dist. v. Missouri State Bd. of Educ., 24 IDELR222 (E. D. Mo. 1996).
Gaskin v. Commonwealth of Pennsylvania, 23 IDELR 61 (Pa. 1995).
Greer v. Rome City Sch. Dist., 905 F.2d 688 (11th Cir. 1991).
Hartman by Hartman by Loudoun Cty. Bd. of Educ., 24 IDELR 1171 (E. D. Va. 1996); 26 IDELR 167
      (4th Cir.1997).
Hudson by Hudson v. Bloomfield Hills Public Sch, 23 IDELR 613 (E. D. Mich. 1995).
Jonathan G. v Lower Merion School District, 955 F. Supp.413 (E. D. Pa. 1997).
Kari H. v Franklin Special Sch. Dist., 23 IDELR 538 (M. D. Tenn.) (1995).
Lachman v. Illinois State Board of Educ., 852 F.2d 290 (7th Cir. 1988).
Mather v. Hartford Sch. Dist. 24 IDELR 231 (D VT. 1996).
Mavis v. Sobel, 839 F. Supp. 968 (N. D. N. Y. 1993).
Monticello Sch. Dist. No. 25 v. Illinois State Board of Educ. 23 IDELR 805 (C. D. Ill. 1995).
Murphyboro v. Illinois State Board of Educ., 41 F. 3d 1162 (7th Cir., 1994).
Oberti v. Bd. of Educ. of the Borough of Clementon School Dist., 995 F.2d 1204 (3d.) (1993).
Poolaw v. Bishop, 23 IDELR 406 (9th Cir. 1995).
S. D. by J. D. v. Independent Sch. Dist. No. 283, 24 IDELR 375 (8th Cir. 1996).
Sacremento City Unif. School District v. Rachel Holland, 14 F.2d 1398 (9th Cir. 1994).
Statum v. Birmingham Public Schools Board of Educ., 20 IDELR 435 (1993).
Student v. Somerset County Board of Educ., 24 IDELR 743 (D. Md. 1996).

3

Changing Tactics: Embedding Inclusion Reforms within General Education Restructuring Efforts

Dianne L. Ferguson
University of Oregon

For more than two decades, special educators in various places of the globe have been pursuing reforms in the design and delivery of special education services and supports (Dalmau, Hatton, & Spurway, 1991; Fullan, 1991; Fullwood, 1990; Gartner & Lipsky, 1987; O'Hanlon, 1995). We have, or have had, mainstreaming, integration, reverse mainstreaming, inclusion, inclusive schooling, inclusive schools, and schools for all. Certainly, these various slogans have meant different things in different countries at different times, and different things over time within single countries. Some initiatives have relied on civil rights discourse to argue against separate, segregated, or variously differentiated forms of schooling. Other reforms have focused more on how to incorporate specially designed, technically different, but needed teaching practices into general education settings and activities. Some reforms emphasized the needs of students with relatively mild but troublesome learning differences; others emphasized the needs of students with significant, even quite severe and multiple disabilities.

Despite differences in meaning and focus, a common vision of what these variously named reforms might mean is clearly emerging. In different ways, some countries have reached the conclusion that people with disabilities have a natural and rightful place in our societies. Schools, as one part of that society, should mirror this broader commitment. Of course, it is the resultant discussions, dilemmas, challenges, and questions that have occupied educators ever since, as they have tried to understand not just what such a commitment might mean, but how to make it happen.

After years of research and effort in pursuit of a greater understanding of inclusion, there is now growing certainty among some educators that inclusive reforms in special education must be pursued in terms of the general education restructuring and improvement (Berres, Ferguson, Knoblock, & Woods, 1996;

NASBE 1990; Pearman, Huang, Barnhart, & Mellblom, 1992; Sailor & Skrtic, 1995; Skrtic, 1995; Tetler, 1995). Indeed, some have argued that unless this merging of efforts occurs, special education reforms will only achieve partial success at best and may even end up reinforcing and maintaining the very assumptions and practices that the reforms seek to change.

The question of what needs to be different in schools seems much larger than inclusion, special educators, or students with disabilities. It is about what schooling should be and could accomplish. As Eisner (1991) put it, the question is "What really counts in schools?" Answering Eisner's question in the day to day life of schooling involves consideration of much more than students with disabilities and special educators.

General educators, too, are realizing that the efforts of renewal and reform that seemed adequate to resolve the educational problems of the past will simply not suffice. Doing better and more efficient schooling work (renewal) or changing existing procedures, rules, and requirements to accommodate new circumstances (reform) will not quiet the need or calls for changes as we approach the next millennium. Instead, educators now argue, schools must begin to engage in the activities that will change the fundamental assumptions, practices and relationships, both within the organization, and between the organization and the outside world, in ways that lead to improved student learning outcomes (Asuto et al., 1994; Conley, 1991; Elmore, 1996). Although many of these fundamental assumptions helped to create the very separateness special education reforms seek to diminish, it is just such fundamental changes that might realize the vision of inclusion.

Yet, in a recent review, Cohen (1995) found "little evidence of direct and powerful links between policy and practice" (p. 11). Schools continue to struggle with an increasing diversity of students who challenge the common curriculum and ability-grouping practices that have been long dominant throughout the system. At the same time, advancements in theories and practices of teaching and learning are leading to a new focus on students' understanding and use of their learning rather than recall of facts or isolated skills. Even more challenging, students must demonstrate use or performance of their learning. How do teachers respond to calls for a single higher standard of achievement? When those uses and performances might vary according to students' particular abilities, interests, and life purposes? In the face of such conflicting messages and challenges, school professionals are also facing rapid erosion of financial support and public respect. Not only are they being asked to "do more with less," but also they are blamed for being incompetent for not accomplishing such an impossible task.

ISSUES AND ACTIONS

As we are beginning to realize, changing schools is both a nonlinear and bi-directional task (Astuto et al., 1994; Clark & Astuto, 1994; Fullan, 1994, 1996). "Top–down" policy changes must be met by "bottom–up" changes in capacity, commitment, and coherence among teachers, students, and families if changes are to become more than superficial accommodations. At the same time, there is no single road map for achieving deeper change. Local events, resources, and personal dynamics combine to create a unique choreography of change for any particular school or district, characterized as much by stepping back as by stepping forward. Teachers and parents must become active co-constructors of new school communities, collaborating with one another, with students, and local community members (Berres, Ferguson, Knoblock, & Woods, 1996; Council of Administrators of Special Education (CASE), 1993; Cohen, 1995; Dalmau et al., 1991; Darling-Hammond, Ancess, & Falk, 1995; Ferguson, 1995). If fundamental change is to occur in teaching–learning for teachers and students, and the dual systems of special and general education merged into a unified system of all students, we must resolve three issues:

Issue 1 *How does special education become an integral part of public schooling? Experience and research have well elaborated the complexity of this issue. One of the most straightforward questions involves how to deliver the specialty and support services long associated with special education. Another involves whether such integration requires specialized personnel or personnel with various specialties. And perhaps most challenging is what to do with the current special educator complement who may not have the capacity to shift to new roles easily?

Issue 2 *How will higher education, various research organizations, educational labs, institutes, and other research organizations in both general and special education need to change? In the same way that relationships in school will need to change, our relationships in higher education and research must be different. Can we learn from each other or are the contingencies in such organizations incompatible with the very kind of cross pollination we are asking of school teachers? Are we asking the right questions, or do we need to refocus our efforts to arenas that are more directly responsive to the "definition of the situation" of people in schools?

Issue 3 *How should families, individual community members, community agencies, and businesses participate in large-scale school change? Many of our reforms have been slowed down, sometimes thwarted, by the families of the students our reforms seek to serve. It seems there is much room for improved communication and involvement with the families and communities in which we expect our students to use their learning. We could also consider the ways in which parents and other community members might contribute both knowledge and resources to school agendas.

This chapter summarizes what my research team and I have learned after 3 years of investigating these three issues in collaboration with schools in three rural districts in Oregon. Our involvement with the schools in the three districts have varied in time as well as tasks. Yet taken together, our efforts are documenting the ways in which schools are working to support the inclusion of students with disabilities along with the gradual restructuring that could result in the kinds of fundamental changes that will lead to better learning for students and teachers alike.

Legislation begun in 1987 and culminating in Oregon's Educational Act for the 21st Century (HB 3565) put Oregon in the forefront of the national calls for comprehensive school reform and restructuring with goals that meet and exceed those of Goals 2000. Hallmarks of the act include an emphasis on identifying high outcome-based standards for all students with grade-level benchmarks, performance-based assessments, common curricular aims, emphasis on essential learning skills, use of developmentally appropriate practices and mixed-age grouping at the elementary level, and a new focus on career development and practice leading to certificates of initial and advanced mastery at the secondary level.

A simultaneous statewide initiative called *supported education* called for local school districts to move toward a flexible and creative array of supportive education services to provide a free and appropriate public education (FAPE) to students with disabilities in general education classrooms. This initiative has been one of five major goals for special education since 1989. Currently, virtually all of the local and regional education service districts have responded by restructuring services to students with disabilities so that they are more fully included in the learning life of the school community. In fact, according to 1995 data, 72% of students with disabilities in Oregon are receiving their schooling in general education classrooms compared to 63% in 1991.

These dual agendas set the stage for our collaborative research agreements with schools and districts to help them blend these initiatives together. The specific opportunity afforded by the reforms was the requirement that all districts, and thereby schools, develop individual school profiles on which to base school improvement plans that would serve as templates for implementation of the various aspects of the comprehensive reforms. A strongly recommended strategy for implementing reforms was to pilot ideas using action research projects and then broadly disseminate successful ideas.

Our Reinventing Schools Research Project (Ferguson, Ferguson, Rivers & Droege, 1994; United States Department of Education [USDOE], H086D90011, 1996) targeted two strands of participatory research activity, each aiming toward a different level of the change effort. The first focused on developing collaborative research agreements with a small number of schools. Our thinking was that we could contribute to their schoolwide profiling and action research agendas and in so doing would learn a good deal about embedding inclusion goals into broader school restructuring goals. Our second strand focused on supporting the efforts of individual teachers through both continuing professional development and practitioner action research. Fig. 3.1 illustrates our activities across both strands by our evolving collaborative strategies that I then briefly summarize.

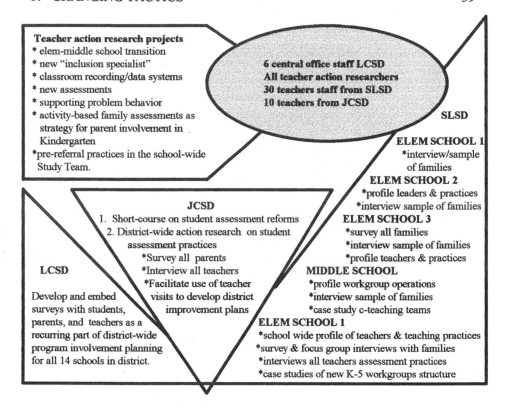

Teacher action research projects
* elem-middle school transition
* new "inclusion specialist"
* classroom recording/data systems
* new assessments
* supporting problem behavior
* activity-based family assessments as strategy for parent involvement in Kindergarten
*pre-referral practices in the school-wide Study Team.

6 central office staff LCSD
All teacher action researchers
30 teachers staff from SLSD
10 teachers from JCSD

SLSD

ELEM SCHOOL 1
*interview/sample of families

ELEM SCHOOL 2
*profile leaders & practices
*interview sample of families

JCSD
1. Short-course on student assessment reforms
2. District-wide action research on student assessment practices
   *Survey all parents
   *Interview all teachers
   *Facilitate use of teacher visits to develop district improvement plans

ELEM SCHOOL 3
*survey all families
*interview sample of families
*profile teachers & practices

MIDDLE SCHOOL
*profile workgroup operations
*interview sample of families
*case study c-teaching teams

LCSD

Develop and embed surveys with students, parents, and teachers as a recurring part of district-wide program involvement planning for all 14 schools in district.

ELEM SCHOOL 1
*school wide profile of teachers & teaching practices
*survey & focus group interviews with families
*interviews all teachers assessment practices
*case studies of new K-5 workgroups structure

FIG. 3.1 Collaborative Research & Professional Development Activities with Three Rural Districts

THREE PROCEDURAL STRATEGIES

Our collaborations have focused primarily on assisting the schools and districts to (a) develop the comprehensive information systems necessary for school improvement planning and action, (b) access needed professional development, and (c) support individual and collective action research efforts.

We have reported the details of our efforts and results elsewhere, although both our results and writing continue (Ferguson, 1995a, 1995b, 1996a, 1996b, Ferguson & Meyer, 1996; Ferguson & Ralph, 1996; Ferguson, Ralph, & Katul, in press).

School Information Systems

As we began negotiating research agreements, it was clear to us that the effort to work together as a whole school was a new challenge for most school faculties. Many individual teachers were experimenting with various aspects of reforms, all related to whole school change, but few efforts were really school reforms—

collective efforts. We also noticed that school improvement planning tended to rely on a relatively small amount of information about student achievement using standardized measures. These traditional measures of both student and school accomplishments satisfied few school personnel, yet along with teacher interests and preferences were the only sources of information guiding school improvement planning efforts. In response to this situation we sought to help schools develop and gradually institutionalize more comprehensive information systems on which to base their improvement planning.

Specifically, we helped schools develop and use qualitative-style surveys of parents, teachers, and students that were user friendly and generated rich information that could be summarized relatively easily with our help. We are continuing to embed the data analysis and summary systems in districts so as to minimize the need for outside collaborators for this step. In one district, for example, parent volunteers have entered the results of student surveys at each school. Staff in the district's central office produce both districtwide and school-specific reports that teams of teachers and administrators analyze and interpret. This is just one way in which parents in this district have become involved in school improvement efforts. Over time, these new roles may be expanded and shared with other community members who might bring computer, writing, planning, and other skills to the overall improvement efforts.

We also conducted in-depth interviews and observations in some schools to gather more information about practices and preferences of school faculty with regard to a variety of reforms. In several schools, we interviewed all school faculty and staff, sometimes multiple times, about their perspectives on school reform efforts, their assessments of the schools capacity for change, and their own personal interests in and contributions toward these efforts. We also spent time observing in each classroom as well as other more collective locations.

Once these profiling data were collected we faced the decision of how to report our findings. We knew that teachers had limited time and inclination for reading reports—that most common and ubiquitous of university products. At the same time, we wanted our reporting to serve as a catalyst for school improvement planning. In the end, we experimented with novel graphic presentation formats in order to improve the accessibility and heuristic nature of our research "reports" (Ferguson, 1996). Our presentations summarized information in ways that encouraged school faculty to create their own collective interpretations that could directly guide school priority setting and action planning.

Not all our efforts are finished. We are still working in and across schools to embed these broader systems of data collection in continuous improvement processes. Perhaps community collaborators and partner schools could assist in the data collection and summary functions required by this more comprehensive school profiling. The point is more that this strategy seems a necessary component of systemic change efforts and one often overlooked by schools and collaborators alike. For us, the information generated from these efforts contributed directly to the content in our professional development offerings, thus tying those efforts directly to empirically based school needs.

Continuing Professional Development

Well-educated and supported teachers have always been the backbone of school reform.   Yet all too often our previous educational reforms have underinvested in teachers (Cremin, 1965; Darling-Hammond, 1995).   Achieving teacher effectiveness, whether in general or special education, ultimately requires attention to more than the technical and content mastery so familiar to both fields of education.   There must also be a broadened definition of teacher roles that includes multitheoretical fluency, creative problem finding and problem solving, reflective and inquiry-based teaching, self-management, and ongoing professional growth (Baumgart & Ferguson, 1991; Goodlad, 1990; Grimmet & Erickson, 1988; Sarason, 1986; Schon, 1983). The dynamic nature of this process suggested to us that the traditional division of teacher education into preservice and inservice components is no longer viable, if it ever was (Ferguson & Ferguson, 1994; 1994b).

In response, we developed a set of professional development activities (Ferguson, & Ferguson, 1992; Ferguson & Ferguson, 1994). The most comprehensive offering has been a four-course sequence that occurred once a week through the academic year, concluding with a 2-week intensive course in June.   Since the Fall of 1992, roughly 250 teachers and other school staff have participated in this course sequence; around 35 to 40 of these participants have been from the districts with which we have also pursued collaborative research. An important component of our professional development efforts has been to achieve as much diversity as possible in our participants.   For example, currently we have 8 graduate students preparing for initial licensure in special education, 13 general educators, 15 special educators, 6 substitute teachers, 4 educational assistants, 4 administrators or district consultants, 2 adult service professionals, and 2 family–school board members.

In two of the districts with which we have collaborated, we have also provided shorter courses on student assessment reforms. These short courses involved five sessions of 2 hours each spread over a 10-week period.   At the end of each short course, participants *peer-taught* the faculty in their own buildings usually in a two-to-three-session format spread over 3 to 5 weeks.

Teaching courses is certainly the currency of universities.   In these instances, however, the agendas and district teachers changed our teaching practice. Over time, we redesigned our use of readings (fewer readings explored in more depth), shifted from making assignments to suggesting a menu of tasks from which students could choose those that best matched their professional development agendas and we adopted more authentic assessments. At first our use of scoring guides and various forms of self- and peer-assessment was difficult for teachers used to "being graded," but eventually the use of assessment practices that aligned with what teachers were demanding of their own students became an advantage for both of us. The effort to use the practices we sought to teach not only made our professional development offerings more accessible but contributed to our increasingly collaborative relations with schools.

Individual and Collective Action Research

Our final strategy for collaborating with the school improvement efforts are three targeted districts involved working with individual teachers to use an action research approach to implementing reforms in their own practice. All of the teachers involved have also participated in the year-long professional development course sequence, and in most cases, their action research efforts targeted using some idea, tool, or approach gleaned from that professional development. In this way the content of the professional development efforts were validated through the individual teacher action research projects.

In Spring, 1997, Junction City School District (JCSD) supported a districtwide action research effort to better inform all teachers about innovative teaching and student assessment practices. Over a period of 2 months, we provided a process for teachers to document and analyze information collected during teacher visits to other schools in preparation for more specific recommendations for district resources allocation to support district improvement targets.

FOCUSING CHANGE IN THREE ACTION ARENAS

Unfortunately, and certainly unintentionally, much of the professional and popular literature about inclusion has focused attention on "all students," which is fast becoming special education advocacy code for trying to ensure the rights of still excluded learners. Yet for the values embedded in the notion of inclusion to ever be obtained in our schools, we must not be misdirected to focus just on all students. Rather, we must enlarge our perspective to all teachers, all curricular reforms, all teaching reforms, all support personnel, all policies, all strategies for student assessment, and so on.

Our experiences with the schools, districts, and teachers involved in our research and professional development efforts suggest that achieving this larger perspective, as well as durable change in the core of educational practice, will involve activity in three action arenas. Indeed, nearly all the specific work in our collaborative research agreements has focused within one or more of these arenas where action and attention is shifting from (a) a focus on teaching to a focus on learning, (b) a reliance on individual teacher practice to group practice, and (c) an effort to deliver service to one of "providing learner supports."

From a Focus on Teaching to a Focus on Learning

Historically, we have cared most about what students know. Teachers must cover content, making sure that as many students as possible remember it all. We have assured ourselves that our schools are doing well by the scores students achieve on tests that measure their acquisition of this content—at least until the test is over. Much teacher work involved introducing new material, giving students various opportunities to practice remembering that content, and assuring all of us of their success by frequently testing memory and mastery in preparation for the official achievement assessments.

The confluence of demands on schools as we move toward the largely unknown challenges of the next century is slowly shifting educators' focus away from what gets taught to what gets learned, and used. Elementary and secondary teachers in all the schools in which we have been working are experimenting with new curricular and teaching approaches that emphasize students' mastery, not just of facts and content, but also of essential thinking skills like problem-solving, analysis, collaboration, and experimentation. Rather than measuring what students have remembered about what we have taught, educators are as interested in how students can demonstrate that they understand and can use whatever they have learned in school and in their various pursuits outside of school.

Many promising curricular and instructional approaches have emerged in general education. Some teachers, for example, design learning unique to each student through the logic of multiple intelligences and learning styles as well as various forms of direct skill teaching.   The technology of brain imaging and related neurological research is supporting a wide range of long-used teaching practice and encouraging the development of new ones (e.g., Sylwester, 1995). Learning is increasingly active, requiring students not just to listen, but to learn by doing. Teachers are turning to projects, exhibitions, portfolios, along with other kinds of curriculum-based information and measurement strategies, to learn what students have learned and can do with their learning (e.g., Darling-Hammond, Ancess, & Falk, 1995; Fogarty, 1995; Harmin, 1994; Valencia, Hiebert, & Afflerbach, 1994). The increasing availability of the Internet offers students an opportunity to access many forms of primary data in ways that are flexible, nonlinear, and responsive to individual student interests and approaches to learning.

The values and logic behind these (and other) approaches can be extremely powerful when extended to all kinds of diverse learners, including special education labeled students. Nevertheless, this is also an area of schooling where the "cross-pollination" between general and special educators has yet to occur very thoroughly. For example, special educators have used activity-based assessment, individually tailored curriculum, and locally referenced, community-based instruction for some time now. They created these approaches precisely because their concern was to use time well for students who might find learning difficult and labor intensive. Directly teaching students in ways that emphasized how they used their learning not only saved valuable time, but for some students, was the only way for them to really appreciate their need to learn. For their part, general educators working with innovative designs of curriculum and teaching stretch their application to only part of the diverse students in schools today. Special education students generally fall outside the pale of such innovations in the minds of most general educators (and special educators familiar with them) even when the ideas and techniques would actually enrich and enable the learning of students with disabilities.

A major stumbling block in the synthesis of approaches that have emerged from both general and special education has been the documentation and reporting of student learning, both because standard grading and achievement measurement practices uncomfortably fit the new curriculum strategies, as well as because annually written Individual Educational Program (IEP) goals and objectives rarely reflect or document all students actually learn in general education contexts.

Standards? or Standardization?

There is great confusion among teachers about the role of higher national standards for learning and the incorporation of diverse learning agendas and accomplishments (Gagnon, 1995; McLaughlin, 1995; Oregon Department of Education Performance Standards, 1996; U. S. Department of Education, Special Education Programs, 1996). Does *standard* mean standardization in the sense of every student accomplishing exactly the same thing to the same picture of mastery, performance, or other measurement? If so, how can any standard accommodate diverse students—especially students with disabilities? If the call for higher national standards means that children really excel—push themselves to do, know, understand just a little more than they thought they could—then how can we compare the achievement of high standards from one student to the next? Never mind, from one school, one district, and one state to the next.

Our work with schools suggests that the entire standards discussion is confusing the requirements of program evaluation (i.e., how well are our schools helping students collectively achieve our articulated standards of learning accomplishment?) with teacher, student, and parent needs for individual student evaluation--how is Sarah accomplishing our articulated standards of learning accomplishment? And how does that make sense for her? Within any group of students, learning accomplishment for some proportion of the group will not necessarily look or be exactly the same as for others in the group. In fact, it would be very surprising if there were not several different patterns of accomplishment in any group of students.

Finding a way to legitimate that some students in any group can accomplish a standard in different ways is at the heart of the standards dilemma. If *accomplishment* can mean different things for different students—certainly a logical outcome of the individually tailored curriculum and teaching practices being encouraged—then the various student accomplishments are difficult to "add up" in any straightforward way. Yet adding up accomplishments against a single defined standard is the essential requirement of program assessment. If everyone is achieving the standards in different ways, how can we know how well our schools are doing collectively?

This dilemma is possible to resolve if the requirements of program assessment are separated from the requirements of student assessment. Interestingly, parents interviewed and surveyed across one district and several other schools in our projects have indicated that the most informative ways for them to learn about their child's learning is through parent–teacher conferences, personal contact with teachers and other school personnel and seeing their children use their learning in their day-to-day lives. Reports, grades, and testing follow, in order of importance and usefulness. Others (e.g., Shepard & Bliem, 1995) investigating parent's preferences for information are also finding that traditional measures are viewed as less informative than some of the emerging performance-based assessments that focus more on individual student growth than acquisition of some standard.

It appears that every student and parent should receive individual feedback about how well the student is learning, how much growth the student has accomplished during some period of time, and how his or her accomplishments compare to the national or community standard established for our students as a group. However, discretion must be possible in letting any individual student know how he or she is doing compared to others. There is no safety in numbers when your own individual achievement is compared. Teachers and parents should have the discretion to filter the comparative message for individual students in ways that encourage and enable interest and effort rather than discourage and disable it. Without interest and effort, learning is shallowly compulsory and soon divorced from use and pursuit.

At the same time, all students' various accomplishments can be summarized in individually anonymous ways to answer the question of how any particular school is achieving whatever the relevant agreed on standard for the students is collectively. In this way, the needs of program assessment and comparison can be met, while leaving the revelations of any particular student's accomplishment in the hands of teachers and parents—surely the best suited to decide. Those students in any group who do not achieve to some collective benchmark might have very good reasons for not doing so while still achieving the more general standard of excellent achievement in a particular area of focus, whether a common curriculum goal, an essential skill, or a learning outcome that emphasizes integration and use of learning in novel ways and situations. The interpretation of the meaning of accomplishment for individual students should rest with those most intimate with the student's learning. An accomplishment rate of 60% to 80% for any group of students on any collective benchmark would likely tell a school that they are teaching everyone well, and that 20% to 40% of their students are accomplishing the benchmark in unique ways (Reynolds, Zetlin, & Wang, 1993). As in all good program assessment, the appropriateness of the collective data is best judged and used by those closest to the operation of the program. It is the teachers, staff, and families that can best determine how the range of results reflects the students with whom they work or whether the collective results should encourage revision of curriculum and teaching practices.

Like changes in curriculum, this shift in focus on student learning and accomplishments will also require restructured teacher planning, new assessment strategies, and less reliance on proscribed curricula. But achieving such changes requires working in two additional arenas.

From Individual to Group Practice

Our current system has created teachers with different knowledge and information that is differently legitimated. General educators sometimes know some important things about the learners with disabilities integrated into their classrooms, but their status as general educators makes that knowledge automatically suspect and illegitimate in the face of the official knowledge possessed by special educators whose labels matched those of the student's. Even though general educators often spend more time observing and interacting with labeled students integrated in their classrooms, their presumed proper role and responsibility is to accept and implement the special educator's expertise as the system's approved specialist in teaching and learning for students with labels. As Sarason (1990) viewed the situation:

School personnel are graduates of our colleges and universities. It is there that they learn there are at least two types of human beings, and if you choose to work with one of them you render yourself legally and conceptually incompetent to work with others. (p. 258)

Our research demonstrates that these assumptions do not hold up in practice, but more importantly, they can easily get in the way of effective learning for students with disabilities (Ferguson, 1996b; Ferguson, Ralph, & Katul, in press; Ferguson & Meyer, 1996; Ferguson, Ralph, Katul, & Cameron, 1997). The nearly 100-year history of sorting and separating both students and teachers has resulted in very little common ground. General and special educators know a few of the same things about schools, teaching, and learning, but most of the knowledge and skills they rely on to fulfill their professional responsibilities seem so unique—even mysterious—that sometimes they must feel as if they are barely in the same profession. Legitimating one teacher's knowledge over another is an artifact of our history that is just as insupportable as creating the separations in the first place. It seems clear to me that rethinking our approach to inclusion as but one dimension of a broader general education restructuring must have as one of its goals to increase the common ground of knowledge and skills between general and special educators.

Having said that, it should be stated that I am not arguing for all educators to become "generalists" or "super teachers" who are presumed to possess all the skills and information needed to serve the learning of all students. I think it very unlikely that anyone could possibly achieve such mastery and competence. Rather, instead of assigning only one teacher to a classroom of 20 or more learners, or to a content area with instructional responsibility for 150 to 250 students, groups of teachers should be collectively responsible for groups of diverse learners. Only through group practice will educators be able to combine their talents and information and work together to meet the demands of student diversity in ways that retain the benefits and overcome the limits of past practice.

These groups of teachers can bring to the task both a common store of knowledge and skills, but also different areas of specialty. In order to achieve a shift from individual to group teaching practice, we must build on the current collaboration initiatives among educational professionals in two ways. If collaboration means anything at all, surely it means that two or more people create an outcome for a student that no individual could have created alone. Group practice creates just such an ongoing, dynamic context, helping educators with varying abilities to contribute to the kind of synergy necessary for effective collaboration.

Replace Restrictive Assignments With Shared Assignments

Current teacher licensure practices tend to be restrictive, limiting the students an educator can teach to specific categories. Of course, some of these categories are broader than others, ranging from specific disabilities (LD or MR certifications for learning disabilities and mental retardation, respectively) to "levels" of students (mild, severe) to disability types and particular ages (secondary severe, or elementary LD). One key feature of mixed-ability group teaching practice, particularly as we await changes in certification requirements to reflect the restructuring of schools, is that teachers share working with all children and youth as part of a team, regardless of their formal preparation or the labels on their certification. This step seems critical because it is one of the most efficient ways for teachers more narrowly educated to cross-pollinate, quickly increasing the size of their common ground. More importantly, shared assignments create the contexts in which genuine collaboration can occur.

We have encountered a number of schools pursuing group practice through shared assignments. A common first step among special educators is to assign various special education support staff within a building—resource room teacher, speech/language specialist, Title 1 teacher, previous self-contained classroom teacher—to a smaller number of classrooms where they can be responsible for students with all the labels they had each separately served across a much larger number of classrooms. Although the previous resource room teacher may feel unprepared to assist the student with significant multiple disabilities, learning how to gather that information from colleagues with different specialties is a step on the way to more complete group practice with general educators.

Other schools we know are beginning to create group practice work groups that include some number of general educators as well as one or more special educators and other certified or classified support staff. Just this year, one of the

South Lane School District (SLSD) elementary schools reorganized into three smaller "vertical" communities. Each community includes classroom teachers from kindergarten to Grade 5 as well as a special educator and a number of classroom assistants previously assigned either to special education or Title 1. These new groups are just beginning to construct the kinds of working relationships that will support their various efforts to change their teaching practices, improve literacy, experiment with multiple intelligences theory, and develop better student assessment systems for what they actually teach, but already there are new roles for the special educators as members of the work groups.

Two of the work groups have already begun designing curriculum together. Because they are part of the discussion from the beginning, the special educators can help tailor the development of the various learning objectives, activities, and assessment tools to better incorporate the unique learning of labeled students. Being part of the design of general education curriculum from the beginning means that special educators no longer have to try to fit labeled students into a completed plan. It also creates opportunities for previous special educators to teach more aspects of the plan to all the students instead of being relegated as helpers for those that might be having trouble or need extra help or support. In one of the work groups the commitment to group practice has allowed them to group all the students into smaller literacy groups, each of the members of the team taking responsibility for several students, regardless of the official title or certification, each member of the team contributing support in his or her own areas of knowledge and interest to others so that students in all the groups experience the best teaching of the collective team.

Other buildings are reorganizing more around grade-level or block teams, where groups meet regularly to share curriculum planning, allocate resources, schedule activities, share teaching tasks (e.g., rotating the class through each of the three or four teachers when doing a unit, each teacher focusing on material according to his or her strengths and interests), and to problem solve issues on behalf of the now "mutually owned" students. In some international schools, teams stay with their students, some for as many as 10 years to achieve maximum benefits of long-term relationships among teachers, students, and families. The schools here are moving toward a 2- to 5-year commitment with the same group of students.

In both elementary and secondary schools, we are also documenting the results of co-teaching efforts. One middle school in particular has relied on this strategy to both share knowledge across general and special educators and to deliver services and supports to very diverse groups of students in block classes. Sometimes these dyadic collaborations have worked. Cross-pollinating their knowledge and skills, teacher pairs have become new forms of educators who benefit both from a shared knowledge base and an appreciation for, and ability to access, others' specialty knowledge. In other situations, the team teachers have not achieved a shared working relationship, but instead recapitulated the history of parallel work relations between general and special educators. Each takes on their own tasks and responsibilities, balanced, but clearly different and differentiated. Students quickly learn the differentiation and respect it with their questions, requests, and responses.

Personnel preparation programs are reflecting a transition to group practice as well. More gradually, but increasingly, initial preparation programs are merging foundational general and special education content and licensure outcomes. Some states are simultaneously shifting from restrictive, stand-alone licensure categories to a greater emphasis on add-on endorsements to initial, usually broader licenses. Innovative continuing professional development opportunities also encourage shared general and special educators to study collaboratively with preservice students as they pursue continuing professional development and specialization (e.g., Baumgart & Ferguson, 1991; Ferguson, 1994a; Goodlad, 1990). In this way, the directions of ongoing professional development can be determined by the needs of a particular group or school to "round out" or increase some area of capacity, say in designing behavioral and emotional supports or extending their use of technology.

From Delivering Service to Providing Learner Supports

The first two shifts together produce a more fundamental shift from structuring education according to a service metaphor to one that relies on a support metaphor. As teachers alter their definitions of learning to not just accommodate, but legitimate, different amounts and types of learning for different students, their relationships with students will necessarily become more reciprocal and shared. Students and their families will become participants not just in the curriculum and teaching enterprise, but also in the definitions and evidences of learning achievement.

Our traditional, ability-based, norm-driven, categorical approaches use differences in students as sorting categories that led students to the matching curriculum and teaching service that their particular constellation of abilities and disabilities might require. The standard curriculum, for example, was the service deemed appropriate to the majority of students—certainly those in the standard range of the norm. If students fell outside that standard range, the curriculum had to be adapted or modified so that the student's learning either approximated or exceeded the learning achieved by most. As student diversity has increased in our schools, the proportion of students for whom the service of schooling must be adapted or modified has burgeoned. As a result, teachers seem quite clear that the "norm," if it ever really existed in the untidy worlds of schools, has nearly disappeared as a useful construct for the design of learning and management of classrooms (Pugach & Seidl, 1995; Putnam, Speigel, & Bruininks, 1995).

Adding the diversity of disability to this mix seems only a small addition. However, the historical baggage that the difference of disability brings to the diversity already present in general education classrooms risks transforming diversity into a deficit rather than transforming disability into just another diversity unless the underlying norm-based assumptions are also transformed (Pugach & Seidl, 1996). Unlike the concept of *diversity*, disability relies on the concept of *norm*. People with disabilities deviate from this single standard. The historical response has been to frame the appropriate educational response as one that either overcomes, or at least attenuates, the power of that deviation.

Diversity, by contrast, challenges the very notion that there is one way to educate, one norm to be sought. Instead, there are different patterns of achievement and social contribution that fit the various cultural, racial, and gender differences that children and youth bring to schooling. The difference of class illustrates the risk that can occur when the norm-laden difference of disability is added to the norm-challenging differences of culture and gender. Too often, the differences of class are viewed in our schools as deficits that impede learning. To be sure, there are experiences children have related to socioeconomic class that can impede learning, such as having too little food, inadequate housing that compromises children's need for rest, and so on. Indeed, the intersection of disability and class has long been established and continues to be evident in the disproportionate number of children of low socioeconomic and minority students served by special education. As a consequence, the life patterns and values of families in some socioeconomic classes—the very same kinds of differences we seek to accommodate and respect for people of other races and cultures—are viewed as in need of remediation rather than respect.

What may help to resolve these contradictions, and to avoid the risk that linking disability and diversity will turn diversity into a deficit, is a new metaphor. The metaphor of support offers a promising alternative. According to the American Heritage dictionary, *support* means "to hold in position," "to prevent from falling, sinking, or slipping," "to bear the weight of, especially from below," and to "lend strength to." The imagery offers not only an appropriate alternative to the norm-based, sorting metaphor of service on which schooling has long relied; it also offers a way to think about diversity as an opportunity for personalizing growth and participation. Any individual's differences are simply lenses through which to see what is required to "hold in position" and "to prevent from falling, sinking, or slipping."

Within the context of schools, the core relationships between teachers and students, the definitions of learning that dominate, and the shared responsibility among educators for achieving student learning all begin with identifying what any student needs to be "held in position" for learning. It supports a shift from viewing any difference or disability in terms of individual limitation to a focus on environmental and social constraints. Support is also grounded in the perspective of the person receiving it, not the person providing it. Thus, all student differences must define the specific opportunities and practices teachers use to support their learning. Various kinds of intensive instruction, physical supports, and accommodations typically viewed as necessary only for some students become opportunities for all students to personalize their learning in ways that mesh with who they are and what they are pursuing as members of their communities.

NEXT STEPS

Our studies have certainly not resolved the issues defined previously. Achieving satisfying and enduring change in schooling is neither simple or quick. Such fundamental changes are arduous, painful and slow in part because the task is large and complex (Fullen & Miles, 1992; Sizer, 1992). The dynamics require engagement in a sociopolitical process that requires people at all levels (individual, classroom, school, district, community, state, and nation) to engage in the "phenomenology of change." We must learn not only how to change our core educational practices, but also to do so with an understanding of how those changes are experienced by students, educators, and community members (Barth, 1990; Fullen & Miles, 1992; Noddings, 1993). I offer the three issues and three arenas of action presented here as a reasonable framework for pursuing this complex task. Although it has emerged from my understanding of our work, as well as the work of many others, I believe it will continue to guide my efforts to understand and support the changes needed in our schools as we approach a new century. Although the task is certainly enormous, it is also necessary.

REFERENCES

Asuto, T. A., Clark, D. L., Read, A. M. McGree, K., & de Koven Pelton Fernancez, L. (1994). *Roots of reform: Challenging the assumptions that control change in education.* Bloomington, IN: Phi Delta Kappa Educational Foundation.

Barth, R. (1990). A personal vision of a good school. *Phi Delta Kappa,* 71: 512—516.

Baumgart, D. S., Ferguson, D. L. (1991). *Personnel preparation: Directions for the Future.* Paul H. Brookes, L. Meyer, C. Peck and L. Brown (Eds.). *Critical Issues in the lives of people with severe disabilities.* Baltimore, Md.: pp. 313–352.

Berres, M., Ferguson, D. L., Knoblock, D., & Woods, C. (1996). *Creating tomorrow's schools today: Stories of inclusion, change and renewal.* New York: Teachers College Press.

Clark, D. L. & Astuto, T. A. (1994). Redirecting reform: Challenges to popular assumptions about teachers and students. *Phi Delta Kappa,* 75(3). pp. 512–20.

Cohen, D. K. (1995). What is the system in systemic reform? *Educational Researcher,* 24(9) 11–17, 31.

Conley, D. (1991). *Restructuring schools: Educators adapt to a changing world.* Eugene: ERIC Clearinghouse on Educational Management, University of Oregon.

Council of Administrators of Special Education [CASE], (1993). *Future agenda for special education: Creating a unified educational system.* Bloomington: Indiana University.

Cremin, L. A. (1965). *The genius of American education.* New York: Random House.

Dalmau, M., Hatton, G., & Spurway, S. (1991). *Assessment in I.S.I. Program—Inclusive Schooling— Integration.* Melbourne, Victoria: Victoria Department of School Education.

Darling-Hammond, L. (1995). The school and the democratic community. *Record in Educational Leadership,* 15(2), 35–41.

Darling-Hammond, L., J. & Falk, B. (1995). *Authentic assessment in action: Studies of schools and students at work.* New York: Teachers College Press.

Eisner, E. (1991). What really counts in schools. *Educational Leadership,* 48(5), 10–17.

Elmore, R. F. (1996). Getting to scale with good educational practice. *Harvard Graduate School of Education,* 66(1).

Ferguson, D. L. (1995a). The real challenge of inclusion: Confessions of a 'rabid inclusionist'. *Phi Delta Kappan* 77(4), 281–287.

Ferguson, D. L. (1995b). *National trends in teacher licensure. Common Ground.* No. Brunswick, NJ: The ARC of New Jersey.

Ferguson, D. L. (1996a). Defining change: One school's five year collaborative effort. *International Journal of Qualitative Studies of Education* 16–37.

Ferguson, D. L. (1996b). Is it inclusion yet? Bursting the bubbles. M. Berres, D. Knoblock, D. Ferguson & C. Woods, *Restructuring schools for all children.* (Eds.), New York: Teachers College Press.

Ferguson, D. L., Dalmau, M. C. Droege C., Boles, S., & Zitek, M. (1994a). *Building capacity for sustainable change: An inservice alternative.* Eugene: Schools Projects, Specialized Training Program, University of Oregon.

Ferguson, D. L., Ferguson, P. M., Rivers, E. & Droege, C. (1994b). *Reinventing schools research project: A collaborative research project on the merger of general and special education school reforms.* Eugene: Schools Projects, Specialized Training Program, University of Oregon.

Ferguson, D. L. & Ferguson, P. M. (1992). *Building capacity for change: Preparing teachers and families to create inclusive schools and community.* Euguen: Schools Project, Specialized Training Program, University of Oregon.

Ferguson, D., & Meyer, G. (1996). Creating together the tools to reinvent schools. In M. Berres, P. Knoblock, D. Ferguson & L. Woods, (Eds.) *Restructuring Schools for All Children.* New York: Teachers College Press.

Ferguson, D. L., Ralph, G., Katul, N., & Cameron, S. (1997). *What's becoming of the special educator?* Eugene: Schools Projects, Specialized Training Program, University of Oregon.

Ferguson, D. L. & Ralph, G. (1996). The changing role of special educators: A development waiting for a trend. *Contemporary Education,* 68(1), 49–52.

Fogarty, R. (1995). *Best practices for the learner centered classroom: A collection of articles by Robin Fogarty.* Palatine, IL: IRI/Skylight Publishing.

Fullan, M. (1991). *The new meaning of educational change.* New York: Teachers College Press.

Fullan, M. (1994). Change forces: Probing the depths of educational reform. *School development and the management of change series, 10,* Bristol, PA: Falmer Press.

Fullan, M. (1996). Turning systemic thinking on its head. *Phi Delta Kappan,* 77(6), 420–423.

Fullan, M. and Miles, M. (1992). Getting reform right: What works and what doesn't. *Phi Delta Kappan,* 74, 745–752.

Fullwood, D. (1990). *Chances and choices: Making integration work.* Baltimore, MD: Paul H. Brookes.

Gagnon, P. (1995). What should children learn? *The Atlantic Monthly,* 276(6), 65–79.

Gartner, A. & Lipsky, D. (1987). Beyond special education: Toward a quality system for all students. *Harvard Educational Review, 57,* 367–395.

Goodlad, J. (1990). *Teachers for our nation's schools.* San Francisco: Jossey-Bass.

Grimmett, P. & Erickson, G., (Eds.), (1988). *Reflection in teacher education.* New York: Teachers College Press.

Harmin, M. (1994). *Inspiring active learning: A handbook for teachers.* Alexandria, VA: Association for Supervision and Curriculum Development.

McLaughlin, M.W. (1995) *Improving education through standards-based reform.* A report by the National Academy of Education Panel on Standards-Based Education Reform. Stanford, CA: The National Academy of Education.

National Association of State Boards of Education, (1990). *Today's children, tomorrow's survival: A call to restructure schools.* Alexandria, VA: NASBE.

Noddings, N. (1993). Excellence as a guide to educational conversation. *Teachers' College Record,* 94(4), 730–743.

O'Hanlon, C., (Ed.). (1995). *Inclusive education in Europe.* London, England: David Fulton.

Oregon Department of Education. (1996). *Performance Standards.* Salem: Department of Education.

Pearman, E. L., Huang, A. M., Barnhart, A. M., & Melblom, C. (1992). Educating all children in school: Attitudes and beliefs about inclusion. *Education and Training in Mental Retardation, 27,* 176–182.

Pugach, M., & Seidl, B. (1995). From exclusion to inclusion in urban schools: A new case for teacher education reform. *Teacher Education, 27*(4), 379–95.

Pugach, M. C., & Seidl, B. L. (1996). Demonstrating the diversity-disability connection. *Contemporary Education,* 68(1), 5–8.

Putnam, J., Spiegel, A., & Bruininks, R. (1995). Future directions in education and inclusion of students with disabilities: A Delphi investigation. *The Council for Exceptional Children*, 61(1), 553–576.

Reynolds, M. C., Zetlin, A., & Wang, M. C. (1993). 20/20 Analysis: Taking a close look at the margins. *The Council for Exceptional Children*, 59, 294–300.

Sailor, W., & Skrtic, T. (1995). Modern and postmodern agendas in special education: Implications for teacher education, research and policy development. In J. Paul, H. Roselli, & D. Evans (Eds.), *Integrating School Restructuring and Special Education Reform*, (pp. 418–433). New York: Harcourt Brace.

Sarason, S. (1990). *The predictable failure of educational reform*. San Francisco: Jossey-Bass.

Sarasan, S. B. (1986). *The preparation of teachers: An unstudied problem in education*. Cambridge, MA: Brookline.

Schon, D. (1983). *The reflective practitioner: How professionals think in action*. New York: Basic Books.

Shepard, L. A., & Bliem, C.L. (1995, November). Parents' thinking about standardized tests and performance assessments. *Educational Researcher*, 25–32.

Sizer, T. (1992). *Horace's school: Redesigning the American school*. Boston: Houghton Mifflin.

Skrtic, T. (1995). *Exploring the theory/practice link in special education*. New York: Teachers College Press.

Sylwester, R. (1995). *A celebration of neurons: An educator's guide to the human brain*. Alexandria, VA: Association for Supervision and Curriculum Development.

Tetler, S. (1995). The Danish Efforts in Integration. In C. O;Hanlon (Ed.), *Inclusive education in Europe*. (pp. 9–23), London, England: David Fulton.

United States Department of Education (1996). *To assure the free appropriate public education of all children with disabilities*: 18th annual report to Congress on the implementation of The Individuals with Disabilities Education Act. Washington, DC: U. S. Department of Education.

Valencia, S. W., Hiebert, E. H., & Afflerbach, P. P. (Eds.). (1994). *Authentic reading assessment: Practices and possibilities*. Newark: International Reading Association.

4

The Inclusion of Students With Disabilities in School Reform and Restructuring: An Analysis of Five Local School Districts

Margaret J. McLaughlin
Kelly Henderson
Lauren M. Rhim
University of Maryland

The educational reforms that have evolved since the 1980s are changing the context of classrooms and the expectations for teachers and students. These reforms have generally been focused on six major policy areas: standards, assessment, accountability, governance, teachers, and finance (Goertz & Friedman, 1996). During this same time period, special education programs have changed in response to efforts to promote inclusion of students with disabilities in general education classrooms, to decrease inappropriate identification of students as disabled, particularly cultural or language minority students, and to improve the educational results for all students receiving special education services. As these general and special education reform initiatives come together in schools and classrooms, they must be defined, negotiated, and adapted to fit existing policies and practices.

Understanding the features of the general education reforms is essential for several reasons. Special education programs operate in the context of the larger educational system and special education policies and resources cannot help but be influenced by larger system priorities. Furthermore, students with disabilities are increasingly receiving their instruction in general education classrooms. According to the U.S. Department of Education (1996), 43% of the students with disabilities receive the majority of their educational program in those environments. Ensuring that these students have meaningful access to the curriculum and instruction provided in general education classrooms requires a sound knowledge of how educational reforms are impacting special education practices. In addition, efforts to reduce costs associated with special education are leading to increased scrutiny of programs and their relative benefits for students with disabilities. Perhaps the most compelling reason for wanting knowledge about general education reform is to provide students with disabilities access to a broad and balanced curriculum and specialized instruction that reflects high expectations, challenging standards, and individually tailored educational goals.

This 3-year qualitative study of local education reform is part of a larger, national study conducted by the Center for Policy Research on the Impact of General and Special Education Reform. The Center has been investigating state and local general educational reform policies with a particular focus on how these policies are interpreted by, or interact with, special education practices. The Center's research includes tracking reforms in 12 states, case studies of 4 states, and the 5 local district case studies. Corollary studies have been conducted relating to charter schools, state policies, and the implementation of assessment accommodations.

This chapter reports the findings of five case studies conducted in local school districts across the country. The following major areas of general education policy and practice were investigated: standards and curriculum, assessment, accountability, and governance. In addition, special education programs were also examined. The demographically representative local districts were selected because of their prominent reform initiatives. Data were obtained through in-depth interviews, focus group discussions, and on-site observations. Traditional qualitative research methods were employed to analyze characteristics of the reform efforts across case studies.

METHODOLOGY

The five local districts were selected on the basis of the prominence of their reform agendas within their respective states, as well as their geographic and demographic characteristics. The districts included a large urban system with a predominately minority-student population (District B); two suburban districts, and a small independent city district (District W); a large countywide system (District D); two rural school districts, and an independent town (District M); and a countywide system (District H).

The qualitative research was conducted using traditional case study methodology (Yin, 1994). Data were obtained during week-long site visits to each of the districts. The primary researcher and three assistants collected data through in-depth interviews, focus groups, and on-site observations.

In District B, interviews were conducted with 15 central office administrators, 8 building principals, 6 special education supervisors, and 45 teachers and other personnel in 9 schools. Of the total 180 schools in the district, 3 middle and 7 elementary schools were site visited. During two visits to District W, 28 interviews were conducted with 47 participants, including 3 central office administrators, 6 building administrators, 4 parents, and a variety of teachers and other school support personnel. The research team visited 6 of the 13 district schools including 4 elementary schools, the middle school, and the high school. Twenty-eight persons were interviewed during the single site visit to District D. These included 12 district administrators and instructional supervisors, as well as 8 school principals, 3 parents and 5 teachers were interviewed. Of the 35 schools, observations were made in 1 high school, 1 middle school, 3 elementary schools, and 2 charter schools. The researchers conducted 18 interviews in District M. These included 3 central office administrators, 4 building-level administrators, 11 teachers, and 3 parents. Site visits were made to 4 of 13 district schools consisting of 2 elementary schools, 1 middle school, and the high school.

Thirty-three interviews were conducted with 44 participants in District H. Five building principals, 7 district-level administrators and program coordinators, 20 teachers, and 6 parents were interviewed. The remaining interviews involved other school personnel, such as special education-related services providers and the director of a youth services center. Researchers visited 5 of the district's 17 schools: the high school, the vocational school, a junior high, and 2 elementary schools. The interviews were conducted using standard protocols. However, all interviews were open-ended and topics could be modified to match the individual characteristics of each district. Interviews were audiotaped and transcribed. Transcripts were then analyzed and sections coded for topical content. The computer program, *Ethnograph 4.0*, was used to assist with analysis of the coded interview data, and common themes across interviews were identified. Secondary document reviews were conducted to triangulate and validate site visit findings. Emphasis was placed on the review of documents pertaining to district demographics, funding, development of new standards and assessment instruments, special education programs, governance, and other reform initiatives specific to each of the five local districts. Examples of these documents include community newspapers and other community information items, state education reform legislation, specific state standards, district mission and goal statements, district special education rules and procedures, curricular documents, individual school plans, and staff development and promotion requirements.

Information gathered from the various sources was used to construct five individual case studies. Each school district contact person was provided a draft copy of the district case study, and encouraged to share the draft and solicit comments on the content. A few minor areas of disagreement were identified and resolved by a reexamination of the transcript data and documents.

Each case study describes individual district initiatives in a broad arena of school reform. A cross-case analysis of the five sites was conducted in the areas of general education reform of standards, assessments and accountability, and governance. In addition, special education issues were examined across the five sites. Each of the categories was first examined to describe and document how districts were designing and implementing specific reforms. Each category was also examined for references to inclusive practice, as well as how the reform overlaps and interacts with district inclusion initiatives.

FINDINGS

The findings are organized to present general observations about how districts were defining and implementing inclusion. This is followed by a discussion of each of the major reforms and their interaction with attempts to increase inclusive practices in classrooms.

What is *Inclusion*

The definition of what in practice constitutes *inclusion* became more salient as information from the five case sites was examined. Within the inclusion literature, certain principles define inclusive practices. Typically, these are defined as placement of *all* students in age-appropriate general education classrooms in neighborhood schools; comprehensive assessment of students' individual learning styles, strengths, and needs; collaboration among families, general education and special education teachers, administrators, and other service providers; systematic arrangement of general education instructional settings and specialized support; adaptations of general education curriculum; and use of age-appropriate settings, activities, and materials provided to students throughout the preschool through postsecondary years (cf. Falvey, Grenot-Scheyer, Coots, & Bishop; 1995). Using these principles as a template, we determined that inclusion is being implemented in very different ways across the five districts and across schools within districts. Not all features exist in all schools in a district nor are all students experiencing inclusive education.

Although none of the districts have a strict, full inclusion mandate, all districts have some special education programs or sites that may generally be considered inclusive, meaning that some students with disabilities are being educated almost exclusively in general education classrooms. Different inclusion policies and degrees of implementation at the individual school level were, in many cases, influenced by site-based governance structures.

For the most part, inclusion in these five districts is a two-tailed process with students with moderate to significant mental retardation and other students with complex needs increasingly being fully included in general education classrooms on a student-by-student basis. These decisions are heavily influenced by parental preference. Students with mild disabilities, such as learning disabilities, tend to be included as a group. This means that one or more general educators and a special educator may decide to co-teach, or engage in some other form of instructional collaboration, and the special education students are either brought as a group into a general education classroom or distributed among several classrooms. These decisions appear to be more influenced by teacher or school decisions. Across all districts, students exhibiting serious emotional and behavior disorders tend to be educated in more segregated settings, such as special classes. However, it should be noted that in some of the case-study districts, teachers still perceived inclusion solely as a change of placement as opposed to a more comprehensive change in a students with disabilities' actual curriculum.

District special education representatives indicated a range of viewpoints on the values of inclusion yet all believed that full inclusion should be an option for certain children based on their needs and parental preferences. Most special educators spoke of the need to change general educators' acceptance of inclusion, and wanted to increase the numbers of inclusive opportunities. All of the special education administrators recognized that they needed to be prepared to offer an inclusive setting to any student whose parents request it. Each administrator also acknowledged the importance of considering how broad systemic changes affect the organizational, curricular, and instructional features of schools and special education's efforts to increase inclusion opportunities. Among the more important reforms that are perceived to be impacting schools are standards, assessments and enhanced accountability, and site-based management.

Standard Setting

Among more prominent reform initiatives being implemented across the states are new content and performance standards. As defined in the federal Goals 2000: Educate America Act (PL 103-227), content standards are "broad descriptions of the knowledge and skills students should acquire in a particular subject area" (Sec. 3(4). Performance standards are defined as "concrete examples and explicit definitions of what students have to know and be able to do to demonstrate that [they] are proficient in the skills and knowledge framed by the content standards" (Sec. 3(9). According to a survey conducted by the Council of Chief State School Officers (1996), 41 states and federal jurisdictions have standards in one or more of the following subject matter areas ready for implementation: math, science, English and language arts, history, and social studies. Several states have additional standards under development. Thirty-five states indicated that their content standards will apply to students with disabilities. An additional 4 states indicated their standards will apply to these students, but local discretion is allowed (Rhim & McLaughlin, 1997). Of the 35 states, 18 allow for some type of exemption from the standards for students with disabilities via a student's Individualized Education Program (IEP). A recent report of the National Academy of Education (McLaughlin & Sheppard, 1995) noted the tremendous variability among states with respect to the conception of curriculum evidenced in the standards, as well as how the standards would be applied. State-level studies conducted by the Center for Policy Research on the Impact of General and Special Education Reform (Goertz & Friedman, 1996) also indicated substantial differences in how states are choosing to implement the standards. Some states have mandated standards, and others are voluntary and articulated through curricular frameworks that may be used by local districts to guide curriculum development as well as assessments. This variation in design was evident among the five local case-study districts.

Local Context. Districts B and H were implementing state standards linked to high stakes state assessments; District M was in the process of integrating its state standards into its curriculum, and was piloting new companion state assessments in a few subject areas; both District D and District W were developing and implementing local standards and assessments. However, District D must ensure its standards meet or exceed the state standards that will be assessed.

The local districts' content standards are referred to *as learning outcomes, essential academic learnings, valued academic expectations,* and *exit outcomes.* They also differ in terms of content addressed. For example, District W has specified nine exit outcomes that students are required to demonstrate prior to graduation. Examples of these outcomes include problem solving, critical thinking, and decision making as well as verbal, quantitative, scientific and technological literacy. The exit outcomes are integrated into specific courses, and are demonstrated through completion of specific course requirements and performance demonstrations. An example of a performance requirement in technology is two authentic demonstrations of word processing ability.

District B is implementing standards in the subject-matter areas of math, science, reading, writing, and social studies, whereas District H's curriculum is guided by 6 state goals and 75 specific student academic expectations developed in December, 1991. District M has state-developed essential academic leanings in reading, writing, communication, mathematics, arts, health and fitness, science, and social studies. The standards incorporate specific skills students are supposed to acquire in school, and are broken down into benchmarks for Grades 4, 7, and 10.

The differences among the district standards are related, in part to their purpose, as well as to the level at which they have been developed. For example, the state standards that District B is implementing were designed to provide only the core goals for local district curriculum. Local districts are encouraged to expand on the standards. Furthermore, they are not designed to be specific enough to form the basis of instruction. Standards in Districts W and D are more detailed, and provide strong pedagogical guidance.

The standards do have several similarities. For example, each district's standards emphasize processes, application of specific facts or knowledge, and subject matter integration. Standards frequently require that students demonstrate, interpret, or apply knowledge or concepts. In addition, communication skills, particularly writing, are emphasized across all of the content areas. A common example is communicating, through written explanation, the reasoning underlying math problem-solving.

Perceived Impact on Classroom Practices.

General and special education teachers were asked if their classroom instruction had changed during the past 5 years in response to standards-based reform. In addition, they were asked whether the state or local standards were influencing what and how they are teaching. Responses to the first question were almost uniformly affirmative. Classroom teachers, at almost all levels, have been implementing curricular changes during the past 10 years. Most notably, primary-level teachers remarked they now stress the writing process and have shifted toward teaching reading through *whole-language* approaches. Middle school and high school math and science teachers reported greater emphasis on application of knowledge through projects or other *hands on* experiences and greater integration of all subject matter content. Many of these changes were attributed to newly developed state or local standards that, in turn, were based on national National Council of Teachers of Mathematics or National Science Foundation standards. Regardless of their origin, the standards are perceived to be impacting what content teachers teach, and how they teach it.

For example, seventh-grade teachers in District H discussed how the state standards and assessments have changed methods for teaching math. One math teacher commented, "We do a lot more group work . . . we're doing a lot more writing in math, which you used to never hear of because you just did facts, basic math . . . Now, it's rewriting the process into questions. So [the standards have] definitely changed the way we teach math a lot."

General education administrators were usually positive about the potential for the standards to increase student learning but teachers' reactions were mixed. On the positive end, most teachers acknowledged that the standards were requiring them to teach more content, and to stress application or "experiential or hands-on stuff." Also, demands to integrate subject matter were requiring teachers to collaborate and to break down departmentalization, most notably at the middle school and high school levels.

Teachers in District W reported that implementation of their new standards-based education initiative is providing a specific integrated focus to the curriculum and fostering collaboration among the school faculty. Outcomes have reportedly encouraged teachers to work with teachers outside their subject area and to view the curriculum in a more integrated fashion. In specific instances, the collaboration extends to individual special education. One social studies performance standard required children to prepare a report on a specific aspect of the Middle Ages. The general and special education teachers worked together to help one fifth grader, with a serious learning disability in reading and writing, prepare a research report on knighthood using CD-ROM and other technologies. The teachers expressed amazement at the facts and concepts the student had mastered.

Concerns about the impact of standards included those expressed by several middle school teachers in two districts, who perceived that standards are forcing them to cover more content in their classes so they cannot teach as deeply or as thoroughly as before. This meant that there was insufficient time to ensure that all students learned the content well. Finding time to teach all of the new content was a big concern to many teachers interviewed across all five sites.

Middle school teachers in District H were struggling with the need to incorporate writing instruction across the curriculum, in preparation for the state-mandated writing portfolios administered in Grade 7. They believed that other content matter was being short-changed. "We've had to drop a lot of science content to find time for other things," stated one teacher. A second agreed, "It's the same thing in math. Basically I feel like it takes me a lot longer to cover the subject matter because we're trying to do so many different things. You know you do [some concept] and spend a week writing about it. So that slows you down and you don't get to cover as much content." The content standards were perceived to value "breadth, not depth." Elementary teachers in District H commented that they are encouraged to use multidisciplinary thematic units to integrate subject matter. In the opinion of one teacher, the thematic units

> are fine for some things. But, as we're looking at the science content scores and the social studies content scores, they're not getting the concept. So they don't understand the democratic principal as much as a third grader should. Or they're not understanding change or interactions with science because they're learning through a thematic unit, which is not stressing one particular thing.

Standards and Students With Disabilities

Opinions about how students with disabilities will fare under the new standards were most often voiced by special education teachers who were actually involved in implementing the new standards. Their opinions were most often influenced by the nature of the students' disabilities. General and special educators are expecting that most students with disabilities will participate in, and be assessed on, new content standards. However, all teachers in District W expressed uncertainty about how to apply the new standards to an increasingly diverse student population. They were particularly concerned about the applicability of all the new outcomes to every student, and questioned the utility of mandating that all students achieve the same outcomes when their long-term goals are so diverse. There were a few concerns expressed about low-incidence students who would require an entirely differentiated curriculum and "[who] will likely require a set of individualized standards." However, for some special educators inclusion in the district standards was an important goal and they believed that all students should be considered to be *in* the standards with appropriate accommodations and modifications. An important issue is the difference between accommodations and modifications. According to definitions proposed by a recent National Research Council report (McDonnell, McLaughlin, & Morison, 1997), accommodations are intended to maintain or even facilitate the attainment of a standard. The skill or knowledge is not changed, but students are given support learning the material. Providing a reader or word processor are examples of accommodations. A modification alters the content or standard, and is likely to change what is really being taught and assessed. For example, a standard that requires obtaining information from a variety of texts can be modified to require reading functional words in isolated phrases.

Most of administrators' concerns centered on students with high-incidence disabilities, such as specific learning disabilities, mild mental retardation, and behavior disorders. Administrators wondered what resources would be required to move beyond rhetoric, and ensure that these and other low-achieving students will meet the new standards. Teachers and administrators in two districts already see problems surfacing at the secondary level because academic demands are greater, and the curriculum is less flexible.

In the districts with state-mandated assessments, general education teachers at all grade levels expressed significant concerns about how to apply standards to all students with disabilities. Generally, these teachers view the standards as absolute criteria that students must master as opposed to generic goals toward which students must work. General education teachers consistently questioned how one set of standards could apply to all learners, particularly those students with cognitive or learning disabilities.

Some special educators voiced optimism about how standards would push all students to realize their potential. Special education administrators in District W stated that the new outcomes and accountability measures helped students with disabilities because it pushed them beyond the expectations outlined in their IEPs. Special education teachers liked the idea of organizing their instruction around the standards because it gave them a focus and a clear framework for collaborating with other teachers, and for organizing their own instruction. One high school special education teacher commented, "I think we're hopeful because [the standards] give us some real concrete direction to work toward when we collaborate with general education teachers." The notion that standards provide a common expectation, and can be used as a basis for designing individualized accommodation and support was very appealing.

The emphasis on experiential learning that was evident in the standards was also generally endorsed by special and general education teachers because they felt that it provided more opportunities for all students to learn important content. In District H, a general education primary-grade teacher reported that the standards-based reforms had made teachers change and modify the curriculum, with a focus on individualization. For example, use of manipulatives had benefited all students, particularly students at risk who may require tactile activities.

Despite many positive comments, special educators generally expressed a wait-and-see attitude regarding standards-based reform and the inclusion of students with disabilities. A prevalent caution was how to incorporate individualized educational goals within a standards framework. Given a finite amount of instructional time, special educators were concerned about how to fit in more functional or nonacademic skills. As one special education administrator noted, "The reason that we have done so poorly with learning disabled students over the years is because we've never had a curriculum. We are now going to have a curriculum. [But] I think that we're going to have to be real careful that we don't still bypass their needs because we are so focused." These concerns about competing priorities were also expressed by parents of students with disabilities. For example, a parent in District W viewed the inclusion of her son in the standards as positive because it increased his opportunity to learn more content and to provide a natural focus to inclusion in general education classrooms. However, this parent also speculated about how her preadolescent son would learn other important skills, such as how to travel around his community. The issue for her son was not where education was taking place as much as what he was learning. A secondary special education teacher in District D raised concerns about the need to modify standards for individual learning needs: "One of the things we've been thinking about is how the decision whether to modify a standard, or to accommodate a standard, is going to be made. Because those are pretty subjective opinions . . . who needs a modification, who needs an accommodation. And if so, what kind and how much? Key questions are: 'what are the important knowledge and skills and who decides where to put the instructional emphasis?'"

Special educators in one high school found groups of their students who needed to be "recycled" through instruction because they were not meeting or coming close to the standards. This reteaching resulted in splitting the groups into several ability groups. The special education teachers did not believe this was inclusive, and believed that this problem is likely to be exacerbated when the standards become even more rigorous, and general content teachers have less tolerance and latitude for modifying or moving their expectations downward.

An administrator from District M reported there is currently "loud discussion about the impact of standards on diplomas" for students with disabilities. Parents are concerned about new assessments and want accommodations to protect their children from failing. Staff in one school in this same district reported they had "an increased number" of parents who have requested referrals for special education assessment, or who were seeking Section 504 of the Vocational Rehabilitation Act accommodation plans because, "They took one look at the standards and said, 'There's no way my kid will meet those.' They want [the child] placed right away."

Overall, however, the tone of most comments was positive. Special educators were willing to engage in the process because they liked the idea of higher expectations and a broader curriculum, as well as the more interactive pedagogy. They remain skeptical, however, about how all students with disabilities will fare in inclusive classrooms that are increasingly centered on higher levels of achievement with an almost exclusive academic focus.

Assessments and Accountability

Assessment and increased accountability for student achievement are among the most visible and controversial reform initiatives. According to recent data from the National Center on Educational Outcomes (Elliott, Thurlow, & Ysseldyke, 1996), 43 states are developing new assessments as part of their overall assessment program. Seventeen of these states have policies linking assessment to graduation. Increasing the participation of students with disabilities in state and local assessments, and ensuring that the results of these students are held to public accountability are major goals of special education policymakers. The recent reauthorization of Individuals With Disabilities Act (IDEA) requires state and local education agencies to develop policies for participation of students with disabilities in assessments, as well as report the number of students participating in them. Several studies have documented that participation rates for these students vary significantly from state to state, ranging from 0 to 100% (Erickson, Thurlow, Thor, & Seyfarth, 1996). In an effort to increase participation, states have been developing guidelines for how decisions should be made and the types of assessment accommodations that should be made available to students with disabilities. Recent state surveys conducted by the National Center on Educational Outcomes revealed that 43 states have written guidelines about the participation of students with disabilities in state assessments (Erickson, Thurlow, & Ysseldyke, 1996). Most of the guidelines rely on the IEP team to make the decision, and only about half of the states require that the decision be documented. In 1995, 39 states wrote policies specifying which accommodations (e.g., most commonly changes in setting, presentation, response mode, or timing) would be permitted in statewide assessments (Thurlow, Scott, & Ysseldyke, 1995). Developing and implementing new assessments and accountability systems were major issues within the five local case-study districts.

Local Context

Districts B and H are in "high-reform" states that implemented new performance-based assessments in the late 1980s. Results of these state-mandated assessments are reported annually on school report cards. Low-performing schools are subject to a variety of state sanctions, and there is significant pressure on principals to get better results. Individual student accountability is not a major feature in these districts, although District B's state requires a minimum competency criterion-referenced test for the high school diploma, has developed new high school standards, and is developing a set of high school end-of-course assessments.

District W has developed a very comprehensive and complex assessment program that includes three nationally norm-referenced assessments administered at different grade levels, criterion-referenced assessments in math and reading administered in Grade 5, a criterion-referenced writing assessment administered in Grades 4 through 6, 8, 11, and 12; and cumulative Kindergarten through 12 portfolios (currently only in place for Grades 9 through 12). The district has continued to develop new assessments to align with their nine new outcomes. The goal is to have an assessment "toolbox" to give teachers options and flexibility. Graduating seniors are responsible for demonstrating successful completion of the nine outcomes via basic course requirements and performance demonstrations that are interdisciplinary projects developed with classroom teachers.

Increased student accountability is an important component of District W's assessment plan. There will be two types of diplomas: a standard diploma requiring 210 credit hours, and a diploma with commendation that will require 224 credit hours. In addition to greater course requirements, students seeking a diploma with commendation are required to complete additional performance demonstrations. There are no state assessments planned.

District D is in the process of developing a system for assessing student attainment of their content standards. Goals for the district's assessment system include providing annual data on student performance as required by the state, providing individual student achievement data for instructional program improvement, providing feedback to students and parents, and presenting evidence that individual students have met matriculation and graduation requirements. Two sources of data will be used in the system including both secured assessments and "bodies of evidence." Secured assessments will be district-administered norm-referenced and criterion-referenced performance assessments. Local schools will also administer secured performance assessments. A "body of evidence" will be collected for each student that documents student progress toward meeting certain benchmarks. The evidence will include such things as essays, teacher tests, personal communication, observations, performance events, and so forth. A body of evidence for a particular benchmark may vary among teachers but the collection process and scoring rubrics will be consistent across the district. Teachers will score their evidence and the judgments will be aggregated across the district, and reported annually in terms of percentage of students attaining each of the benchmarks. Beginning in 1996, the state administered the first of several state proficiency tests to a sample of Grade 4, 8, and 10 students. Beyond public reporting of scores, there will be no consequences attached to the assessments.

District M is currently in the process of developing local assessments and integrating state-developed assessments in conjunction with the standards. The local assessments are being developed as interim assessments geared toward making staff "assessment literate" and in preparation for the state assessments that are currently being piloted by subject area. At this time, the district has not developed any specific attrition or retention policies based on satisfactory completion of the standards or the new performance assessments.

Perceived Impacts

As might be expected, conversations in Districts B and H that were implementing state-mandated assessments and high-stakes school accountability were almost exclusively focused on how to increase scores. Principals interviewed in these districts clearly understood the consequences of the assessments and talked about the need to raise scores and focus their school improvement efforts on raising scores. However, principals' understanding of what it would take to raise scores varied. Principals in these districts recognized that improved assessment results would require changes in content and pedagogy, and that student performance reflected a cumulative acquisition of knowledge and skills. Accordingly, middle school principals in each of the two districts had initiated efforts in their feeder schools to improve curriculum opportunities. In one school, the principal was using his Title I-funded teacher to help fifth and sixth grade teachers in feeder elementary schools to implement a new science curriculum. Science was the area in most need of improvement according to his eighth grade assessments.

Some principals in other schools in both Districts B and H appeared less clear about how to improve test scores. Several principals talked about the need to increase cooperative learning (some of the state assessments are administered to groups) or parent involvement. Increasing the amount of time spent on writing was a common comment made by several principals in these districts. However, the understanding that deep changes would be required in curriculum and instruction was not evident across all those interviewed in the districts.

Teachers in Districts B and H also varied in terms of their enthusiasm for the assessments. Although many teachers in District H understood and supported the adoption of state standards and assessments, they also commented on teacher anxiety caused by such high-stakes reforms. One high school teacher noted:

> I think most of the anxiety came over the fact that we were going to be measured as a school. Not that the students would not [improve], or that we wouldn't figure out a way to move the students towards what needs to be done, but could we do it fast enough? Could we boost enough of them out of [the lowest] category into [higher performance levels] to keep the school out of trouble?

Teachers at the specific grade levels where the state assessments are administered expressed particular stress. These teachers felt that assessment results reflected on them and their teaching.

Districts D and W, with locally developed assessments, had a much more flexible and less threatening approach. Also, because the programs were not fully implemented at the time of this study, there was less anxiety about student performance and more willingness to reflect on the merits of the system. There were teacher and administrator concerns about how to manage the paper associated with cumulative portfolios and other collections of student work. Teachers were extremely concerned about the time required to develop and score some of the new assessments. A District D administrator referred to this as "reform fatigue" and the district is now rethinking its assessment approach.

District W teachers generally supported the standards and accompanying high school assessments. They liked the accountability. "It's really nice to have some outlines so the students who come to us have the same experiences and so we have some accountability about what they're supposed to leave us knowing." This district offers a great deal of flexibility and support for students. They are permitted to take the tests as often as they want and have numerous special remedial classes. One administrator shared a story about permitting a student to take one competency exam on the afternoon of graduation day to give her one last chance to graduate. She passed.

State and local assessments are currently being developed and piloted in District M, so it is premature to assess their impact. However, teachers and administrators expressed some reservations about the proposed new assessments and accountability. One administrator in this district expressed concern about the possible future use of school report cards that may not necessarily reflect the population of students in the school. In addition, teachers were concerned that new standards and assessments aimed to push all students to the same level without apparent sensitivity to student differences. Finally, administrators expressed concern that high-stakes testing would cause teachers to limit what they teach and really narrow the curriculum to what is on the test. There was a great deal of confusion or lack of understanding about how the assessment results might be used and a general wariness about increasing accountability. However, there was a general acceptance that standards and assessments were necessary to increase student learning and accountability.

Across all five districts, strategies for changing instruction and improving scores were being actively explored. For example, some principals spoke of how they had moved grade by grade to get teachers to examine current curriculum and classroom practice. Schools in each of the districts used professional development funds to permit teachers to work through the summer with consultants to help align their curriculum. The state allowed District H to reduce the number of student instructional days by 4 to increase staff development days, so teachers could work on curriculum alignments, portfolio development, and other assessments. However, the use of professional development days is largely determined by individual schools and not all schools have used the days for these purposes.

Assessment and Accountability and Students with Disabilities

General and special education teachers and administrators expressed concern about assessing students with disabilities, and being held accountable for their progress. Although special education teachers appreciated the curricular structure provided by the content standards, the assessments set the performance expectations, and these teachers generally had doubts about how all students with disabilities, particularly those with moderate levels of cognitive disabilities, will meet them. The 1997 IDEA amendments require that students with disabilities who are not participating in the state or local assessments have an alternative assessment. Yet, there was little understanding of what these assessments might look like or how they could be used for school improvement planning. In the two districts with state-mandated assessments, one required all students with disabilities to be included in statewide assessments, including an alternative assessment and to have results reported. The second district has been under increased pressure from the state education agency to include more students with disabilities in the state assessments. Numbers of exemptions from state assessments are now published on the school report cards.

Teachers in District H were generally supportive of the inclusion of students with disabilities in the assessments. Many saw the positive impact assessments had on instruction, but they were also cognizant of the modifications necessary for success of students with special needs. One general education middle school teacher mused, "It's amazing how much knowledge [special education students] do have, and it really wouldn't have been reflected if they had not had help and had [to participate] in the assessment."

District M teachers were not overly concerned with either assessments or accountability at this time. However, conversations with district administrators reveal that, as the assessments are piloted and become operational, serious discussion about accommodations, and the implications of including of students with disabilities are starting to bubble up in the community.

District W is very informal about the inclusion of students with disabilities in their assessments. Although a few concerns were expressed by general educators. One administrator noted that, "When you bring that accountability piece into inclusive classes [teachers] all say, 'Accountable to what degree and for what?'". Increasing accountability while increasing the diversity of classrooms was problematic to all teachers. A teacher in District W questioned "how to include to enhance accountability yet keep the assessment appropriate for the long-term development of the student?" The general philosophy of most general and special education teachers and administrators in District W is to evaluate these students on their improvement or progress as opposed to against a set performance criteria. A parent and several central office administrators supported increased accountability because it pushed teachers and students with disabilities.

District D is just beginning to develop its assessments and accountability plan. Staff had few specific concerns about how students with disabilities will participate. Central office administrators indicated that they expect 90% of students with disabilities to fully participate in the assessments. The district has deliberately been very low key and nonthreatening about how assessments will be used. They want principals to become focused on using student performance data for decision making as opposed to becoming fixated on raising scores. However, as the district has become more data-driven, there is evidence that some principals are attempting to walk away from accountability by pointing to students' socioeconomic status or disability as influencing scores.

Assessment Accommodations

All five districts permitted students with disabilities to receive assessment accommodations. Four of the districts (Districts B, D, H, M) were in states that provided comprehensive state guidelines for accommodation. District W has no guidelines. Regardless of the specificity of state guidelines, individual assessment accommodation decisions are made at the school level through the IEP process or by a building team. Two of the districts require that accommodations be noted on the IEPs and one district flags assessment results when certain accommodations are considered to change the nature of the test. For example, large print assessments would not be flagged but extended time would be.

There is no evidence that decisions to provide an assessment accommodation are scrutinized, nor are individuals or teams held accountable for the decisions. Several teachers noted that accommodation decisions were unsystematic and varied widely among students with similar disabilities and functional abilities. However, all teachers generally believed that accommodations were critical to even the playing field and help the child. Their concerns appear to be centered more around the welfare of the child than raising scores. Nonetheless, the overriding goal of assessment accommodations was to include more students with disabilities in the assessments. In fact, inclusion in assessments appeared to be an end as opposed to the means to achieve greater accountability for student learning. In other words, it was good to test all of the students, but maybe not as good to report the scores or be held accountable for them. Issues related to the impact of accommodations on assessment validity were rarely mentioned by assessment directors.

Site-Based Management

Four of the five case-study sites had instituted formal site-based management (SBM) models in their schools. This reflects a national trend toward changing governance structures to decentralize school management and the devolution of fiscal and programmatic decision making to individual school sites. Site-based management is among the most widely adopted school improvement strategies. Although not new, SBM greatly expanded during the mid-1980s such that more than one third of the nation's schools, including the 10 largest, had implemented these new governance models by 1990 (Cawelti, 1994).

Typically, SBM transfers authority to local school sites and requires that principals, teachers, parents, community members, and occasionally students make critical decisions about budgets, staffing, curriculum and instruction, and professional development. However, schools and school districts differ widely in terms of how much authority is divested to schools, and how able and willing local buildings are to assume more control over important decisions. The extensive research on the outcomes of SBM is mixed. For example, some studies have found greater innovation in school practices (U.S. Government Accounting Office, 1994). Other research, however, concluded that SBM has limited effect on changing control and authority at the school level (Malen, 1994; Wohlstetter & Odden, 1992).

Research related to the impacts of SBM and special education is very limited (see Rabb, 1993; Schofield, 1996). These programs and the students with disabilities who are served by them have largely been ignored in the evaluations and discussions of SBM.

Local Context

Among the four local districts that were formally implementing SBM, only District B had begun the process in the last several years. The other three districts, D, M, and H, had begun the process between 5 and 10 years ago. District W, although not formally implementing SBM, is small and has always had participatory management and strong community involvement. Principals and teachers in that district agree that they are empowered and are included in various strategic planning activities and committees at the district and school levels, and do not need formal SBM procedures. Districts M and H both had former superintendents who had instituted SBM in the late 1980s. Administrators and staff in both districts believed that the primary reason their district had become known throughout the state as reform-oriented is because of the their early involvement with SBM. District H now has a state mandate that requires site-based decision making in every school, and specifies who must participate, as well as the boundaries of decision making. District D has both a local and state-required site-based team in each school, although some schools have merged these teams. The district administration encourages wide community involvement in all decisions, including day-to-day operational decisions. The district also has a very flat central office organization. Key central administrators include the superintendent and three assistant superintendents. Each of the latter is also the director of one of the three administrative areas. They support and supervise principals in their respective areas and collaboration and shared decision making occur naturally.

In general, all schools within the five districts had broad decision-making powers in areas related to the organization of curriculum and instruction, staffing, and professional development. All of the four SBM districts had a district curriculum or standards that guide what knowledge and skills students were expected to attain, but schools could decide how they wanted to implement that curriculum. This included how classrooms were organized, which texts and materials to use, and so forth. Hiring, and other staffing decisions, could also be made by local schools. However, all districts had some level of central-office control over determining eligibility for positions. Budget and staffing decisions were also left to local schools, with some restrictions, as were professional development issues.

SBM and Students With Disabilities

Site councils in each of the five districts had received no formal training in the area of special education policy, or current approaches or practices. Some site councils had a special education teacher as a member; few had parents of students with disabilities. According to data from the five local case studies decisions relating to special education were rarely made by site councils primarily for four reasons: Special education is not a priority for councils that are responding to more pressing issues such as curriculum decisions, staffing, or budgets; SBM council members lack knowledge and confidence in their decision making in this area; the council is not clear about who has responsibility for making which special education decisions (e.g., central office or school site); and site councils lack special education advocates.

In two districts, individual school site councils had made decisions about how special education inclusion would be implemented. In one instance, a council made the decision regarding inclusion. They decided to cluster all special education students in specific classrooms so that the special education teachers would be able to co-teach with specific general educators for extended blocks of time. This decision was not supported by the local special education director who felt that students with disabilities might be better served if distributed proportionately across all general education classes. Interestingly, in this case the decision was influenced by a parent of a student with a disability who was on the site council. In addition, the special education directors lacked control over the professional development agendas and teacher release time in buildings. Local special education directors fear that the specialized professional development needs required to implement inclusive education will become secondary to the needs of other classroom teachers in a school building and inclusion will get lost as a priority.

In District M, special education decisions made by the informal school site councils are monitored by the central administration, which strives to maintain what it characterized as a consultant type relation with schools. According to one special education administrator, "We went out and said, 'Hey, we're not going to tell you what to do, but these are some of the parameters you have to operate within.'" The parameters were primarily driven by state and federal regulations for students with disabilities and did not dictate program models. Thus, inclusive practices tended to be defined building by building, and to respond to the philosophical influences of the staff in a building. On the one hand, some teachers perceived that controlling special education decisions at the building level had a positive effect on teachers and administrators. One teacher commented: "What that got for our children with disabilities was ownership of those students and their programs." On the other hand, administrators feel that they can only ensure legal and procedural consistency across buildings, and that special education practices will be increasingly varied. Parents in two districts reportedly shop around for a school that has the type of program they want for their child and then request a transfer, which the local administrator honors.

Summary and Conclusions

This chapter has presented selected findings obtained from case studies of educational reforms implemented in five local school districts and their perceived interactions with inclusion. The general education reform areas selected for review are among the more prominent initiatives being implemented in the local districts. For special educators in each of the districts, the focus was how to create more inclusive classrooms. However, these efforts were generally separated from the overall reform agenda, and tended to concentrate on placement of students with disabilities as opposed to changes in their curriculum. During the site visits, the researchers were directed to inclusive classrooms, and received a great deal of information about various general and special education collaboration models that were being implemented. Yet, there was little discussion about how this collaboration related to larger issues of inclusion of students with disabilities in standards, curriculum, frameworks, and assessments. In only one district had special education personnel begun to critically examine the IEP processes and forms to determine how to align these with new standards and assessments.

Findings point to some key challenges to promoting inclusion. For example, the development and implementation of new standards and resulting curriculum reform are clearly changing the context of classrooms in the five school districts. Not only are basic beliefs about the way in which children learn being challenged, but earlier conceptions of content scope and rigor are also being confronted. The development of standards and new assessments have encouraged schools to accept increased accountability for the outcomes of their students with disabilities. New approaches to governing schools are also impacting the education of students with disabilities. Local districts have adopted SBM, and choice options such as charter schools and magnet programs. Although these programs provide greater flexibility, they also pose challenges to creating inclusive schools.

There was great variability among special educators in all districts in terms of their level of knowledge of standards, assessments, and other district-reform initiatives. Special education administrators appeared to be focused with a number of issues specific to students with disabilities that may or may not relate to larger system reforms. Moreover, special education's endorsement or opposition to a specific initiative appeared to have little influence on the direction that a reform might take. Larger political and professional forces are shaping what standards look like, and how assessments will be used to ensure greater school accountability. The attention to students with disabilities in this decision-making process varied across the five states and local districts. Four of the five sites had specific guidelines or statements regarding how a student with a disability would be expected to participate. However, the implementation of the guidelines, such as when a student is exempted from an assessment, or given an assessment accommodation, or when a standard is modified, is very much under the control of special education teachers in local school buildings who are operating with little or no accountability for their decisions.

The lack of authority over individual schools resulting from changes in governance structures appeared even more trying for special education directors who wanted to maintain consistency across schools in the types of programs and procedures or to promote inclusive schools. They also wanted to ensure that their staff was not ignored in the site-based governance process. The directors in several districts expressed frustration at their lack of influence over the decisions of the site-based councils. Although no single director specifically addressed this issue in relation to standards, assessment, or accountability, it does cause one to question the effectiveness or inclusiveness of various state or district guidelines and policies concerning participation of students with disabilities in standards-based reform. Without accountability for key decisions such as those discussed here, it is unlikely that teachers or IEP teams will implement the policies consistently.

A major question raised by these case studies is whether standards-based reform works for students with disabilities. Do the reforms promote or impede the development of critical outcomes? Obviously, there is no definitive answer. Much depends on how the reforms are defined and implemented: What are the standards, how will student performance be measured, and who will be held accountable for meeting them? In addition, it is critical to determine how these reforms will interact with special educations' goal of creating more inclusive classrooms. The answer to this lies in part in how standards change the focus of instruction in classrooms and expectations about students, as well as the demands of new assessments and accountability requirements. Results of our case studies suggest that there are positive aspects as well as challenges in what schools are implementing. Current policies or proclamations regarding full participation of students with disabilities in reforms need to be examined and interpreted for building staff and parents to ensure that individuals know how to prioritize individual educational goals, and set expectations of what is important for students to know and be able to do as they leave school.

ACKNOWLEDGEMENTS

This research was supported by the Center for Policy Research on the Impact of General and Special Education Reform, a consortium of the Institute for the Study of Exceptional Children and Youth at the University of Maryland, the National Association of State Boards of Education, and the Consortium for Policy Research in Education at the University of Pennsylvania, funded by the Division of Innovation and Development, Office of the Special Education Program, U. S. Department of Education. The views expressed in this chapter do not constitute an official endorsement of the U. S. Department of Education.

This study has begun to identify key questions and issues for general and special education policymakers, administrators, teachers, and parents regarding how to implement the concepts of current *reform-challenging standards* and *increased public accountability* in an environment that respects the learning goals of all students, and honors their right to be educated in inclusive schools and communities.

REFERENCES

Cawelti, G. (1994). *High school restructuring: A national survey.* Arlington, VA: Educational Research Service.

Council of Chief State School Officers, State Education Assessment Center (1996). *Key state education policies on K–12 education: Content standards, graduation, teacher licensure, time and attendance.* Washington, DC: Author.

Elliott, J. Thurlow, M., & Ysseldyke, J. (1996). *Assessment guidelines that maximize the participation of students with disabilities in large-scale assessments: Characteristics and considerations.* (Synthesis Rep. No. 25). Minneapolis: University of Minnesota, National Center on Educational Outcomes.

Erickson, R., Thurlow, M. L., Thor, K., & Seyfarth, A. (1996). *1995 state special education outcomes.* Minneapolis: University of Minnesota, National Center on Educational Outcomes.

Erickson, R., Thurlow, M. L., & Ysseldyke, J. E. (1996). *Neglected numerators, drifting denominators, and fractured fractions:Determining participation rates for students with disabilities in statewide assessment programs.* Minneapolis: University of Minnesota, National Center on Educational Outcomes.

Falvey, M. A., Grenot-Scheyer, M., Coots, J. J., & Bishop, K. D. (1995). Services for students with disabilities: Past and present. In M. A. Falvey (Ed.), *Inclusive and heterogeneous schooling: Assessment, curriculum and instruction (pp. 23–29).* Baltimore: MD P. H. Brookes LC4031.I52, 1995.

Goals 2000: Educate America Act of 1994, Pub. L. No 103-227, 103rd Congress.

Goertz, M., & Friedman, D. (1996). *State education reform and students with disabilities: A preliminary analysis.* New Brunswick, NJ: Rutgers University, Consortium of Policy Research In Education and Center for Policy Research on the Impact of General and Special Education Reform.

Malen, B. (1994). Enacting site-based management: A political utilities analysis. *Educational Evaluation and Policy Analysis, 16(3),* 249–267.

McDonnell, L. M., McLaughlin, M. J., & Morison, P. (1997). Education One and All: Students with disabilities and Standard & Basic Reform. Washington, DC: National Research Council.

McLaughlin, M. W., & Sheppard, L. A. (1995). *Improving education through standards-based reform: A report of the National Academy of Education panel on standards-based reform.* Stanford, CA: The National Academy of Education.

Rabb, E. T. (1993). *Selected elementary school principal's perceptions of the issues related to special education in the school restructuring movement.* Unpublished doctoral dissertation, University of Maryland, College Park.

Rhim, L. M., & McLaughlin, M. J. (1997). *State policies and practices: Where are students with disabilities,* (Center for Policy Research on the Impact of General and Special Education Reform). Alexandria, VA: National Association of State Boards of Education.

Schofield, P. (1996). *School-based decision making: Perceived effects on students in special education.* Unpublished doctoral dissertation, University of Maryland, College Park.

Thurlow, M. L., Scott, D. L., & Ysseldyke, J. E. (1995). *A compilation of states' guidelines for including students with disabilities in assessment.* (Synthesis Rep. 17). Minneapolis: University of Minnesota, National Center on Educational Outcomes.

U.S. Department of Education, Office of Special Education Programs. (1996). *To assure a free appropriate public education of all children with disabilities: The Eighteenth Annual Report to Congress on the Implementation of the Individuals with Disabilities Education Act.* Washington, DC: Division of Innovation and Development.

U.S. General Accounting Office. (1994). *Education reform: School-based management results in changes in instruction and budgeting.* Washington, DC: Author.

U.S. National Research Center. (1996). *Third international mathematics and science study.* (Rep. No.7). East Lansing: Michigan State University, Author.

Wohlstetter, P., & Odden, A. (1992). Rethinking school-based management policy and research. *Educational Administration Quarterly, 28*(4), 529–549.

Yin, R. K. (1994). *Case study research: Design and method* (2nd ed.). Thousand Oaks, CA: Sage.

5

Characteristics of Elementary School Classrooms Where Children With Moderate and Severe Disabilities are Included: A Compilation of Findings

Martha E. Snell
University of Virginia

"Inclusion does not mean trying to 'fit' students with special needs into the mainstream; instead it means creating a mainstream where everyone fits" (Snell & Janney, 1993, p. 245). What is involved in this creation? What might classrooms and schools look like during and after the transition to inclusion? This chapter focuses on some of these structural and cultural changes that schools and classrooms undergo when children with disabilities are integrated into school, and included in general education classrooms. I draw heavily on my current research in Virginia as well as on the work of others.

EDUCATIONAL CHANGE

School reform poses many challenges: assessing the needs, specifying the outcomes, matching methods to needs and outcomes, involving the stakeholders, initiating the change, and sustaining its beneficial effects. Fullan's (1991) review of change in schools cited lengthy commitment periods of 5 to 10 years from initiation to stable establishment. Clark and Astuto (1994) reminded us that the improvement of schools is like individual learning. It must be an "interactive, mutually reinforcing activity" that builds from a grassroots approach and relies on the collaborative efforts of all the local stakeholders in a supportive environment (p. 516). Successful reform cannot be standardized reform, a mandate handed down from above, nor a "quick fix," but instead must build on a foundation of teacher collaboration, center on students, and be developed cooperatively in a particular community.

Several studies have analyzed the factors that promote and constrain change efforts in schools. For example, when change is initiated by someone who is in the role of a chief administrator and experienced with the content of the change, the probability for its success is increased (Huberman & Miles, 1984; LaRocque & Coleman, 1989). In fact, without specific pressure, both to implement the changes and to support them, Huberman and Miles found that adopted changes fail. Whether the location for this pressure and support to change must be in central office or could be in an individual school community with site-based management, a research update is needed. In cases when teachers did not have a commitment to the change, Huberman and Miles reported on the strong effects of having teachers practice the skills required by the innovation while providing needed assistance and support. Assistance-supported practice not only increased teachers' effort and skill, but also their commitment. Their study of 12 schools' experiences with change further indicated that initial applications of an innovation characteristically was described as being "rough," due to the new teacher and administrator responsibilities and the skills required. In fact, when the initial application of an innovation was described as being "smooth," the innovation rarely became permanent. Thus, although guided practice of needed skills contributes to the successful achievement of change, its initial implementation appears unpolished and crude, and requires real work to achieve meaningful outcomes.

There appear to be some advantages of setting preliminary goals for achieving localized or incremental school reform rather than aiming initially for systemic reform. These advantages have included fewer staff conflicts when a system agrees to pilot a reform on a smaller scale, respect for professional choice (e.g., the option for participation or for observation from a wait-and-see position by those not involved), and the opportunity to learn from observation of colleagues' positive involvement (Bredo & Bredo, 1975). Schools considering complex change, such as required by inclusion may want to plan for early incremental reform as it may assist rather than hinder a school's overall progress toward systemwide commitment to that reform.

INTEGRATION AND INCLUSION AS SCHOOL CHANGE

There has been substantial concern regarding the practice of providing special education via a continuum of services and its impact on children (Gartner & Lipsky, 1987; Lytle, 1988; *Oberti v. Clementon*, 1993; Skrtic, 1991; Taylor, 1988). When school systems restructure their programs so that children with special needs receive individualized services and supports in general education classrooms in their neighborhood schools, significant effort is required for widespread impact (McLaughlin & Warren, 1992). Making special education a support service rather than a location for services involves many changes in the roles and responsibilities of teachers and administrators. The studies of school reform cited here did not focus on the change from a pull-out model to an inclusion model for providing special education. However, those studying educational change suggest that the specific innovation or change that a school undertakes may be less important than the fact that a school system is attempting to incorporate any significant change into their operation and policy (Fullan, 1991; Huberman & Miles, 1984; Sarason, 1990). Thus, those involved in inclusion should benefit from knowing this research. Recent studies of inclusion lend evidence to the existence of similarities in the process by which schools seem to evolve through change regardless of the specific change. These studies of children with disabilities who have been included in general education alongside their peers not only contribute to the position that inclusion can produce desirable outcomes for both students and schools, but they also emphasize the complexity of the change process and its similarity to other efforts of improving schools (Evans, Salisbury, Palombaro, Berryman, & Hollowood, 1992; Ferguson, Meyer, Jeanchild, Juniper, & Zingo, 1992; Giangreco, Dennis, Cloninger, Edelman, & Schattman, 1993; Kozleski & Jackson, 1993; Salisbury, Palombaro, & Hollowood, 1993;   Stevens & Slavin, 1995; York, Vandercook, Macdonald, Heise-Neff, & Caughey, 1992).

For some schools with traditional pull-out models of delivering special education, the integration of special education students into general education classes involves significant redefinition of professional roles, increased interactions between teachers, as well as some preparatory and ongoing skill development. Yet, integration of students with nondisabled peers does not necessarily mean that students with special needs attend their neighborhood school, nor that they spend much of their day alongside their peers, nor that all students with disabilities are involved, nor that individualized adaptations and supports are provided in the general education setting. *Integration* is an umbrella concept that, when applied to disability and schools, generally means that students with disabilities simply spend time with their nondisabled peers. *Mainstreaming*, also under the broad umbrella of integration, is an older term that primarily has concerned students with mild disabilities attending general education classes, although more often without systematic and meaningful support, such as individualized accommodations and curricular adaptations (Rogers, 1993). Instead, mainstreaming often has meant that students must earn the opportunity and then must simply "sink or swim" in the mainstream. Inclusion, by contrast, means that students with disabilities attend their neighborhood school in proportions natural to the region, and that individualized accommodations, curricular adaptations, and other supports follow students into the general education classroom and into schoolwide activities (lunch, music, bus transportation, assemblies, etc.). Inclusion is individually planned for each student and relies upon collaborative teaming between general and special educators and others on the student's team. Inclusion does not preclude the use of pull-out services such as resource room or community based instruction, and its implementation includes planning not only for strategies to produce learning and social acceptance, but also for the transition between grades, teachers, and schools. Primarily due to special education staffing considerations, inclusion is a more complicated change in service delivery than is integration or mainstreaming. Current research reflects these three approaches to inclusion, although researchers may not differentiate clearly between them nor describe what version operated in the schools studied.

Since the 1980s, we have learned many things about promoting the inclusion of students with severe disabilities in schools and inclusion's effect on students and staff. Attending one's home or neighborhood school appears to contribute positively to the conditions for establishing and maintaining meaningful relationships with peers (Brown et al., 1989; Fryxell & Kennedy, 1995), whereas   partial integration, particularly early in school, does not seem to promote membership in a class, nor establish the conditions for reciprocal relationships or friendships to develop (Schnorr, 1990). Preschoolers across a range of disabilities, and older students with more severe disabilities, appear to demonstrate more improvements in social and behavioral outcomes when they are enrolled in integrated school settings with special education services than when they are enrolled in segregated school settings and classrooms (Buysee & Bailey, 1993; Cole & Meyer, 1991; Fryxell & Kennedy, 1995). Fryxell and Kennedy found that included elementary students with severe disabilities had significantly higher levels of social contact with nondisabled peers, more social supports, and larger friendship networks than did similar students enrolled in self-contained classrooms. However, research to the contrary exists as well for elementary-aged students with mild disabilities (Sale & Carey, 1995) and for preschoolers with speech and language disabilities or emotional disturbance. These contradictory findings may that social benefits are not automatic for children with disabilities when they are included among nondisabled peers, and that the social benefits are not necessarily better in inclusive classrooms than in self-contained classrooms with primarily mildly delayed children and trained teachers (Sontag, 1997).

Improvements on academic outcomes have far less support, although it is likely that we are less knowledgeable about curriculum adaptation, and how to bridge the diverse range in academic needs between students with severe disabilities, and their typical peers. Some recent research has shown that active engagement and learning by children with moderate to severe disabilities and by their nondisabled classmates, depends in part on the skilled use of teaching arrangements like cooperative groups (Hunt,   Staub, Alwell, & Goetz, 1994), the avoidance of   whole-class instruction (Logan, Bakeman, & Keefe, 1997), and the circumvention of social barriers created by overzealous or protective teaching assistants assigned to individual children with disabilities (Giangreco, Edelman, Luiselli, & MacFarland, 1997; Schnorr, 1997).

The primary rationale for integration and inclusion of these students with moderate and severe disabilities concerns the social and attitudinal benefits they accrue. Their presence in general education classrooms has been shown by some researchers to have benefits for peers and teachers. Researchers have demonstrated that, when included students have the proper supports, typical peers and classmates tend to experience positive personal growth and may develop meaningful relationships with those who have disabilities (Evans et al., 1992; Hall, 1994; Helmstetter, Peck, & Giangreco, 1994; Kishi & Meyer, 1994; Peck, Donaldson, & Pezzoli, 1990). For general education teachers, the current research on inclusion seems to indicate that, when they have the proper individualized supports for included students, the experiences teachers have with such a student in their classroom tend to lead gradually to   (a) feelings of ownership for that student, (b) positive views of inclusion, (c) comfort in interacting with and teaching the student, and (d) a willingness to learn about inclusion approaches from their typical students (Ferguson et al., 1992; Giangrego et al., 1993; York et al., 1992).

Some evidence of inclusion's effect on peer learning has been presented that indicates that the effects may be neutral, and thus not negative (Staub & Peck, 1995) or positive (Hunt, Staub, Alwell, & Goetz, 1994). This relation between the presence of students with disabilities in general education classrooms, and learning by students with and without disabilities is a complex one with many factors having an influence on learning (e.g., design and implementation of inclusion, quality of the teachers involved, use of instructional arrangements and adaptations). For example, Logan, Bakeman, and Keefe (1997) reported that the amount of engagement students with moderate to profound disabilities had in general education classrooms was related to the instructional arrangement teachers used: one-to-one, small group, and independent work arrangements resulted in more engaged behaviors than did whole-class arrangements. With additional precise research on the outcomes for students with and without disabilities across the range of special education service delivery models, we can better assess the impact inclusion has on student learning and weigh the attitude and social benefits that have been reported by peers, parents, and teachers.

TEACHERS WORKING TOGETHER TO INCLUDE STUDENTS WITH DISABILITIES

The research I describe next was built on these findings just reviewed, and was conducted in schools applying either an integrative or an inclusive service delivery model with students having moderate and severe disabilities. Almost all the research I discuss has been conducted with my colleague Rachel Janney. The research has relied on qualitative analyses of many data sources: formal and informal interviews with teachers and administrators; conversations with paraprofessionals, peers, parents, related services staff; direct observations in classrooms and other school settings and at meetings; fieldnotes taken on these observations; meeting summaries, student performance data; and teacher planning documents. I review some of the trends in our findings across several studies giving particular attention to (a) teachers' understandings of implementing change, (b) changes in roles and responsibilities, (c) teachers' means of accommodating differences, (d) teachers' use of peer interactions to promote inclusion, and (e) child-focused problem-solving between teachers.

Teachers' Understandings of Implementing Change

In our first study (Janney, Snell, Beers, & Raynes, 1995a), we interviewed 26 elementary to high school general education, classroom teachers from five school districts where planned change had been undertaken toward integrating students with moderate and severe disabilities into general education. These school districts had not attempted inclusion, but aimed to improve their programs so all the focus students were served in age-appropriate, general education schools and had at least several daily opportunities to be part of classes and other school activities with nondisabled peers. Our interviews focused on these teachers' beliefs and attitudes toward the integration efforts in which they had directly participated in their schools and the resultant changes. We found that teachers viewed four aspects of these efforts and changes as most important to them: their purpose, the clarity, the effort or work involved, and the rewards.

The teachers' initial reaction to the integration effort was uncertainty about the purpose. They wondered what they could offer these students who had been segregated from their peers. They commented on their lack of training: "I'm not trained in working with the kids, and their ability levels are miles from what we do in here every day. We're really at this point working on the socialization . . ." (Janney et al., 1995a, p. 102). However, the rationale that these students would accrue social benefits from being included with peers appealed to them. Following their experience with individual students, these teachers learned that the socialization rationale was applicable as well to their students without disabilities.

Even though all teachers involved volunteered to participate in the integration effort, they expressed early concerns about a lack of clarity on their role and their responsibilities with the included students. What would they teach the students who were "miles below what we do in here" (Janney et al., 1995a, p.102)? They credited special education teachers with alleviating their initial fears (more work, and having to teach these students they had not been trained to teach) by giving them practical information on the students' needs and skills, and credited the process of getting to know the student as further clarifying what the change would entail. The general education teachers acknowledged the respect that special education teachers and administrators had for their autonomy, such as letting them choose to be involved or not and seeking out and using their ideas.

Teachers' criteria for success of the change to integration was whether students had fit in, both socially and in instructional activities. Their initial fears of ridicule and isolation were replaced by judgments that the students with disabilities had been accepted by peers and that positive relationships had resulted. Students were either integrated primarily for socialization or were integrated for classes. This former group's "real learning" continued to be addressed by special education, whereas the latter group was viewed as needing minimal adaptations, which typically were easily implemented by the special education teacher. Thus, special educators were a reliable source of support, while peers became an unexpected source of support to teachers with their practical help, their attention, and their ideas. This design for integrating students with disabilities meant that general education teachers' fears of having to do more work were not realized, but this design also meant that the change was incremental in nature, and did not extend beyond the included students or the affected classrooms.

Finally, teachers expressed benefits far beyond the included students: for their typical students, for themselves, and for the school community. Similar to the findings of Giangreco et al. (1993) on the transformation of general education teachers by inclusion, the teachers we interviewed not only expressed their goal for included students "being a part" (p.106) of their classes but talked about that goal being realized along with the unanticipated rewards that emanated from their own interactions with the students themselves. Classroom teachers discovered that their students with disabilities had personalities and skills and could learn. In turn, teachers were motivated by their own unexpected discoveries.

We found that several elements favorable to change were operating within the classrooms in which these teachers taught: (a) Teachers accepted socialization as a valid purpose for the change; (b) teachers obtained clarity about the change through in-service training and through having a choice to participate and the opportunity to influence the process; (c) their concerns were addressed by receiving support that matched their concerns; and (d) the outcomes of the change fueled their motivation for it. The changes that occurred as a result of these integration efforts were incremental in nature. Not all teachers or students participated; socialization, not academics, was the primary focus for most; and change did not occur in the teachers' primary roles, nor in the classrooms' basic goals or structure. Even though the changes were incremental, they provided positive experiences that could stimulate further change. For example, teachers reported that they talked to, asked questions of, and cooperated more with each other, a characteristic many identify as essential to any educational improvement. However, to ensure that incremental changes remain positive and advance over time, school leaders need to become involved, organizational structures must be modified to provide the foundation, and school cultures need to become collaborative in nature (Fullan, 1991; Skrtic, 1991).

Changes in Roles and Responsibilities

In several studies, we have learned more about how teachers and administrators implementing integration and inclusion perceive their changing roles and responsibilities. One of the primary modifications teachers described that accompanied the shift to delivering special education in the general education classroom was the addition of full- or part-time special education teaching assistants or teachers to the general education classroom (Janney & Snell, 1997; Janney, Snell, Beers, & Raynes, 1995b). With this modification, the general educator was still regarded as the primary teacher who planned the schedule, lessons, and activities and established classroom rules and routines (see first part of Table 5.1).

When the included student was part of a class activity and treated the same as classmates, the classroom teacher took primary responsibility, although an assistant might be available to facilitate the child's involvement, or the involvement of other children with the focus child. When special education staff were in the classroom, the class teacher still maintained this primary role.

The special education teacher's influence and responsibility was most visible when the included student was treated differently from peers. For example, special education staff attended to children's health and physical needs (medication, eating toileting) when these needs differed from their classmates, and made sure children went to and from therapy when pull-out therapy was employed. Special education staff

TABLE 5.1.
Three Types of Classroom Modifications

Type and Purpose of Modification	Requirements, Critical Features
1. Teacher Role Modifications: Modify teachers' roles so that student belongs to the classroom teacher but receives assistance from special education teacher and assistant.	**Classroom Teacher Responsibilities:** (i) treat focus student same as the group as much as possible (ii) provide selected supports/adaptations (e.g., maintain proximity, assign peer helpers, provide cues) **Special Education Staff Responsibilities:** (i) maintain agreed on presence (ii) attend to physical/health needs (iii) adapt materials (iv) provide parallel instruction (v) assist other students and classroom teacher
2. Classroom RoutineModifications Modify classroom routines and physical environment to keep student situated near peers and in similar seating.	Adults and peers provide physical help and cues to stay with the group. Provide adaptive equipment, positioning Change timing and/or location of activities as necessary.
3. Instructional Activity Modifications: Maintain topical connections with class learning activities. Degree of participation varies:	
a. **Academic Adaptations:** Achieve active academic and social participation in class lesson and provide instruction in individualized learning goals.	Same activity with modified methods, input or response mode, objectives, criteria, and/or materials planned by special educator; implemented by special education teacher, classroom teacher, assistant, or peer.
b. **Social Participation Strategies:** Maintain connections to group through social participation, but not to achieve active academic participation.	Same activity, same or adapted materials Additional staff not required Primarily for students with severe disabilities
c. **Parallel Activities:** Conduct instruction in classroom and generally nearby classmates, yet separately from classroom group; maintain topical similarity to class lesson, but social participation minimized.	Different activity, similar lesson topic Designed and delivered by special educators More during reading and math

Note. From "How teachers include students with moderate and severe disabilities in elementary classes: The means and meaning of inclusion," Janney, R. E. & Snell, M. E. (1997). *Journal of the Association for Persons with Severe Handicaps, 42*(2), p. 163. Copyright © 1997 (by) The Journal of the Association for Persons with Severe Handicaps Reprinted [or adapted] with permission.

also taught and assisted others in the class, although their main roles centered on the included student and assisting the classroom teacher (Table 5.1).

In another study (Janney, Snell, Beers, & Raynes, 1995b), we interviewed 54 teachers and administrators from 10 schools involved in integration efforts, and queried them for the advice they would offer other educators facing a change to integration. They offered numerous suggestions that related to roles and responsibilities. Principals were advised to make known their positive attitude toward integration in the school and to bolster teacher input by promoting a collaborative teaming approach for planning integration and resolving problems with its implementation. Starting implementation with teachers who volunteered was viewed as a way principals could respect teachers' autonomy. Principals were relied on for arranging orientation and training sessions relevant to integration, involving all staff, managing the logistics of schedules, staff adjustments, obtaining needed materials, and making the building accessible. Educators championed the practices that principals start small and build on success, but also grant teachers collegial support and the freedom to implement integration using their own ideas.

Special education teachers were advised to provide interpersonal supports to general education teachers in a manner that could be characterized as being harmonious, flexible, enthusiastic, and nonintrusive. The second type of supports special education teachers were urged to give general education staff were task-related supports: Information about the included students' strengths and needs, along with ideas for including them meaningfully in their classes. Interviewees agreed that special education teachers could not work alone, but needed to practice mutual planning and teamwork. Thus, special education teachers were recommended to seek the classroom teacher's ideas on when and where to include the student and whether assistance in staffing or materials preparation was needed.

Finally, general education teachers were cautioned not to bend to their fears about integration, but to "go in with an open mind" (Janney et al., 1995b, p. 435). Most interviewees confessed to having early fears about integration, but described the strong positive attitudes that replaced these fears after getting to know a student with disabilities on an individual basis. Furthermore, general education teachers were urged to work in teams to resolve problems, ask questions, brainstorm, and experiment. Helping the student with disabilities belong was a final theme of advice for general education teachers. Specific suggestions were to model this philosophy of treating the student like others for peers to learn by, teach peers to interact with the included classmate, and take actions that would foster positive relationships between these focus students and their nondisabled peers.

A third, but less extensive interview study with teaching staff and administrators in one elementary school where inclusion was practiced, yielded evidence for many of these same role changes (Snell et al., 1995). A strong collaborative emphasis was evident in the responsibilities described for all staff. Several additional responsibilities were added to those previously mentioned for special education teachers: Respect the classroom teacher's role, base curricular adaptations on the teacher's lesson plans and schedule, collaborate with others who teach the student (e.g., art, music, library, etc.), train and supervise special education teaching assistants while coordinating with the classroom teacher, develop and assist in implementing any programs involving problem behavior by the included student, and work with classmates to involve the included student in a positive and age-appropriate way. The role characteristics of teaching assistants were unanimously described as being team members who integrate into the classroom like any other teaching adult. Assistants who hovered over the focus student, or failed to help the focus student participate as a class member, were judged to discourage successful peer interactions. Finally, all staff shared in common the responsibility for fostering the involvement of classmates in the effort. Specifically, staff were advised to answer peers' questions sensitively, to serve as models for interaction, to engage peers in problem-solving around the included child, and, at least initially, to monitor, but not stifle, interactions. Table 5.2 sets forth some of the major findings regarding staff roles.

Table 5.2
Changing Roles in Inclusive Schools (Snell et al., 1995)

Responsibilities of General Educators	**Responsibilities of Teaching Assistants**
Treat the child like other students	Self-initiate
Model for peers	Work with other students
Develop and use adaptations	Be part of the team
Function as a team member	Know and work well with the focus child
Serve as the child's primary teacher	Help the child fit into the class
Be flexible	
Responsibilities of Special Educators	**Responsibilities of Related Services Providers**
Serve as the inclusion facilitator and case manager	"Don't pull out the kids; do your work in the context of the class activities"
Work with general education teachers	Provide equipment that helps the child participate
Collaborate	in class activities
Make curricular adaptations	Have flexible schedules that allow therapy to be
Teach and supervise the teaching assistant	provided during the most relevant times (e.g.,
Provide information on the child	physical therapy during physical education)
Develop, assist in implementing, and supervise behavior programs	Obtain lesson plans from the teacher and weave the child's therapy objectives into the
Work with peers	planned class activities
	Come prepared with adaptations and "be able to jump in and do whatever the class is doing"
Responsibilities of the Principal	Be sensitive enough to know when to stay and when to leave
Give teachers a choice about participating	**Promoting Peer Involvement**
Initiate and be active in a school integration committee	
Prepare teaching staff for the change to inclusion	Answer the questions
	Model appropriate interactions
Provide teacher support when needed	Use peer planning groups
Address the concerns of parents and others about inclusion	Monitor interactions and help peers problem-solve
Participate in problem-solving around specific children	Assign buddies
Handle the logistics that affect inclusion	Use cooperative learning groups

Note: From Source: Changing roles in inclusive schools: Staff perspectives at Gilbert Linkous Elementary., Snell, M. E., Raynes, M., Byrd, J. O., Colley, K. M., Gilley, C., Pitonyak, C., Stallings, M. A., VanDyke, R., William, P. S., & Willis, C. J. (1995)., *Kappa Delta Pi Record, 31*, 104 - 109. © 1995 by Kappa Delta Pi Record. Reprinted (or adapted) with permission.

Means of Accommodating Differences

Regardless of the severity of the disability, multiple strategies appear necessary to accommodate the differences in learning objectives that exist between students with disabilities and their nondisabled peers, as well to achieve their social belonging among peers or their classroom membership (e.g., Deno, Foegen, Robinson, & Espin, 1996; Giangreco et al., 1993; Jenkins et al., 1994; Kozleski & Jackson, 1993; Salisbury, Mangino, Rainforth, & Syryca, 1994; Stevens & Slavin, 1995). We also have found that multiple strategies are necessary for inclusion to be meaningful, but have extended our focus to examine the ways teachers work together to plan these accommodations and to implement them.

In a recent study of seven classrooms (kindergarten to third grade) in four elementary schools (Janney & Snell, 1997), we studied the ways that teachers worked together to include students with extensive disabilities in their general education classes, and found similar practices among elementary general and special education teachers for making modifications to include these students. The three school systems from which they were drawn used different models for including students with moderate to severe disabilities ranging from full inclusion (neighborhood school, enrolled in general education class all day), to full integration (clustered school, all day), to partial integration (clustered school, part of the day). Table 5.1 lists the three types of classroom modifications these teachers used to include students with moderate to severe disabilities: teacher role modifications, classroom routine modifications, and instructional activity modifications. In the previous section of this chapter, I briefly described the first modification: the ways general and special educators agreed to change or not change their routine responsibilities in order to include the child with disabilities. To reiterate, classroom teachers continued to have primary authority for the class and for the included child when treated the same as others, whereas special education teachers and assistants had primary responsibility for special services (when the focus child was treated differently from classmates for health, physical needs, or learning) and also served to assist the classroom teacher and nondisabled students. Furthermore, we found that teachers set several things forth in unwritten inclusion agreements between them: (a) their assumptions about inclusion (e.g., as possible, keep the focus student near their peers, treat them the same, and provide them with the same or similar activities and materials); (b) the specifics of who would do what to include the child; and (c) some individually defined duties of what the general education teacher would and would not do.

At times, general and special educators made adaptations in classroom routines, or in the school environment for the purpose of keeping focus students situated near their peers. These classroom--routine modifications included having peers hold the hand of a focus student on the way to physical education class, or pushing a wheelchair to keep the child with the class; making room for adaptive equipment so a student could lie on the floor amid his or her peers at story time; and using adapted seats the same height as peers' chairs at an art activity and when using the computer.

Sometimes the scheduled time or location of a class activity was moved, so the child's inclusion with the group was facilitated.

We observed three general types of modifications made to instructional activities: academic adaptations, social participation strategies, and parallel activities. As described in the third section of Table 5.1, these three types of modifications meant that one or more characteristics of an instructional activity was changed for students with disabilities in contrast to their nondisabled peers. Changes may have been made in the types of materials used by a focus child (adapted or not adapted), the curricular theme or topic of lesson for a focus child (same, related, or different from peers'), the actual task or activity participated in by the focus child (same or different from peers'), the amount of participation by the focus child (a little to a lot), the type of participation by the focus child (academic, social, or both), proximity of focus student to peers, and the effort required by staff (planning, preparation of materials). Academic adaptations allowed for both active participation in the academic task, and social participation in the group of classmates due to their proximity and involvement in the same activity. Focus students were with their peers (whole class or in a group) and involved in the same activity, but often with some modification made to enable their participation. Adaptations required some planning by teachers, at least initially, and involved adjustments in response (listen to a tape instead of reading), objectives (simplified content), criteria (half the amount of spelling words), or materials (sandpaper letters, adapted scissors).

Sometimes instructional activities were modified only to the extent that enabled a focus student to participate socially. This meant that the student remained with the group and had the same or modified materials, but did not achieve participation that could be described as "academically active," although they participated socially with their peers (e.g., sat alongside, held similar materials, received hand-over-hand prompting to turn pages). Strategies to promote social participation had the advantage of not requiring additional staff or extensive planning: a nonreading student with disabilities sat by a peer at music and shared a music book, but did not sing. The disadvantage was that student participation was often minimal or limited to "being there," making one question whether the focus child was learning.

Finally, we observed what we call *parallel activities*, when special education staff worked with one or two students with special needs and conducted individualized instruction apart from peers though in the same classroom. These parallel activities usually were topically similar to the lesson peers worked on nearby (e.g., peers worked on subtraction problems while focus students counted coins), but, because of the physical separation, social participation with peers was minimal. We found that parallel activities required the presence of special education staff, occurred more often in Grades 2 and 3 (in contrast to kindergarten and Grade 1), and happened when activity-based instruction was less easy (during reading and math, rather than science and social studies).

Both social participation strategies and parallel activities were easier to create and implement than academic adaptations due to a lack of collaborative planning time or, in the case of social participation strategies, no extra staff. The unwritten inclusion agreement between the teachers did not state that the entire classroom would be redesigned, nor that the classroom teacher needed to adjust the teaching methods to facilitate inclusion. Instead, what we observed in these five classrooms was a containment approach to change. The modifications that were made to promote individualized social and academic participation were focused on the child with disabilities, whereas, the teaching focus for classmates remained unchanged. An emphasis on academic participation, not social belonging, without individualization, but driven instead by a grade-level curriculum applied to an entire class.

One way to extend social belonging support for students with disabilities beyond the teachers is to involve peers in that process. Several researchers have described approaches for teaching nondisabled peers to become social supports for their classmates with disabilities. These interventions involved multiple components such as a "buddy" or peer group system to match peers to a classmate, regular peer support meetings to provide information and engage in problem-solving, facilitation of social interactions to prompt and interpret communication as needed, the selection of mutually interesting activities or media as the content for social exchange, and communication skill instruction for the student with disabilities (Haring & Breen, 1992; Hunt, Alwell, Farron-David, & Goetz, 1996; Vandercook, (1991). Another way to overcome the contained change that we observed, and to extend social support to all students, is to build cooperative school environments (Salisbury, Galucci, Palombaro, & Peck, 1995).

Using Peer Interactions to Include Students with Disabilities

In another study of the same classrooms, we focused on the ways teachers used interactions with peers as the means for including young children with moderate to severe disabilities in kindergarten through Grade 3. We found that the norms of independence and competition seemed to dominate school activities for students without disabilities unless cooperative activities were in place (and more often in most kindergarten activities). Work requirements and behavior expectations were fairly uniform for typical students, and helping each other was not encouraged. By contrast, the norms were different for nondisabled peers interacting with the students who had moderate to severe disabilities. Peers were encouraged to help these classmates and did so by pushing wheelchairs, holding their hands to guide them places, giving prompts for them to perform, getting equipment or needed articles, supervising or monitoring their behavior, and brainstorming adaptations. Teachers indicated that peer assistance was needed to support the focus students, and viewed peer assistance as a strategy to promote peer interaction.

> Our analyses of the fieldnotes and informal interviews with staff and students
> indicated two sets of information about these new norms for peer helping:
> Teachers had rules for when peers could help and when they could not help,
> and teachers taught lessons (incidentally and sometimes directly) on how to
> help and how to interact with their classmates who had disabilities. These

rules included three guidelines for when to help classmates with disabilities: Students could help when,

1. One was chosen as the peer helper of the day (*"I'm* supposed to be helping," a kindergartner said vehemently to a peer who was helping the focus child without having been chosen as the day's helper, (p. 76)
2. One was asked to help by school staff,
3. One volunteered to help, but at the right time (not "when I'm teaching the lesson," said a third-grade teacher; but when "we're not working," said a first grader, (p. 76).

Helping peers was discouraged at times when teachers were teaching priority activities or, in some cases, if focus students indicated they did not want help. However, sometimes peers did not give focus children an opportunity to indicate whether they wanted help or not, but simply imposed their assistance.

The lessons teachers gave on how to help and how to facilitate socialization fell into four categories: (a) "Don't do it for him," (b) "Just another student," (c) Age-appropriate interactions, and (d) "Back off." The first category of how to give help, *"Don't do it for him,"* concerned the provision of support without hindering the child's independence: helping in a way that lets focus students participate as much as they can on their own. At the same time, staff were observed to ignore this advice, and make decisions for focus students rather than supporting them to make such decisions more independently (e.g., first-grade teacher asked peers to think about what Kim could do during field day, but did not look to Kim for her reaction, nor did she try to give Kim choices).

The lesson entitled *"Just another student"* rested on teachers' belief that focus students be treated the same as their peers as much as possible. Evidence of peers learning this lesson were prevalent: Peers greeted and sat close to focus students, joked with them, played games with them, shared personal information, and assumed they would be included in all activities even when they weren't. Peers reacted as if the rules for behavior were the same (e.g., a peer gently pushed Peter's head down on his desk after the teacher scolded the students for their noise, and told them to put their heads down); and teachers verbalized that class rules applied to everyone in the class. Teachers expressed pleasure when they observed typical students treat focus students like each other rather than differently.

Teachers also agreed that focus students should be treated age-appropriately and were encouraged to look and act in ways that reflected their chronological age. For example, teachers tried to normalize several students' appearances by encouraging jeans over short frilly dresses in a second grader and planning to fade out over-sized crayons and use an age-appropriate adaptation for a child who could not grasp easily. Some children learned through teachers' direct corrections: Focus students were their age peers, not "babies." Teacher's lessons in this area seemed potent as most of the interactions we observed between peers and focus students were both equitable and age-appropriate.

Finally, the lesson of "backing off" was a strategy adults used to encourage peers to socialize without hampering their interactions. Teachers expressed agreement that hovering over students as they socialized prevented them from being themselves and doing "kid stuff" (Janney & Snell, 1996, p. 78). Thus, we observed staff setting up a play situation in the sandbox by getting Daniel (who had extensive cerebral palsy) well-situated on a waterproof mat near his peers, and then moving back when the children appeared and started to interact with him.

These rules for helping, and lessons to teach nondisabled classmates to socialize with the focus children, were evident in all five classrooms, kindergarten through third grade. Although general education teachers appeared to have fairly uniform expectations for typical students in learning and to minimize their differences, they willingly worked with special education teachers to make unique modifications that encouraged academic and social participation in students with disabilities. The challenges posed by these focus students were that their developmental levels were moderately different to highly different from their peers. Teachers tried to accommodate for the differences in these students through academic and social adaptations, but they also implemented rules for socialization and helping that promoted their focus students' similarity with peers, which teachers seemed to believe was necessary for them to "belong."

What seemed to result from these practices was the existence of two cultures in these classrooms: one for the nondisabled students that we regarded as being competitive (competition between students, goals of independence, and uniform treatment of students by adults), and one for the focus children that we saw as being cooperative (cooperation students encouraged, goals of interdependence, and accommodation and adaptation for individual differences). However, two of the helping practices just described seemed to be counterproductive to the cooperative culture that operated for focus children. First was the practice of teachers asking peers to be tutors of focus students or to supervise their behavior in other adultlike and nonreciprocal ways. Second was the fact that the rules for helping each other were based on ability and disability rather than defined by the situation, and thus, helping was usually one-way: from nondisabled student to the student with disabilities. Still, it was true that the clear majority of peer interactions we observed were positive, even when these interactions involved helping.

Our observations raise several questions about the existence of these dual cultures. Can teachers implement classroom rules for helping each other that are based less on "wishing to do good to others" or benevolence, and more on working together for the mutual benefit? Can the individual who helps and the individual who is given help be defined by the situation rather than by the presence of ability and disability? Many have commented on the benefits that would result for all students if a cooperative culture replaced the competitive culture that seems to prevail in general education classrooms (Salisbury, Palombaro, & Hollowood, 1993; Sapon-Shevin, 1992; Van der Klift & Kunc, 1994).

Problem-solving Between Teachers

A current study has been directed toward teachers and their ways of working together to include young children with disabilities in the primary grades (Snell & Janney, 1998). Over a 13-month period, we observed teachers and school staff interacting in teams to problem-solve issues and design supports for three children with more extensive disabilities who were fully included in two kindergartens and a first-grade class. The length of study allowed us to observe the changes in teachers' perceptions of inclusion and how their working arrangements evolved over time.

We found that teachers and support staff repeatedly interacted on three main areas of concern regarding the focus students: their abilities, their participation in class activities, and their class membership. For example, the primary concern for one kindergartner was his ability to communicate, which also influenced his participation in class activities (indicating what he wanted to do, and when he wanted a change or needed help). Another student's concern was her difficulty attending to and completing activities. Many issues for the third student involved his ability to walk and move around the room and school. Teaching staff held these informal, problem-solving discussions frequently, in groups of two or more, in many situations (recess, while children worked or played independently, over lunch, etc.), at many times of the day (before and after school and during the day), and at planned (sit down) and unplanned ("on-the-fly") meetings. At these discussions, school staff primarily involved with the focus child (classroom and special education teachers, teaching assistants, related services staff, "specials" teachers for music, library, and physical education, and principal) focused on a single child at a time and primarily addressed child concerns rather than concerns about the team members or team functioning. These discussions tended to follow a problem-solving cycle of six steps:

1. Identify your concern: The problem was named or described.
2. Watch, think, and talk: Staff observed the focus child to see the problem, then thought and talked about it among themselves.
3. Throw out ideas: Staff brainstormed solutions, reviewed what had been tried or could be tried.
4. That sounds good or that won't work: Staff judged these potential solutions as workable or not, while also modifying or combining some ideas to improve their expected success.
5. Give it a shot: Staff tried out the agreed on solution with the focus child.
6. More watch, think, and talk: Staff observed the outcomes, thought about, and discussed the results.

A cycling through these six steps may have taken several days or just part of a day, but the discussions were often hurried and curtailed by the time available, and sometimes lengthened when more team members needed to be consulted or simply continued without input from all needed team members ("We usually try to work it out ourselves because Maggie's [special education teacher] not here all the time, and Nate [student] is, so you can't wait for Maggie," (Snell & Janney, 1998, p. 18). We found that the same problem or concern was tackled repeatedly. However, with each recycling through the problem-solving steps, staff started with a redefinition or refinement of the problem, and then moved to design a revision and refinement of the solution. Teachers described themselves as working as a team using an active process of talking and trying things out: "We talk, we try something, we talk again, and we revise our plans" (Snell & Janney, 1995a, p. 86).

For these teachers and school staff, collaborative teaming was more often done "on the fly" between two or three staff members before or after school, during transitions in activities, between classes, at lunch, and during recess. Given these characteristics, special effort had to be made to communicate with all involved. This responsibility belonged primarily to the special education teacher. Formal team meetings with parents were held about every 6 weeks, but were not frequent enough to serve the often daily need for problem-solving. The special education teacher's schedule, which was divided between two schools and several classrooms, was formalized so teachers could count on his or her presence for direct student support, assessment, "touching base" on current progress, problem-solving, and team teaching.

We also noted that sometimes the topic of discussion shifted from child-centered concerns to adult- or team-centered concerns such as (a) disagreement about a child's goals or problem identification (e.g., the special education teacher viewed hugging the focus child as a problem of age-inappropriate behavior, whereas another staff member did not); (b) coordination problems (e.g., having time to talk and plan, scheduling meetings and related service staff, etc.); (c) implementation and evaluation problems (inadequate solutions or staff skills, partial team decision rather than consensus); and (d) communication problems (disagreement and hurt feelings, inadequate communication, trust). When the focus of team discussions shifted away from child concerns to adult concerns, it seemed that progress on child concerns were postponed until the difficulties that sidetracked collaboration were resolved.

In inclusive schools, many agree that collaborative teaming is "the glue that holds it all together." Yet most recognize that traditional school environments do not promote the teacher interdependence that is required by collaboration, or as Little (1990) called it: the "joint work" between teachers that involves taking "a single course of action in concert" (p. 519). These observations support the belief that inclusion requires teaming between general and special educators and suggests specific aspects of the problem-solving process involved. It appears that teachers were motivated to work together in part because they required each others' talents in order to succeed with including a child with disabilities in a general education classroom. Neither teacher could accomplish this goal alone nor without the cooperation of the other.

CONCLUSIONS

Although our knowledge about inclusion is expanding, it is still rather imprecise about the ways that special and general education teachers come to understand their work with each other around individual students with disabilities, and how teachers define and resolve issues of including students who are highly diverse from their typical peers. We know that successful inclusion of students requiring extensive support is possible under rather ordinary circumstances, and that inclusion can be both beneficial to students with and without disabilities, and be viewed with favor by teachers and parents. But it is also clear that successful inclusion involves some elaborate improvements in schools, including changes in teachers' roles and skills, some novel combinations of instructional strategies and staff scheduling, and collaborative teaming. These improvements need to come together in a cooperative and supportive work environment. Some researchers have worried that the very complexity of inclusion makes it too difficult to undertake (Reeve & Hallahan, 1994). Others strongly suggest that the benefits of enhanced learning opportunities in the general education settings do not fulfill the promises of achievement that can be obtained with a continuum of services (Zigmond, et al., 1995). Others hold that inclusion often fails due to the absence of one or several of the multiple elements that make it possible to successfully include children with disabilities. These omissions may be the reason that inclusion has not always been found to be beneficial for students with disabilities or for their typical classmates, and that not all general and special education teachers have found inclusion of students with disabilities in general education classes to be feasible or desirable. Despite these criticisms, inclusion cannot be quantified into a generic recipe, or a uniform set of "things" that are added to a school or to a child' program. Inclusion must be designed to suit individual students.

Probably the ultimate challenge to those seeking to make educational change, such as the change to inclusive service delivery models, lies in the ordinary fact that teachers try to fulfill their jobs as they understand them, and that these understandings can be modified by the positive and personal experiences they have with new approaches. The first steps of meeting this challenge are to identify new approaches that have been found effective, and then to individualize these approaches so that they fit other settings, but still achieve the desired outcomes. Individualizing the plan for educational change so it works beyond the pilot classroom or research site cannot be done without some trial and error, nor without an investment of effort by school staff and administrators. Implementation is another major phase of change that involves sharing the needed knowledge, providing models, giving guided experiences, and lending the support necessary for school staff to do things in different and improved ways. The last phase, sustaining the momentum that comes through these experiences requires that teachers have continued the opportunity to refine, expand, and apply new skills in a supportive organization. Changes in classrooms must be supported by changes in the school organization, and changes in the school must be supported by changes in the school system, or the results will be temporary, limited to individual teachers, and narrow groups of students and classes. Successful educational change depends both upon an individualization of the reform by those involved to suit the setting, and continued attention to that reform over time.

Future researchers should continue to unravel the workings of teachers and students in inclusive classrooms and schools, while also examining the background factors: those organizational structures and cultures that facilitate novel ways of thinking about serving nontraditional students, or serving all students. Skrtic (1991) described adhocratic schools as places where their organization makes collaborative teaming and novel outcomes possible. By contrast, conventional school organization depends on specialization, isolated teaching, and standardization of methods and products. The bright part of the findings reviewed in this chapter are that the cooperative and collaborative school atmosphere, which current research has found to be associated with successful inclusion, is also conducive to other school improvements, like heightened teacher morale and positive student outcomes (Clark & Astuto, 1994; Fullan, 1991; Sarason, 1990; Skrtic, 1991). Today's educators, under pressure to improve learning, should neither bypass inclusion as a strategy unrelated to the improvement of learning, nor fear its complexity. A "classify and separate" approach that led to the widespread exclusion of students with disabilities since the 1970s has been used by some in today's charter and alternative schools for "nontraditional" students. As with students having disabilities, the outcomes are highly mixed and generally have not produced durable improvements. Our energy as educators should be devoted first, to refining our common research questions concerning the improvement of learning in diverse student populations, and our tools for measuring these outcomes. Based on these broader understandings, we could examine the essential elements involved in successfully including nontraditional students so that the resulting intervention processes and strategies are grasped with more clarity and can be applied to a wider range of school settings and children.

ACKNOWLEDGEMENT

I thank Rachel Janney of Radford University for her critical review of this manuscript, describing the research we have conducted together, and her thoughtful suggestions for its revision

REFERENCES

Bredo, A. E., & Bredo, E. R. (1975). Effects of environment and structure on the process of innovation. In J. V. Baldridge & R. E. Deal (Eds.), *Managing change in educational organizations* (pp. 449–467). Berkeley, CA: McCutchan.

Brown, L., Long, E., Udvari-Solner, A., Davis, L., VanDeventer, P., Ahlgren, C., Johnson, F., Gruenewald, L., & Jorgensen, J. (1989). The home school: Why students with severe intellectual disabilities must attend the schools of their brothers, sisters, friends, and neighbors. *Journal of the Association for Persons with Severe Handicaps, 14,* 1–7.

Buysse, V., & Bailey, D. B. (1993). Behavioral and developmental outcomes in young children with disabilities in integrated and segregated settings: A review of comparative studies. *The Journal of Special Education, 26,* 434–461.

Clark, D. L., & Astuto, T. A. (1994). Redirecting reform: Challenges to popular assumptions about teachers and students. *Phi Delta Kappan, 75,* 513–520.

Cole, D. A., & Meyer, L. H. (1991). Social integration and severe disabilities: a longitudinal analysis of child outcomes. *The Journal of Special Education, 25,* 340–351.

Deno, S., Foegen, A., Robinson, S., & Espin, C. (1996). Commentary: Facing the realities of inclusion for students with mild disabilities. *The Journal of Special Education, 30,* 345–357.

Evans, I. M., Salisbury, C. L., Palombaro, M. M., Berryman, J., & Hollowood, T. M. (1992). Peer interactions and social acceptance of elementary-age children with severe disabilities in an inclusive school. *Journal of the Association for Persons with Severe Handicaps, 17,* 205–212.

Ferguson, D. L., Meyer, G., Jeanchild, L., Juniper, L., & Zingo, J. (1992). Figuring out what to do with the grownups: How teachers make inclusion "work" for students with disabilities. *Journal of the Association for Persons with Severe Handicaps, 17,* 218–226.

Fullan, M. G. (1991). *The new meaning of educational change* (2nd ed.). New York: Teachers College Press.

Fryxell, D., & Kennedy, C. H.(1995). Placement along the continuum of services and its impact on students' social relationships. *Journal of the Association for Persons with Severe Handicaps, 20,* 259–269.

Gartner, A., & Lipsky, D. K. (1987). Beyond special education: Toward a quality system for all students. *Harvard Educational Review, 57,* 367–395.

Giangreco, M. F., Dennis, R., Cloninger, C., Edelman, S., & Schattman, R. (1993). "I've counted Jon": Transformational experiences of teachers educating students with disabilities. *Exceptional Children, 59,* 359–372.

Giangreco, M. F., Edelman, S. W., Luiselli, T. E., & MacFarland, S. Z. C. (1997). Helping or hovering? Effects of instructional assistant proximity on students with disabilities. *Exceptional Children, 64,* 7–18.

Hall, L. J. (1994). A descriptive assessment of social relationships in integrated classrooms. *Journal of the Association for Persons with Severe Handicaps, 19,* 302–313.

Haring, T. G., & Breen, C. G. (1992). A peer-mediated social network intervention to enhance the social integration of persons with moderate and severe disabilities. *Journal of Applied Behavior Analysis, 25,* 319–333.

Helmstetter, E., Peck, C. A., & Giangreco, M. F., (1994). Outcomes of interactions with peers with moderate or severe disabilities: A statewide survey of high school students. *Journal of the Association for Persons with Severe Handicaps, 19,* 263 –76.

Huberman, A. M., & Miles, M. B. (1984*). Innovation up close: How school improvement works.* New York: Plenum Press.

Hunt, P., Alwell, M., Farron-David, F., & Goetz, L. (1996). Creating socially supportive environments for fully included students who experience multiple disabilities. *Journal of the Association for Persons with Severe Handicaps, 21,* 53–71.

Hunt, P., Staub, D., Alwell, M., & Goetz, L. (1994). Achievement by all students within the context of cooperative learning groups. *Journal of the Association for Persons with Severe Handicaps, 19,* 290 301.

Janney, R. E., & Snell, M. E. (1996). Using peer interactions to include students with extensive disabilities in elementary general education classes. *Journal of the Association for Persons with Severe Handicaps, 21,* 72–80.

Janney, R. E. & Snell, M. E. (1997). How teachers include students with moderate and severe disabilities in elementary classes: The means and meaning of inclusion. *Journal of the Association for Persons with Severe Handicaps, 22, 42,* 159–169.

Janney, R. L., Snell, M. E., Beers, M. K., & Raynes, M. (1995a). Integrating students with moderate and severe disabilities: Classroom teachers' beliefs and attitudes about implementing an educational change. *Educational Administration Quarterly, 31,* 86–114.

Janney, R. E., Snell, M. E., Beers, M. K., & Raynes, M. (1995b). Integrating students with moderate and severe disabilities into general education classes. *Exceptional Children, 61,* 425–439.

Jenkins, J. R., Jewell, M., Leichester, N., O'Connor, R. E., Jenkins, L. M., & Troutner, N.M. (1994). Accommodations for individual differences without classroom ability groups: An experiment in school restructuring. *Exceptional Children, 60,* 344–358.

Kishi, G. S., & Meyer, L. H. (1994). What children report and remember: A six-year follow-up of the effects of social contact between peers with and without severe disabilities. *Journal of the Association for Persons with Severe Handicaps, 19,* 277–289.

Kozleski, E. B., & Jackson, L. (1993). Taylor's story: Full inclusion in her neighborhood elementary school. *Exceptionality, 4,* 153–175.

LaRocque, L. & Coleman, P. (1989). Quality control: School accountability and district ethos. In M. Holmes, K. Leithwood & D. Musella (Eds.), *Educational policy for effective schools* (pp. 168–191). Toronto: OISE Press.

Little, J. W. (1990). The persistence of privacy: Autonomy and initiative in teachers' professional relations. *Teachers College Record, 91,* 509–536.

Logan, K. R., Bakeman, R., & Keefe, E. B. (1997). Effects of instructional variables on engaged behavior of students with disabilities in general education classrooms. *Exceptional Children, 63,* 481–497.

Lytle, J .H. (1988). Is special education serving minority students? A response to Singer and Butler. *Harvard Educational Review, 58,* 116–120.

McLaughlin, M. J., & Warren, S. H. (1992). *Issues and options in restructuring schools and special education programs.* College Park: University of Maryland and Westat, Inc.

Oberti V. Clementon, 995 S.2d 1204 (3d Cir. 1993).

Peck, C. A., Donaldson, J., & Pezzoli, M., (1990). Some benefits nonhandicapped adolescents perceive for themselves from their social relationships with peers who have severe handicaps. *Journal of the Association for Persons with Severe Handicaps, 15,* 241–249.

Reeve, P. T., & Hallahan, D. P. (1994). Practical questions about collaboration between general and special educators. *Focus on Exceptional Children, 26 (7),* 1–12.

Rogers, J. (1993). The inclusion revolution. *Research Bulletin of Phi Delta Kappa, 11,* 1–6.

Sale, P., & Carey, D. M. (1995). The sociometric status of students with disabilities in a full-inclusion school. *Exceptional Children, 62,* 6–19.

Salisbury, C., Gallucci, C., Palombaro, M., & Peck, C. (1995). Strategies that promote social relationships among elementary students with and without severe disabilities in inclusive schools. *Exceptional Children, 62,* 125–137.

Salisbury, C. L., Mangino, M., Rainforth, B., & Syryca, S. (1994). Promoting the instructional inclusion of young children with disabilities in the primary grades: A curricular adaptation process. *Journal of Early Intervention, 18,* 311–322.

Salisbury, C. L., Palombaro, M. M., & Hollowood, T. M. (1993). On the nature and change of an inclusive elementary school. *Journal of the Association for Persons with Severe Handicaps, 18,* 75–84.

Sapon-Shevin, M. (1992). Celebrating diversity, creating community. In S. Stainback & W. Stainback (Eds.), *Curriculum considerations in inclusive classrooms,* pp. 19–36. Baltimore: Paul H. Brookes.

Sarason, R. B. (1990). *The predictable failure of educational reform.* San Francisco: Jossey-Bass.

Schnorr, R. F. (1990). "Peter? He comes and he goes...": First graders' perspectives on a part-time mainstream student. *Journal of the Association for Persons with Severe Handicaps, 15,* 231–240.

Schnorr, R. F. (1997). From enrollment to membership: "Belonging" in middle and high school classes. *Journal of the Association for Persons with Severe Handicaps, 22,* 1–15.

Skrtic, T. M. (1991). The special education paradox: Equity as the way to excellence. *Harvard Educational Review, 61,* 148–206.

Snell, M. E., & Janney, R. E. (1993). Including and supporting students with disabilities within general education. In B. S. Billingsley (Ed.), *Program leadership for students with disabilities,* (pp. 219–262). Richmond: Virginia Department of Education.

Snell, M. E., & Janney, R. E. (1998). *Teachers' problem solving about young children with moderate and severe disabilities in elementary classrooms.* Manuscript submitted for publication.

Snell, M. E. & Raynes, M., with Byrd, J. O., Colley, K. M., Gilley, C., Pityonak, C., Stallings, M. A., Van Dyke, R., Williams, P. S., & Willis, C. J. (1995). Changing roles in inclusive schools: Staff perspectives at Gilbert Linkous Elementary. *Kappa Delta Pi Record, 31,* 104–109.

Sontag, J. C. (1997). Contextual factors in influencing the sociability of preschool children with disabilities in integrated and segregated classrooms. *Exceptional Children, 63,* 389–404.

Staub, D., & Peck, C. A. (1995). What are the outcomes for nondisabled students? *Educational Leadership, 52*(4), 36–40.

Stevens, R. J., & Slavin, R. E. (1995). The cooperative elementary school: Effects on students' achievement, attitudes, and social relations. *American Educational Research Journal, 32,* 321–351.

Taylor, S. J. (1988). Caught in the continuum: A critical analysis of the principle of the least restrictive environment. *Journal of the Association for Persons with Severe Handicaps, 13,* 41–53.

Vandercook, T. (1991). Leisure instruction outcomes: Criterion performance, positive interactions, and acceptance by typical high school peers. *The Journal of Special Education, 25,* 320–339.

Van der Klift, E., & Kunc, N. (1994). Beyond benevolence: Friendship and the politics of help. In J. S. Thousand, R. A. Villa, & A. I. Nevin (Eds.), *Creativity and collaborative learning* (pp. 391–401). Baltimore: Paul H. Brookes.

York, J., Vandercook, T., Macdonald, C., Heise-Neff, C., & Caughey, E. (1992). Feedback about integrating middle-school students with severe disabilities in general education classes. *Exceptional Children, 58,* 244–258.

Zigmond, N., Jenkins, J., Fuchs, L. S., Deno, S., Fuchs, D. Baker, J. N., Jenkins, L., & Couthino, M. (1995). Special education in restructured schools: Findings from three multi-year studies. *Phi Delta Kappan, 76,* 531–540.

6

Factors for Successful Inclusion: Learning from the Past, Looking toward the Future

Dorothy Kerzner Lipsky
Alan Gartner
The City University of New York

In looking to the future of public education for students with disabilities, we begin with the baseline of the current practices of school districts. School districts across the country are increasingly implementing inclusive education programs. Two national studies conducted by the National Center on Educational Restructuring and Inclusion (NCERI) provide evidence of this development (*National Study*, 1994, 1995). Inclusive education activities are taking place in school districts in every state they are in urban, suburban, and rural school districts they are involving students with the full range of disability conditions identified in The Individuals With Disabilities Act (IDEA), at all levels of severity and they take place at all grade levels, Kindergarten through Grade 12. Between the 1994 and 1995 studies, there was a threefold increase in the number of school districts reporting inclusive education programs, and NCERI's ongoing work indicates continuing expansion in the number of school districts initiating inclusive education, increasingly as part of broader school restructuring efforts, (For a full treatment of these developments, see Lipsky & Gartner, 1997, esp. chapters 10–12, and 14).

EMERGING NEW PRACTICES

As school districts across the country implement inclusive education programs, they have moved from "first-generation" to "second-generation" inclusion issues. Table 6.1 contains two columns or stages of inclusive education implementation, first-generation issues and issues related to the second-generation. Only to some extent are the generations time-based; whereas the second generation represents the cutting edge of current practice, many (perhaps most) current inclusive education programs are characterized by first-generation practices and attitudes.

Table 6.1 is meant to be introductory and preliminary, not final and definitive. Furthermore, it is limited in that it neither includes those issues that came before the first generation (i.e., the largely segregated placements of the period well into the 1980s) or the practices that are yet to be implemented in a consistent manner.

Table 6.1
TABLE 1: Stages in the Implementation of inclusive Education

First Generation Issues	Second Generation Issues
· Should we do inclusive education?	· How do we do inclusive education?
· Inclusion viewed as a special education issue..	· Inclusion as a schoolwide/districtwide issue..
· Implementation of inclusion the responsibility of special education administrators and staff.	· Implementation of inclusion the responsibility of general education administrators and staff, along with special educators.
· Students placed in general education classes must be "ready".	· Including all students regardless of the intensity of their disability.
· Providing elaborate modifications when a student is included.	· Providing only those supports and accommodations that are educationally necessary.
· Individual paraeducators assigned to students who are included.	· Paraeducators assigned to support all students in the inclusive classroom.
· Inclusive education seen as parallel to general education reforms.	· Inclusive education initiatives are entwined with general education reform.
· Students perceived as "belonging" to general or special educators.	· Special and general education assuming a shared responsibility for all students.
· Assessment focused in student's individual progress.	· Assessment tied to overall curriculum and instruction..
· Teachers who implement inclusive education should be volunteers.	· The teaching of students with disabilities is a normal part of all teacher's' role.
· Staff development focused on transfer of special education skills to general educators.	· Staff development emphasizes development of the discrete and shared knowledge of general and special educators and the development of collaboration between them.
· Emphasis is on helping the student with special needs adjust to general education.	· Emphasis is on empowering all students
· Focus is on inclusive education at the elementary grades.	· Focus widens to include middle and high school.
· Honoring of parents' due process rights.	· Beyond due process to engagement of parents as partners.
· Related services provided outside of regular classroom.	· Related services integrated into the regular program activities.
· Funding tied to placement.	· Funding follows the child.

(Continued)

First Generation Issues	Second Generation Issues
· Does inclusion benefit the special education student?	· Does inclusion benefit all students.
· Students remain in inclusive environments the entire day.	· General education classrooms provide a common learning base for all students and service delivery and placement decisions are individualized and crafted for children with and without disabilities.

THE RENEWAL OF IDEA

Neither *inclusion* nor inclusive education are part of the language of IDEA, as it was initially enacted more than 10 years ago, and as it was reenacted in 1997 (nor were they a part of P.L. 97-142 when it was enacted in 1975). Given the stridency of some attacks, it is worth noting that there was never any consideration during the nearly 2 years of consideration of IDEA's renewal by the Congress or the president of limiting the law's least restrictive environment (LRE) commitment as part of IDEA's renewal. Indeed, several changes in IDEA have the consequence of strengthening the presumption that students with disabilities are to be served in general education settings, with the needed supplemental aids and support services. These include changes concerning participants in the Individualized Education Program (IEP) meeting, participation of students with disabilities in standardized testing programs, funding formula issues, and parental involvement. These legislative changes are discussed in various sections of this chapter, some as forces in the development of future opportunities for inclusive education, and others as possible limits to inclusive education and school restructuring.

FACTORS FOR SUCCESSFUL INCLUSION AND RESTRUCTURING

Analysis of the reports from some 1,000 school districts on their inclusive education programs in the *National Study* (1994, 1995) identifies seven factors for success: visionary leadership, collaboration, refocused use of assessment, support for staff and students, funding, effective parental involvement, and the implementation of effective program models and classroom practices. These seven factors are congruent with the factors identified in a study of 12 inclusive schools conducted by the Working Forum on Inclusive Schools (*Creating schools,* 1995), convened by 10 national organizations.

Visionary Leadership

The statement of a Vermont special education director underscores the importance of this component.

> Some years ago, we came to view inclusion as a subset of the restructuring of the entire educational system. From this perspective, we no longer view special education as a means to help students meet the demands of the classroom, but as part of the classroom services that must be available to accommodate the learning needs of all children in a restructured school. (*National study*, 1995)

Based on a study of 32 school sites (in Arizona, Illinois, Michigan, New York, Ontario, and Vermont) that were implementing inclusive educational opportunities for students, Villa, Thousand, Meyers, and Nevin (1993) reported that among general and special educators, the degree of administrative support emerged as the most powerful predictor of attitudes toward full inclusion.

Although traditionally (and appropriately) we think of leadership as emanating from the school superintendent, in districts across the country the initial impetus for inclusive education has come from many sources: superintendents, principals, teachers, other school personnel, parents, and on occasion, from a university or state-level project. The issue is less the initiator, but more a recognition that, for inclusive education to be successful, ultimately all stakeholders must become involved.

Collaboration

Reports from school districts indicate that the achievement of inclusive education presumes that no one teacher can be, or should be, expected to have all the expertise required to meet the educational needs of all the students in the classroom. Rather, individual teachers must have available to them the support systems that provide collaborative assistance, and that enable them to engage in cooperative problem solving. Building planning teams, scheduling time for teachers to work together, recognizing teachers as problem solvers, conceptualizing teachers as front-line researchers—these means were all reported as necessary for collaboration.

Kentucky, which as part of its comprehensive reform of education has implemented the most extensive programs to serve all students in an integrated setting, has developed a wide array of program designs for collaboration among the full array of personnel who serve students. Moll (1997) made the point that the development of a collaborative system requires change and growth in every aspect of the educational environment, including personnel, curriculum, instructional strategies, and school structure and organization. (A brief discussion of the Kentucky program model follows.) She cites five elements that characterize a collaborative school:

1. The belief that the quality of education is largely determined by what happens at the school site.
2. The conviction that instruction is most effective in a school environment characterized by norms of collegiality and continuous improvement.
3. The belief that teachers are responsible for the instructional process and accountable for outcomes for all students.

4. The use of a wide range of practices and structures that enable administrators, parents, and teachers to work together on school improvement.
5. The involvement of teachers in decisions about school goals and the means for implementing them. (p. 7)

Refocused Use of Assessment

Two issues are addressed here: (a) the use of assessment as a screening device (to determine which students require special education services, and what services are appropriate), and (b) to measure student progress. As a screening device, numerous studies have documented the inadequacy of this screening. The seminal work here is that of Ysseldyke. For a discussion of these issues, see Lipsky and Gartner (1997). In the measuring of student progress, inclusive education schools and districts are reporting moving toward more authentic assessment designs, including the use of portfolios of students' work and performances, and generally working to refocus assessment.

In the renewal of IDEA there are new requirements regarding the assessment of student learning. These include:

·   States (and thus local school districts) were to establish, by January 1, 1998, performance goals, consistent with the goals for all students in the state, and develop indicators to judge student progress.
·   By January 1, 1998, students with disabilities were to be included in state and district assessments of student progress, with individual modifications and accommodations as needed.
·   For those students who cannot participate in such assessments (with modifications and accommodations), alternative assessments are to be developed and conducted by July 1, 2000.
·   By January 1, 1998, states were to report to the U.S. Department of Education and to the public the assessment performance of students with disabilities, including those participating in alternative assessments.

These requirements will require major changes in practices, in perspective, and in philosophy. These reforms recall the debate of 20 years ago, during the deliberations prior to the passage of PL 94–142. At that time, there was contending testimony among professionals as to which students could benefit from education. Finally, the Congress—more as a matter of belief and ideology than based on research findings—indeed, tired of the professionals' disputes, declared that *all* students were to be served, because *all* students could benefit. In the 1997 IDEA amendments, the Congress declared that the learning of *all* students must be measured, that the starting point for that is the learning expected of students in general, and that the outcomes of their learning count, that is, are a matter of public concern and are to be incorporated in the overall results for a school, a district, and a state. As James Ysseldyke, a noted researcher, said, "We value only what we measure, and if [students with disabilities] are not in the picture, then people assume that they're not responsible for educating them. Out of sight is out of mind" (cited in "National Study," 1995, p. 3). Of course, it is equally true, that we only measure what we value!

Support for Staff and Students

Two support factors are essential for successful inclusive education programs: systematic staff development and flexible planning time for special and general educators, classroom, and other personnel. These two factors must work together.

From the vantage point of students, supports for inclusion often mean supplementary aids and support services. Districts report that these include assigning full- or part-time school aides, short- or long-term; providing needed therapy services integrated into the general school program peer support "buddy systems" or "circles of friends" and effectively using computer-aided technology and other assistive devices.

As noted previously, there have been significant changes in the character and nature of supports. From the earlier practice of elaborate modification, the newer trend is to modify only as much as needed (to avoid, in McKnight's powerful phrase, the provision of "disabling help"); the use of paraeducators assigned to a class, not "velcroed" to an individual child; the recognition that related services are supposed to be educationally necessary, not all that is needed to meet a child's other than educational needs; and that computers are to be integrated into the regular work of the classroom, as opposed to being fancy gadgets in a special room. Giangreco and colleagues developed a number of designs that provide the basis for this new approach, especially as it relates to the integration of related services (Giangreco, 1995; Edelman & Giangreco, 1995; Giangreco, Edelman, Luiselli, & MacFarland, 1996; Giangreco, Edelman, Dennis, Prelock, & Cloniger, (in press).

Funding

Special education funding formulas have often favored restrictive placements for students in special education. The IDEA renewal now requires that states adopt policies that are "placement neutral," that is, ones that do not contravene the law's program mandate as to LRE placement. Funds must follow the student, regardless of placement, and must be sufficient to provide the services necessary. Districts report that, in general, inclusive education programs are no more costly than segregated models. ("Does inclusion cost more?", 1994; McLaughlin & Warren, 1994; Parrish, 1997) However, districts must anticipate one-time "conversion" costs, especially for the necessary planning and professional development.

Effective Parental Involvement

Inclusive schools report the importance of parental participation. They encourage parental involvement by providing family support services, as well as the development of educational programs that engage parents as co-learners with their children. Programs that bring a wide array of services to children in the school settings report at least two sets of benefits—direct benefits to the children, and the opportunities for parents and other family members to become involved in school-based activities. As the child in an inclusive school becomes a part of the fabric of the school along with her or his nondisabled peers, so, too, the parents of children with disabilities become less isolated.

The IDEA renewal enhances parental participation. It does so by requiring their participation in all eligibility and placement decisions involving their child and by requiring that they be informed about their child's progress, no less frequently than is the district's practice for nondisabled children.

 Use of Effective Program Models and Classroom Practices

There are many models of inclusion that have been successful. These include:

- A co-teaching model, where the special education teacher co-teaches alongside the general education teacher,
- Parallel teaching, where the special educator works with a small group of students from a selected special education population in a section of the general education classroom,
- A co-teaching consultant model, where the special education teacher provides assistance to the general educator, enabling her or him to teach all the students in the inclusive class,
- A team model, where the special education teacher joins with one or more general education teachers to form a team, sharing responsibility for all the children in the inclusive classroom,
- A methods and resource teacher model, where the special education teacher, whose students have been distributed in general education classes, works with the general education teachers, providing direct instruction, modeling of lessons, and consultation,
- A dually licensed teacher, that is, one who holds both general and special education certification and, thus, is equipped to teach all of the students in an inclusive classroom.

Schools have been successful with each of these designs. Factors in adopting a particular model most often depend on local decision making and teacher preference. In Kentucky, the state that has developed most fully restructured and inclusive classrooms, three designs are used:

- Complementary instruction, whereby the general education teacher takes the overall responsibility for the subject matter, and the strategic teacher (i.e., special education teacher, a teacher of the gifted, a speech-language pathologist, Chapter I teachers, remediation teachers) works with the mastery of specific skills based on the subject matter.
- Role-reversal teaming (dual certification), whereby both the general education teacher and the strategic teacher are certified in elementary

education. Here the teachers jointly develop instruction and implement it according to their individual strengths and preferences.

- Supportive learning style, whereby both teachers share responsibility for planning. The general education teacher provides basic instruction on the essential content, and the strategic teacher designs and implements supportive and supplementary materials, activities, instruction, and so forth.

Basic to each of these designs is a strong professional development component, both prior to the initiation of the program, as well as ongoing technical assistance.

Effective classroom practices, as reported by districts implementing inclusive education, have two over-arching characteristics. The first is that the adaptations appropriate for students with disabilities benefit all students. And, second, is that the instructional strategies used in inclusive classrooms are practices recommended by educational reformers and researchers for general education students. Indeed, the most common statement from teachers in the NCERI *National Study* (1994, 1995) was, "Good teaching is good teaching is good teaching."

Cooperative learning has most often been identified as the most important instructional strategy supporting inclusive education. Well over half of the districts implementing inclusive education included in the *National Study* (1994, 1995) reported using cooperative learning. Instructional strategies cited by one quarter or more of the districts include: cooperative learning, curricular adaptations, students supporting other students, using paraprofessionals/classroom aides, and using instructional technology. (For a full discussion of the use of these instructional strategies, see Lipsky & Gartner, 1997, especially Chap. 12.)

EARLY CHILDHOOD AND PRESCHOOL INCLUSIVE PROGRAMS

The rapid growth in the numbers of students with disabilities served in early childhood inclusive programs indicates a significant trend. The passage of PL 99-457, the Education of the Handicapped Act Amendments of 1986, began the national provision of special education services for preschool children. Begun as a program in which states could voluntarily participate (and, ultimately, all 50 did), the most recent federal data (*Eighteenth annual report*, 1996,) report that the early childhood programs served nearly 200,000 children. Both programs have requirements for services to be provided in integrated settings, for the Part H programs the term is *natural environments*, whereas for the Section 619 programs it is IDEA's *LRE language*. This legal emphasis on integration is echoed by the leading professional group, the Division of Early Childhood (DEC), Council for Exceptional Children (CEC). Its 1993 "Position on Inclusion" states as follows:

> Inclusion, as a value, supports the right of all children, regardless of their diverse abilities, to participate actively in natural settings in their communities.

[T]o implement inclusive practices, DEC supports (a) the continued development, evaluation, and dissemination of full inclusion supports, services, and systems so that options for inclusion are of high quality; (b) the development of preservice and inservice training programs that prepare families, administrators, and service providers to develop and work within inclusive settings; (c) collaboration among key stakeholders to implement flexible fiscal and administrative procedures in support of inclusion; (d) research that contributes to our knowledge of state-of-the-art services; and (e) the restructuring and unification of social, education, health, and intervention supports and services to make them more responsive to the needs of all children.

This statement was endorsed in November 1993 by the leading early childhood organization, the National Association for the Education of Young Children (NAEYC).

There is no single best program model or design for preschool programs; however, a set of eight quality indicators that characterize inclusive early childhood programs has been identified by Bruder (1997). These include the following:

1. A program philosophy for inclusive early childhood services,
2. A consistent and ongoing system for family involvement,
3. A system of team planning and program implementation,
4. A system of collaboration and communication with other agencies that provide services to young children with disabilities and their families,
5. A well-constructed IEP or Individualized Family Service Plan (IFSP) that dictates the instructional content for each participating child,
6. An integrated delivery of educational and related services,
7. A consistent and ongoing system for training and staff development,
8. A comprehensive system for evaluating the effectiveness of the program.

In a comprehensive publication, *Planning for Inclusion*, the National Information Center for Children and Youth with Disabilities (NICHCY) identified the following components that inclusive early childhood programs should work toward achieving:

- Establish a philosophy that supports appropriate inclusionary practice,
- Plan extensively for inclusion,
- Involve the principal or program director as a change agent,
- Involve parents,
- Develop the disability awareness of staff and students,
- Provide staff with training,
- Ensure there is adequate support in the classroom,
- Provide structure and support for collaboration,
- Make adaptations,
- Establish policies and methods for evaluating student progress,
- Establish policies and methods for evaluating the inclusion program. ("Planning," 1995, pp. 5–8)

These components run parallel to the factors for successful inclusion identified by the school districts in the *National Study* (1994, 1995), cited previously.

The evaluation database for inclusion in early childhood and preschool programs has a longer history and is more extensive than that for school-age children. Nisbet (1994) stated that "over the past 25 years, there has been an extensive body of research and preschool integration" (p. 153). Citing several summaries of this research, Nisbet offered the following conclusions:

- First, it is clear that integration has positive effects on the social competence and interactions of preschoolers with disabilities. Findings include more time playing with peers, more positive interactions with peers, and more verbalization with peers.
- Second, integration opportunities also appear to have positive effects on other behavioral outcomes, such as more sophisticated play with toys.
- Third, integration opportunities also appear to have positive effects on other behavioral outcomes, such as more sophisticated play with toys. Fourth, no negative outcomes have been reported for normally developing children. (p. 153)

This summary is echoed by a report of the Early Childhood Research Institute on Inclusion (Odom et al.,1995):

> At least four reviews of research occurring over the last 15 years have
> concluded that children with disabilities in inclusive preschool programs
> make at least as much progress on standardized assessments of cognitive,
> language, motor, and social development as do children enrolled in non-
> inclusive special education preschools. (p. 8).

As we have noted, inclusive early childhood programs have been growing rapidly. In the years to come, several factors combine to offer the potential for even greater growth. These include:

- Language in the renewal of IDEA,
- Welfare reform at the federal level and the consequent changes at the state level, including the provision of day-care services for the children of persons who have been on welfare,
- Actions by the legislatures in several states,
- Public and private innovations in child-care financing.

IDEA Renewal

There are changes in both the early intervention program (formerly Part H) and the preschool program, Part B. Part H has been replaced (effective July 1, 1998) by a new part C, with a higher level of authorization (up from $229 million to $400 million), assuring each state no less funding in Fiscal Year 1998 and 1999 than it received in Fiscal Year 1994, unless there was a decline in the number of disabled infants and toddlers. In terms of eligibility, states have been provided with greater flexibility: for serving *at-risk* infants and toddlers; through expanding collaborative efforts; to establish links with public and private identification and evaluation groups; to pay for services and personnel; and to refer at-risk children to nonPart C services. The mandated IFSP now must include a statement about the natural environments in which early intervention services will be provided, including a justification for the services that are not to be provided in inclusive settings. In addressing the need for additional staff (in the anticipation of program expansion), greater flexibility is provided in the employment of trained paraprofessionals to help provide early intervention services, and for the employment of persons whose training is as yet not completed.

The program for children and youth 3 years to 21 years of age, permanently authorized, has been strengthened in a number of ways to support inclusive education. Appropriations for programs for children 3 years to 5 years old are increased from $360 million to $500 million. Substantive changes, as discussed in the following section, address issues of the participation of general educators in the IEP meeting, inclusion of students with disabilities in state- and districtwide assessments tied to the general education curriculum, a requirement that state-funding formulas that do not support the LRE requirement be revised, and various steps to enhance parental involvement.

Welfare Reform

The implementation of the national welfare reform program ("Personal Responsibility and Work Opportunity Reconciliation Act of 1996") will have significant consequence for day-care programs, with the requirement to provide child-care assistance for the children of former welfare recipients.

Expanded Preschool Programs and Innovations in Child-Care Financing

In a number of states, responding both to overall school reform efforts and the recommendations of several national studies of early education (e.g., *Years of promise*, 1996), there has been significant expansion of preschool programs. Illustrative, for example, are steps in New York, including offering of prekindergarten classes for all 4-year-olds, all-day kindergarten for districts that have been providing half-day programs, and smaller class sizes in the early grades. And in many states, new financing arrangements, both public and private, support expansion of child-care programs. For example, in Colorado, there is a tax check-off option for child-care and tax credits for individuals as well as businesses. In Minnesota, there is an income tax credit that specifically benefits low-income families, and a bond program to support the building of child-care facilities. In Maryland, there is a loan guarantee program to help child-care centers secure loans for facilities. In Texas, there is increased funding for child-care linked to the need for school readiness. Finally, North Carolina's Project T.E.A.C.H., which leverages funds from several sectors to support educational scholarships and wage increases for child care practitioners, is being replicated in Florida, Georgia, and Illinois.

The great opportunity here is in connecting these developments: the expansion, per IDEA, of programs for young children with disabilities, along with a strong emphasis on inclusion, with the broader expansion of early childhood programs, as part of welfare and educational reform efforts.

LOOKING TOWARD THE FUTURE

As we consider the future of inclusive education, there are potential concerns and opportunities.

Potential Concerns

Perhaps the greatest potential problem is inclusion done poorly. A school district seeking to implement inclusive education "on the cheap," not devoting sufficient time and resources to achieve all the factors for success (discussed previously), not involving all stakeholders, or expecting instant success, is doing little more than "dumping." And, too many districts call what is little more than dumping, "inclusion."

Additionally, the treating of inclusion as a new program or innovation, rather than as part of the fabric of the school restructuring efforts, can significantly decrease the effectiveness of inclusive education programs. School districts reporting successful inclusive education programs have recognized the program as having consequence for all school activities, including curriculum, instructional strategies, assessment, student grouping, personnel utilization and deployment, parental participation, pupil transportation, fiscal affairs, and building and district organization.

In the IDEA renewal, new disciplinary procedures have the potential consequence of limiting inclusion opportunities. However, as the law does not allow for the cessation of services nor does it revoke the student's right to a free appropriate public education (FAPE) in the LRE, these changes should have limited consequence as regards inclusive education opportunities. The actual effect will have to await the issuance of regulations by the Department of Education and, then, the implementation in school districts across the country.

Future Opportunities

The components of the renewed IDEA provide further impetus for the expansion of inclusive education opportunities for all students with disabilities. In the "Findings" section of the law, the Congress states,

The education of students with disabilities can be made more effective by:

- having high expectations for students and ensuring their success in the general curriculum,

- strengthening the role of parents and ensuring that families have meaningful opportunities to participate in the education of children at school and at home,
- coordinating this Act with other local, educational service agency, State, and Federal school improvement efforts in order to ensure that such children benefit from such efforts and that special education can become a service for such children rather than a place where they are sent,
- providing appropriate special education and related services and aids and supports in the regular classroom to such children, whenever appropriate,
- supporting high quality, intensive professional development for all personnel who work with such students in order to ensure that they have the skills and knowledge to be prepared to lead productive, independent lives to the maximum extent possible,
- providing incentives for whole-school approaches and prereferral intervention to reduce the need to label students as having disabilities to address their learning needs,
- focusing resources on teaching and learning while reducing paperwork and requirements that do not assist in improving educational results.

Without ever using the word *inclusion*, the Congress has dramatically supported it. The new law has the potential to change education for students with disabilities equal to IDEA's predecessor, PL 94–142. Just as that 1975 law brought students with disabilities (then called *handicapped*) into the school house, the 1997 amendments provide the basis for making them full members of the school community. In the years to come, we are less likely to hear about LRE and more about FAPE. In the future, school policies and practices will need to focus on the goal of appropriateness—understood as providing the basis for achievement, consonant with that expected of students in general—in the context of full participation. Outcomes less than those for other children, and services apart from them will no longer be accepted as the norm but rather, will become matters to be explained and justified.

Illustrative of the potential here is the reissuance by New York's State Commissioner of Education, Richard P. Mills, of the Board of Regents *Least Restrictive Environment Implementation Policy Paper* (1997), emphasizing the strengthening of the law's LRE requirements. In his transmittal memo, Mills stated, "I am issuing an updated version of this paper to underscore the commitment the Education Department has to implementing our responsibilities in this area and to remind all stakeholders of the importance of these policies. It is essential that school districts review their local policies in preparation for the new IDEA amendments," (*Least Restrictive*, 1997, 1–2).

Mills directed local districts to examine their policies and practices regarding the appropriateness of the regular education program; the provision of supports to enable students to participate in general education services; students attending the school that they would attend if not disabled, except if otherwise required by the IEP; providing an explanation for why a student would not participate with nondisabled students; notice to the student's parents about each program and placement option considered for the student and a rationale for rejecting those options; and documentation of the consideration of the general education programs and placement options considered in the development of the IEP. Although New York State's record in this area is particularly woeful, ranking among the lowest of the 50 states in the placement of students in regular education classrooms (*Eighteenth annual report*, 1996, Table AB1), the areas identified by Mills are ones appropriate for all the states and their school districts.

The language of the renewed IDEA encourages relation of inclusive education to broad school reform. In some instances, districts implementing inclusive education programs have already recognized the importance of this. In the nation's two largest school systems, New York City Public Schools and Los Angeles Unified School District, propelled in the former by a Memorandum of Understanding signed with the Office of Civil Rights and in the latter by a consent decree each has committed to undertake steps that involve both restructuring and inclusion.

Parental support for inclusive education for their children with disabilities provides a significant opportunity for quality program expansion. Their support is manifested in numerous ways, including policy statements by parent organizations (e.g., the ARC, TASH, UCP), the establishment of organizations that promote inclusion (e.g., National Parent Network on Disabilities, The PEAK Parent Center, SAFE), and the initiatives taken by the federally funded Parent Training and Information Centers (particularly noteworthy here is the work of, the Statewide Parent Advocacy Network in New Jersey [SPAN]). Often as a last extreme, parents use the courts to achieve the inclusive placement that they believe their children need. At the appellate level, the four "full inclusion" cases, in each of which the parents' demand for an inclusive placement prevailed over the school districts' refusal (Lipton, 1994), are the governing decisions. Subsequent cases, decided at the district court level, have generally but not always supported parental demands for inclusive placements, especially in the cases of older children.

Increasingly, leaders in the disability rights movement have come to see the importance of their involvement in the promotion and implementation of inclusion, for the sake of the children involved and as part of their larger civil rights agenda. Along with parents, they can be a powerful force for change.

Developing a critical mass of school districts implementing inclusive education programs means that programs are becoming more successful and serve as resources for other districts (see table of "second-generation" activities, shown earlier). The *National Study* (1995) identified a threefold increase in districts reporting inclusive education programs within one year. In the late 1970s, Edmonds (1979) said about the education of poor and minority students, "We can, whenever and wherever we choose, successfully teach all children whose schooling is of interest to us. We already know more than we need in order to do this" (p. 29), so, too, today, about educating students with disabilities in inclusive settings. Again, as Edmonds (1979) said, "Whether we do it must finally depend on how we feel about the fact that we haven't done it so far" (p.29).

112 6. FACTORS FOR SUCCESSFUL INCLUSION

REFERENCES

Bruder, M. B. (1997). Inclusion for infants, toddlers and preschoolers: Participation in natural environments. NCERI *Bulletin*, 1–7.

Council for Exceptional Children.(1995). *Creating schools for all our students: What twelve schools have to say.* Reston, VA: Author.

Does inclusion cost more? (1994). *Inclusive Education Programs*, 1(5), 4–5.

Edelman, S.W., & Giangreco, M. F. (1995). VISTA: A process for planning educationally necessary support services. *Language Learning and Education*, 2 (2), 17–18.

Edmonds, R. (1979). Some schools work and more can. *Social Policy*, 9 (5), 25–29.

Giangreco, M. F. (1995). Related services decision-making: A foundational component of effective education for students with disabilities. *Occupational and Physical Therapy in Educational Environments*, 47–67.

Giangreco, M. F., Edelman, S. W., Dennis, R. E., Prelock, P. A. & Cloniger, C. J. (1998). *Getting the most out of support services. Quick guide to inclusion: Ideas for educating students with disabilities.* Baltimore: Paul H. Brookes.

Giangreco, M. F., Edelman, S. W., Luiselli, T. E., & MacFarland, S. Z. C. (1996). Support service decision making for students with multiple service needs: Evaluative data. *JASH, 21* (3), 135–144.

Lipsky, D. K., & Gartner, A. (1997). *Inclusion and school reform: Transforming America's classrooms.* Baltimore: Paul H. Brookes.

Lipton, D. (1994). The "Full Inclusion" court cases: 1989–1994. NCERI *Bulletin, 1* (2), 1–8.

McLaughlin, M. J. & Warren, S. H. (1994). *Resources implications of inclusion: Impressions of special educators at selected sites.* Palo Alto, CA: Center for Special Education Finance.

Moll, A. (1997, July). *ASK: HOW can we work collaboratively to ensure success for ALL students: NOT: Do we HAVE to work together to serve students with disabilities?* Paper presented at Summer Institute on Collaboration and Inclusion: Rhetoric to reality.

National Center on Educational Restructuring and Inclusion, The Graduate School and University Center, The City University of New York. *National study of inclusive education.* (1994, 1995). New York: National Center on Educational Restructuring and Inclusion, The Graduate School and University Center, The City University of New York.

National study shows states exclude disabled from tests. (1995, May 8). *Educational Daily, 1*, p. 3.

Nisbet, J. (1994). Education reform: Summary and recommendations. In (Eds.) *The national reform agenda and people with mental retardation: Putting people first* (pp. 151–165). Washington, DC: President's Committee on Mental Retardation.

Odom, S. L., Peck, C. A., Hansom, M., Beckman, P. J., Kaiser, A. P., Lieber, J., Brown, W. H., Horn, E. M., & Schwartz, I. S. (1995). *Inclusion of preschool children with disabilities: An ecological systems perspective.* Nashville, TN: Early Childhood Research Institute, Vanderbilt University.

Parrish, T. (1997). In D. K. Lipsky & A. Gartner, (Eds.), *Inclusion and school reform: Transforming America's classrooms.* (pp. 275–298). Baltimore: Paul H. Brookes.

Planning for inclusion. (1995, July). *NICHCY News Digest, 5* (1), 1–31.

The State Education Department. (1997). Least Restrictive *Environment Implementation Policy Paper.* Albany, NY: Author

U.S. Department of Education. (1995). *Seventeenth annual report to Congress on the implementation of The Individuals with Disabilities Education Act.* Washington, DC: Author.

U.S. Department of Education. (1996). *Eighteenth annual report to Congress on the implementation of The Individuals with Disabilities Education Act.* Washington, DC: Author.

Villa, R., Thousand, J. S., Meyers, H., & Nevin, A. (1993). *Regular and special education teachers and administrator perceptions of heterogeneous education.* Unpublished manuscript.

The Report of the Carnegie Task Force on Learning in the Primary Grades. (1996). *Years of promise: A comprehensive learning strategy for America's children.* New York: Carnegie Corporation.

7

Parents and Inclusive Schooling: Advocating for and Participating in the Reform of Special Education

Leslie C. Soodak
Rutgers University

Several recurring themes emerge from recent discussions of educational reform, one of which is the importance of parental involvement in the education of their children. Research has shown that parental involvement benefits children's learning and school success (Chavkin, 1993; Eccles & Harold, 1993; U. S. Department of Education, 1994). The notion that schools would be more effective if parents participated in the education of their children is appealing. However, establishing meaningful partnerships with parents remains an elusive goal in many schools. Even when parental participation in decision making is mandated, as in the education of students with disabilities, collaborative decision making is often difficult to achieve (Hilton & Henderson, 1993; Turnbull & Turnbull, 1997). In special education, parents' rights to participate as members of the team responsible for decisions pertaining to the diagnosis, placement, and instruction of their children are protected by federal mandates that were initially included in PL94-142 (later renamed the Individuals with Disabilities Education Act [IDEA]). The rights of parents of children with disabilities have been reaffirmed and strengthened in the 1997 reauthorization of IDEA. However, although proponents of school improvement advocate for parental involvement in education, and parents of children with disabilities have secured the right to participate in decisions pertaining to their children, parents' perspectives on their children's education are not always adequately understood or sufficiently considered in educational planning. The former situation calls for greater understanding of parents' perspectives; the latter suggests the need to rethink policies and practices supporting (or hindering) collaboration.

Parents' perspectives on inclusive education can provide rich information regarding what parents value in the education of their children, and what they perceive their role to be in obtaining the desired schooling for their children. The move toward inclusive education is an important and relevant context within which to explore parents' perspectives for several reasons.

First, parents are among the primary stakeholders in the success of inclusive education. Whereas parents have the most to gain in terms of their children being accepted as respected members of their schools and communities, they also risk losing access to educational services that they fought hard to obtain for their children. Interestingly, despite their concerns, most parents support the goals of inclusive education, and feel strongly that children with and without disabilities will benefit from shared educational experiences (Erwin & Soodak, 1995; Guralnick, 1994; Ryndak, Downing, Jacqueline, & Morrison, 1995; Turnbull, Winton, Blacher, & Salkind, 1982). In fact, parent advocacy has been largely responsible for the move toward inclusive education in many schools throughout the country (Lipsky & Gartner, 1997).

Second, proponents of inclusive education maintain that effective schooling is a collaborative endeavor involving all stakeholders, including parents (Lipsky & Gartner, 1997; Stainback & Stainback, 1996). Inclusive schools are characterized by collaborative problem solving reflecting a belief that professionals are not the only experts in the education of diverse student groups. Thus, parental participation in inclusive schools is not limited to consent giving. Rather, parents are considered to be an integral part of school planning and service delivery.

Parents' perspectives on inclusive education are also revealing because, despite general support for the values underlying inclusive schooling, parents have assumed diverse roles in its implementation. Whereas some parents have served as catalysts for reform, other parents have assumed less active roles in initiating change. Variability in parents' involvement in their children's education may reflect underlying differences in their beliefs about themselves, their children, and their children's schooling. Hoover-Dempsey and Sandler (1997) proposed a model of parent involvement in which they suggest that parents elect to be involved in their children's education based on their construction of the parental role; their sense of efficacy for helping their children succeed; and their perceptions of the school's willingness, demands, and opportunities for parental participation. According to Hoover-Dempsey and Sandler, these three constructs have an additive effect on parents' decisions to become involved, (i.e, parents must first believe they should be involved, and they must feel both capable of helping their children, and welcome to participate.) The unique experiences of parenting a child with disabilities may complicate this model. Mandates requiring parent involvement in special education may encourage parents to be involved or, as MacMillan and Turnbull (1983) suggested, may place them in an inappropriate, unrealistic, or overly professionalized role. Furthermore, the issues that limit the participation of some parents may be exacerbated when parents from minority backgrounds and those new to the U.S. educational system are involved (Harry, Allen, & McLaughlin, 1995). Therefore, to understand parents' perspectives on inclusion, and to understand why some parents may take greater initiative than others in pursuing change, it is necessary to explore the reasons underlying their beliefs and actions.

Parents' perspectives on inclusion are not only likely to be diverse, but due to the dynamic nature of reform, are also likely to change over time. Clearly, the movement toward inclusive education is a process involving considerably more than the placement of children in general education classes. In inclusive schools, individual differences in all children are recognized and accepted, and instructional methods vary to meet the needs of all students. Attitudes, expectations, and classroom practices change slowly, and changes in thinking and behavior are influenced by a number of personal and situational factors. For example, parents may be more willing to place their children in inclusive settings following positive experiences with students and teachers in heterogeneous classrooms. On the other hand, parents may become disillusioned following negative experiences with inclusion. An understanding of changes in parents' perspectives may shed light on the nature of the reform process, and may provide direction for developing strategies to facilitate collaboration.

In this chapter, I explore the beliefs, motivations, and concerns of parents who have advocated for inclusion, as well as those who have served as participants in this reform. Parents' perspectives on their child's schooling, and their role in their child's education, are explored as dynamic phenomena in which roles and responsibilities are likely to change over time. In the first section, I focus on the reasons underlying parents' decisions to advocate for inclusive education for their children, their experiences in doing so, and their perceptions of the outcomes of their efforts. The second section synthesizes research on the perspectives of parents who may be effected by, but who have not advocated for, inclusion. Specifically, parents' perspectives on the benefits and drawbacks of inclusive education are explored and factors underlying differences in attitudes toward inclusion are discussed. In the last section, I draw on the research presented in the prior sections to reflect on how schools may facilitate collaboration with parents. Several key questions guide this chapter:

- What do parents value in the education of their children with disabilities?
- How and why do parents differ in their support of, and advocacy for, inclusive education?
- How do parents' perspectives on inclusion change over time?
- What are parents' perspectives on the outcomes of inclusive education?
- How can parental involvement in inclusive education be fostered so as to benefit students and their families?

PARENT SATISFACTION, INVOLVEMENT, AND ADVOCACY

Parents of children with disabilities have been a major force in making inclusive education possible for their children. Although many parents recognize the benefits of educating their children in general education classrooms, few parents take on the role of advocate and reformer. What motivates parents to move from a concerned parent to advocate for change? Of the many factors that are needed to inspire advocacy, parents' dissatisfaction with special education is the most documented explanation for parents' involvement in their child's education (Meyers & Blacher, 1987; Plunge & Kratochwill, 1995) and in their advocacy for inclusion (Bennett, Deluca, & Bruns, 1997). In a survey of 200 parents of children receiving special education services, Plunge and Kratochwill found a negative relation between parents' level of involvement in their child's education and their level of satisfaction with their child's educational plan, special education services, and school personnel. The 18 parents who participated in follow-up interviews unanimously agreed they had become more involved in their child's education as a result of their dissatisfaction, and to ensure that their child received adequate services. Similarly, Meyers and Blacher's study of 99 families of school-age children with disabilities indicated that the least satisfied parents were among those who were most likely to be highly involved in school activities, suggesting that parents seek to address perceived inadequacies through their involvement. In a more recent study of 48 parents of children with disabilities in preschool programs through Grade 7, Bennett and his colleagues (1997) found that parental advocacy for inclusion increased as positive experiences with members of the multi-disciplinary team responsible for educational planning decreased.

Inclusive education may be an appealing option for parents who are dissatisfied with their child's education because of the high priority placed on the social and emotional development of their children, and their belief that segregated special education classes hinder such growth. Research suggests that parents regard social integration as a primary goal for their children, irrespective of the child's age or disability. Plunge and Kratochwill (1995) selected parents for their study so as to represent the characteristics of all children receiving special education in the school district. When questioned about their concerns, parents indicated that they were least satisfied with the lack of opportunities for social integration. Parents of children with reading disabilities who were interviewed by Green and Shinn (1994) considered affective factors, such as self-esteem, as being more important than skill acquisition in their evaluation of their child's progress in the resource room. Parents of preschool children have consistently cited opportunities for interaction with same-age peers without disabilities as the primary factor in their support of inclusive education (Bailey & Winton, 1987; Green & Stoneman, 1989; Guralnick, 1994; Guralnick, Connor, & Hammond, 1995).

Thus, parental involvement is related to parents' dissatisfaction with their children's education, and those dissatisfied with special education may seek inclusive education in order to promote the goals that they value for their children. Although results of these studies offer a possible explanation for parental involvement, the relation between satisfaction and involvement is unclear because the findings were based on correlation data only. Thus, parental dissatisfaction may motivate parents to become advocates for inclusion or, conversely, their dissatisfaction may have resulted from their having assumed adversarial positions. Furthermore, these studies considered several degrees of involvement, ranging from support for inclusion to advocacy for reform, making it difficult to understand the unique experiences of parent advocates, (i.e., those who actively pursue systems change). The factors that underlie parents' decisions to advocate for inclusive education, their experiences in "taking on the system," and the degree to which their efforts lead to satisfaction with their child's education, are explored more fully in the following section.

PARENTS AS ADVOCATES FOR REFORM

Two research projects have been conducted to explore the motivations and experiences of parents who have actively pursued, and obtained, inclusive education for their children. In Soodak and Erwin (1995), we interviewed nine parents who advocated for inclusion to understand their perspectives on special education and their experiences in pursuing inclusive education (Erwin & Soodak, 1995). Similarly, Ryndak and her colleagues interviewed 13 parents who advocated for inclusion regarding their perceptions of their children's education in self-contained and integrated settings (Ryndak, Downing, Morrison, & Williams, 1996), and their perceptions of the outcomes of having their children in general education classes (Ryndak, Downing, Jacqueline, & Morrison, 1995). Parents in both research projects were recruited through parental advocacy organizations and were not identified through schools. Thus, both samples were intentionally biased to include parents who were extremely knowledgeable about inclusion, and who were actively involved in promoting inclusive education, at least for their own children.

The nine mothers who participated in the Soodak and Erwin Research lived in New York City and the surrounding suburbs, and were from diverse ethnic and socioeconomic backgrounds. All but one of these mothers were married and employed. Their children ranged in age from 5 to 19 years old, and were reported to have disabilities in the moderate to severe range. Five of the nine children spent some or all of the school day in special education classes. Of the four children who were in general education classes, one child was in a class with his same-age peers, and three children were in classes with students who were between 1 to 2 years their junior.

The 13 participants in the study conducted by Ryndak and her colleagues lived in western New York. They were white, comprised two-parent families, and were from diverse socioeconomic backgrounds. Children of parents in this study ranged in age from 5 to 19 years old, attended schools in urban, suburban, and rural districts, and were considered to have moderate, severe, or multiple disabilities. All of the children had been in inclusive educational settings between 1 and 5 years, and had previously spent between 0 and 13 years in self-contained, special education classrooms. Five children were in classes with same-age peers and the remaining eight students were in classes with students who were 1 to 2 years younger than themselves. All of the children attended their neighborhood school or school of choice.

There are interesting similarities among the participants in both studies. First, almost all families were comprised of two parents, and, although the researchers in both studies invited mothers and fathers to participate, it was primarily mothers who elected to be interviewed. (Three fathers participated with their wives in the interviews conducted by Ryndak and her colleagues.) Perhaps the large representation of two-parent families suggests that specific resources are needed for advocacy, such as emotional and financial support. The large representation of mothers is consistent with previous observations that, traditionally, mothers are more involved than fathers in their children's education (Hoover-Dempsey & Sandler, 1997). In fact, the mothers that were interviewed described themselves as the parent who more actively pursued inclusion, (i.e., attended meetings, visited classrooms, even when both parents were equally supportive of it). A second similarity among the participants in both studies is that all parents described their children as being moderately, severely, or multiply disabled. Perhaps parents of children with severe disabilities are more likely to advocate for inclusion. However, it is also possible that parents of children with more challenging behaviors were more likely represented in the particular advocacy organizations through which participants were recruited.

Parents' Perspectives on Their Motivations for Advocating for Inclusion

There was considerable consistency among the parents in the two studies regarding their reasons for becoming advocates for inclusion. The two primary reasons underlying parents' decisions to pursue inclusive education were their desire for their children to fit in as members of their communities, and their negative perceptions of their child's experiences in special education (Ryndak et al., 1996; Soodak & Erwin, 1995). Parents wanted their children to "have the same opportunities that we've given everybody else" (Soodak & Erwin, 1995, p. 265). However, they felt that school personnel did not see the need for their children to have natural support networks or interactions with nondisabled peers. Parental dissatisfaction with their child's participation in segregated special education classes emerged as an important theme in both studies. Parents did not want their children to attend schools apart from their own siblings or neighbors, and they resented special education classes being situated in undesirable locations within the school. Several parents drew parallels to racial segregation. One mother remarked: "How far have we come? So we've had the segregation of the races at one point. It is exactly the same thing" (Soodak & Erwin, 1995, p. 266). Thus, according to parents, inclusion is based on the a fundamental right of all children to the same opportunities, and experiences and the belief that this right is violated by the practice of educating students in segregated, special education classes.

Parents were motivated to integrate their children into general education because they felt that educators maintained a deficit orientation toward children in special education. Specifically, parents indicated that special education teachers held low expectations for their children, focused on problems that the parents did not recognize as being important, and provided far too much supervision for their children. Whereas these problems were noted by parents of children of all ages, the issues were most pronounced when discussed in relation to older students. For example, one mother remarked: "There was open lunch for the other high school kids [without disabilities]. The kids in the special education class, though, stood and waited in line . . . What message does that give to the other professionals the other students when you have to take a 17-, 18-, 19-, or 20-year-old kid to the bathroom?" (Ryndak et al., 1996, p. 115). Furthermore, parents who advocated for inclusion felt there was a pervasive lack of individualization in special education, and they cited examples in which all students attending the same program received identical related services, students were assigned goals irrespective of their needs, and goals were repeated regardless of student progress.

An additional area of concern for parents in both studies pertained to their own roles in their child's special education. Parents described feeling powerless when interacting with school personnel, leaving them to defer to "expert judgments" even when they disagreed with the decisions being made. One mother commented that she "had absolutely no control over what schooling [her son] was getting" (Soodak & Erwin, 1995, p. 270). The Individualized Education Program (IEP) meeting was particularly difficult for many of the parents. During these meetings parents were consistently outnumbered by school personnel, and were often unable to understand the professional jargon being used. The interactions between parents and professionals, as described by these parent advocates, are consistent with what Biklen (1992) referred to as the "myth of clinical judgment" in which parents' options for recourse are limited by shared and erroneous assumptions regarding the accuracy of professional expertise.

Findings of these studies support the notion that parental advocacy results, in part, from parents' perceptions of the incongruity between the goals they have for their children and what the perceive to be the goals of special education. Consistent with the findings of research on parent satisfaction and involvement cited earlier, parents who strongly advocate for inclusive education are extremely dissatisfied with the services their children receive in special education, and the limited opportunities they have to collaborate with school personnel in the planning of their child's education. Although caution is needed in the interpretation of findings based on a limited number of parents (23 mothers) and a limited data source (each parent was interviewed once), the consistency of findings within and across studies suggests that, at least for this group of parents, issues of equality and acceptance led them to pursue changes in their child's education.

Parents' Perspectives on the Pursuit of Inclusion

Parents in both studies stood up to the system in order to make inclusive education available to their children. In doing so, each took a unique and difficult journey that not only had an impact on their child, but on their families, and on their perceptions of themselves. Despite sometimes powerful resistance from professionals, parents employed numerous strategies to obtain what they believed to be best for their children. These strategies, detailed in Erwin and Soodak (1995), included involving schools in due process hearings, obtaining media attention, lobbying key players in the school district, becoming involved as a parent member of the interdisciplinary team, removing their children from school, and relocating their families to an area with a more receptive school district. Many parents used multiple strategies simultaneously. For example, one mother kept her child out of school for several years in order to accept no less than an inclusive education for the child. While providing home instruction for her child and being employed full-time, this parent sought media attention, engaged in due process hearings, and tried to educate school personnel about the goals of inclusion. For all parents, the pursuit of inclusive education was undertaken at great expense, in terms of time, money, and emotional well-being.

Despite parents' willingness to fight for what they believed to be best for their children, many grew to resent the role they felt forced to assume. Many parents were angry and frustrated at having to devote significant time and energy to obtain an appropriate education for their children. One parent felt that the pursuit of inclusion had been more difficult for her to endure than dealing with complications arising from her son's medical condition: "Sometimes you have to fight for medication. To me, it is a right. I should not have to fight for this — it's his right." (Erwin & Soodak, 1995, p. 143). However, despite their anger and frustration, many parents noted they had developed an awareness of their own strengths as a result of their advocacy efforts. Several comments reflected the personal transformations that had been experienced. For example, one mother remarked that the experience of advocating for the inclusion of her child "probably affected me more than any one thing in my whole life" (Erwin & Soodak, 1995, p. 143). Another mother concluded that the experience left her feeling good about herself, whereas another attributed her satisfaction to making others "stop and think" (Erwin & Soodak, 1995, p. 143).

Thus, parents who strongly desire inclusive education for their children are willing to struggle long and hard to obtain it. However, regardless of the parents' success in securing inclusive education, they feel angry at having to assume the role of advocate. Similar findings were reported by Hanline and Halvorsen (1989) in their study of parents' perception of the transition from special to general education. Seven of the 13 parents in this study who were considered to be the prime advocates for the inclusion of their children in general education expressed resentment at having to assume the role of advocate. One mother commented that "One of the hardest parts is having people not like you. . . . Parents should not have to go through some of the things we've had to go through" (p. 488). Furthermore, several parents felt that the role of advocate was more appropriately assumed by school personnel, as noted in one parent's question: "Why wasn't it done by the people who's job it is?" (p. 489). Hanline and Halvorsen suggested that educators who feel powerless to make changes in service delivery may encourage parents themselves to pursue inclusion rather than work collaboratively with them to ensure that districts provide integrated services.

Parents' Perspectives on the Effects of Their Advocacy Efforts

Parents who advocated for, and obtained, inclusive education for their children readily reflected on the positive outcomes of their efforts. All parents who participated in the research conducted by Ryndak and her colleagues cited benefits of having their children in inclusive settings. Unlike the parents in this study, however, most of the parents who participated in the research conducted by Erwin and me had not yet secured inclusive education for their children at the time of the initial interviews. Rather, these parents were still actively in pursuit of the expected benefits of inclusion. Follow-up interviews that were conducted 3 years after the initial interviews (Soodak, 1997) indicated that nearly all of the nine parents who participated in the original study had secured inclusive educational placements for their children within that time and that many of them also felt that their children were benefiting from the experience in general education. At the time of the follow-up interviews, seven of the parents reported their children were in general education classes full time (three of whom were in age-appropriate classes), one child was spending a half day in general education, and one child had "aged out" of school. Only half of the school-age children were attending classes in their neighborhood schools.

Parents who successfully advocated for inclusive education cited specific benefits of such placements both to their children and to their families. Ryndak et al. (1995) found that parents were satisfied because they felt that their children had increased opportunities to interact with nondisabled peers, and had greater access to the general education curriculum when in inclusive settings. Each of the parents reported that their children had made significant gains in the acquisition of academic, communication, and social skills. Positive effects of integration on the children who were included were also reported by the parents interviewed by Hanline and Halvorsen (1989). Specifically, parents in this study (the majority of whom had advocated for their child's integrated placement) reported that their children had enhanced their social skills and self-esteem as a result of their participation in general education. I also found parents to be satisfied with their child's inclusion in general education. Almost all the parents interviewed felt their children were benefiting socially and academically from their involvement in general education. The only parents who were unable to identify benefits of inclusion for their children were those who also indicated that their child's placement was not truly inclusive (i.e., the child was only attending general education classes part time or was not placed in a class with his or her age-mates).

Positive effects of inclusion on families were also noted by parents. The mothers and fathers interviewed by Hanline and Halvosen indicated that their own expectations for their children had been raised after the children had participated in integrated settings. One father stated that expecting any less than "a perfectly normal life" for his 9-year-old daughter would be his own "artificial barrier" (Hanline & Halvorsen, 1989, pp. 490–491). Parents in this study also noted that their families had benefited from integration, in that siblings were less concerned about issues of long-term care and that the families' focus had shifted away from the child's disability. For these families, community acceptance of children with disabilities reinforced their commitment to inclusion, encouraged parents to be less overprotective of their children with disabilities, and strengthened family ties.

The follow-up interviews conducted indicated that the roles parents assume in their child's education change once inclusive education is made available to their children. Although no less committed to inclusion, many of the parents interviewed noted that their advocacy efforts had diminished the longer their children participated in general education. Several parents no longer actively participated in advocacy organizations, and instead were involved in established and mainstream parent organizations, such as the parent–teacher association and the local school board. The more secure parents were that the school was truly committed to inclusive education, the more they were able to retreat from their advocacy roles. However, they did not terminate their involvement in their child's education. Parents indicated they remained involved to ensure their children were given a reasonable opportunity to learn and interact in general education.

In summary, studies that have explored the motivations and experiences of parents who advocate for inclusion indicate that parents' commitment to inclusive education overrides their reluctance to challenge the system. In fact, parents who advocate for inclusion seem willing to persist in their efforts to seek change in their child's education despite the financial and emotional costs to themselves and their families. Furthermore, parents who advocate for inclusive education, or at least those who had agreed to participate in these studies, are likely to be successful in securing inclusive education for their children, and to be generally satisfied with the effects of inclusive education on their children and their families. However, despite the success of their advocacy efforts, parents unanimously agree that they should not have had to challenge schools to be more inclusive.

PARENTS AS PARTICIPANTS IN REFORM

Although the progress made toward inclusive schooling during the 1990's has been attributed, in part, to parent advocacy, there are far more parents who assume less active roles in this movement. Research on parents' perspectives on inclusive education suggests that differences in parents' involvement is not a function of differences in attitudes toward inclusive education. In fact, the most consistent finding to emerge from 10 years of research is that most parents of children with disabilities are supportive of the goals of inclusion. Parents want their children to learn and socialize with typically developing children, and they believe that all children are likely to benefit from integration. However, parental support for inclusion is tempered by their perceptions of barriers to successful inclusion. In this section, research on parents' attitudes toward inclusive education is reviewed to understand parents' expectations and concerns regarding the education of their children, and to identify factors that mediate their perspectives on this initiative.

Perceived Benefits Of Inclusion

Considerable support for inclusive education is found among parents of children ranging in age and ability. Interestingly, the largest body of research to emerge on this topic pertains to the attitudes of parents of preschool children. The preponderance of data pertaining to the inclusion of preschoolers, and specifically parents' responses to inclusive education, may be due to the relevance of this issue to children entering the educational system. As children enter school, parents are able to see their children in a new context, one that incorporates a given set of goals and expectations for their children that may or may not match their own. In addition, research on parents of preschoolers may have flourished because of the specific focus on parental involvement at this level of service.

Parents of preschoolers with disabilities consistently support inclusive education for their children. Positive attitudes toward inclusion have been found among parents with children in segregated programs (Diamond & LeFurgy, 1994; Guralnick, 1994; Miller, et al., 1992), those with children in the process of transitioning to integrated preschool programs (Bailey & Winton, 1987; Reichart, et al., 1989), and those with children who have participated in inclusive preschool programs (Bailey & Winton, 1987; Diamond & LeFurgy, 1994; Guralnick, 1994; Miller et al., 1992). Most of these studies surveyed more than 100 parents, and employed questionnaires to assess parental attitudes toward integration. Regardless of the specific instrument employed, the vast majority of parents in each study were found to be supportive of inclusive education. For example, approximately 85% of 222 mothers surveyed by Guralnick (1994) indicated they perceived either probable or definite benefits of inclusion to children with and without disabilities. Specifically, parents noted that inclusion would promote the acceptance of children with disabilities, prepare children for real-world experiences, and provide children with greater opportunities for learning. In addition, Miller and her colleagues (1992) found that parents of preschoolers with disabilities were optimistic about the integration of children with disabilities into school-age programs, suggesting that parents of preschool children believe that the benefits of inclusion will endure as children continue their education.

Parents of school-age children are also supportive of inclusive education. Interviews with parents of children ages to 20 years with moderate to severe disabilities have demonstrated that both parents who have had their children in inclusive settings, and those who have not, are able to cite benefits of integration (Bennett et al., 1997; Reichart et al., 1989; Ryndak et al., 1995; Turnbull et al., 1982). A recent study of 48 parents of school-age children with a broad range of disabilities who were participating to varying degrees in general education indicated that parents felt strongly that inclusion represented a positive change in the educational system, and that it would likely benefit all children (Bennett et al., 1997). Furthermore, parents' positive attitudes were associated with their having had positive experiences with inclusion. Nearly two thirds of the parents whose children were in inclusive settings indicated that they were generally satisfied with their child's experiences in these settings.

Parents of children with mild disabilities who receive special education services in resource-room programs also hold positive attitudes toward inclusion. However, it is noteworthy that parents and professionals representing students with learning disabilities have been among those who are most resistant to the idea of full inclusion (Skrtic, 1995). Research indicates that, although parents believe that reintegrating students from pullout programs into general education classrooms will likely improve the academic abilities of children with learning disabilities (Abramson, Willson, Yoshida, & Hagerty, 1983; Mlynek, Hannah, & Hamlin, 1982), they are less likely to perceive benefits of inclusion for their own children (Abramson et al., 1983; Green & Shinn, 1994; Simpson & Myles, 1989). It seems that parents of children with learning disabilities are in agreement with the goals inclusive education, but that they are not confident that their own children will benefit from the experience. Green and Shinn (1994) suggested that parents' reluctance to include their children with reading disabilities in general education may be a function of parents' satisfaction with the pull-out services their children have received, and conversely, their fear of relinquishing services that they feel have been beneficial to their children.

Although parents of children with mild disabilities may be reluctant to include their children initially (or more accurately, they may be less likely to recognize the benefits of doing so), their hesitancy seems to diminish as inclusion moves closer to becoming a reality. Specifically, parents are more likely to endorse inclusion once they have been informed that their children will begin receiving instruction in the regular classroom (Green & Shinn, 1994), and following their child's involvement in integrated settings (Lowenbraun, Madge, & Affleck, 1990). Although it is unclear whether parents held more favorable attitudes as a result of the inclusion of children in general education classes, or whether changes in parental attitudes played a role in their child's move to inclusive education, attitudes among parents of children with learning disabilities seem to become more favorable over time.

There is considerable consistency among parents regarding their perceptions of the benefits of inclusion. The two reasons parents offer most often for their support of inclusion are increased opportunities for friendships with nondisabled children, and increased opportunities for learning (Bailey & Winton, 1987; Guralnick, 1994; Reichart et al., 1989; Turnbull et al., 1982). Specifically, parents feel that interactions among students with differing abilities will facilitate the acceptance of children with disabilities, and will provide opportunities for friendships among children. Furthermore, parents feel that the availability of role models will be an asset to their child's education and social development. In terms of academic benefits, parents believe that their children will be exposed to, and benefit from, a richer and more varied curriculum in general education. Parents are also supportive of inclusive education because they feel that integrated educational experiences will provide better preparation for participation in mainstream activities outside of school, and in later life. Indeed, research on parental perspectives of the outcomes of inclusion indicate that, for most parents, the expected benefits are realized. Although there have been only a limited number of studies that directly explore parents' perceptions of the success of inclusion, parents of children who have experienced inclusive education readily identify gains made by their children in integrated settings (Bennett et al., 1997; Guralnick, 1994; Guralnick et al., 1995; Shinn, Powell-Smith, Good, & Baker, 1997; Ryndak et al., 1995; Soodak, 1997). Parents of preschoolers report their children show gains in social, communication, and motor skills after participation in integrated programs. Parents of school-age children report their children benefit in terms of social skills, preacademic and academic skills, and communication skills. In all studies, parents specifically noted that, much to their satisfaction, inclusion facilitated the development of friendships, and promoted acceptance of their children among their peers.

Sources Of Concern

There are two concerns that predominate parents' thinking about the integration of their children. First, parents are concerned about the possibility of their children experiencing rejection, and second, they are concerned about the quality of the education their children will receive in integrated programs. Issues pertaining to attitudinal barriers are important to both parents of preschoolers (Bailey & Winton, 1987; Diamond & LeFurgy, 1994; Guralnick, 1994; Peck, Hayden, Wandschneider, Peterson, & Richarz, 1989), and parents of school-age children (Bennett et al., 1997; Green & Shinn, 1994; Hanline & Halvorsen, 1989; York & Tundidor, 1995). Interestingly, these concerns reflect the same values that underlie parents' perspectives on the potential benefits of inclusion. In other words, whereas parents long to have their children fit in with typically developing children, they also fear that those in the mainstream, (i.e., students and teachers), may be less than welcoming to their children.

As is the case with all parents, parents of children with disabilities desire to protect their children from social isolation and ridicule. Although parents' concern about their child's rejection in inclusive settings is an important and recurring theme, it is a concern that may not be consistent with what actually happens in integrated classes. In fact, research indicates that integrated settings promote positive peer relationships among children with and without disabilities (Green & Stoneman, 1989; Guralnick et al., 1995). However, it is presently unknown whether children with disabilities are more likely to be rejected in integrated settings than in segregated settings, and if so, what strategies may be employed to minimize problems for children. Regardless of the basis for parents' fears, efforts must be made to address parents' concerns about their child's sense of security in integrated settings. As suggested by parents in one study, perhaps children with special needs in integrated programs should have access to others with similar abilities to reduce feelings of isolation, and encourage greater tolerance of differences (Guralnick et al., 1995).

Parental concerns about the educational opportunities provided to their children in integrated settings must also be addressed. Presently, not all parents believe that the individual needs of their children will be adequately addressed in inclusive settings. Specifically, at issue is the availability of instructional and related resources, and teachers' ability to adapt instruction to the needs of the child with disabilities. In addition, parents of typically developing children are concerned that the inclusion of children with disabilities will limit the educational resources (such as teacher attention) available to their children. Because of these concerns, teachers are seen by parents as being vital to the success of inclusion (Reichart et al., 1989; York & Tundidor, 1994) Interestingly, the concerns parents have regarding their child's access to instruction with the necessary adaptations, supports, and related services are most often cited by parents of children who have not yet been included. Parents of children who have participated in inclusive settings, on the other hand, often perceive adequate learning opportunities for their children (Bennett et al., 1997; Ryndak et al., 1995; Shinn et al., 1997). Therefore, it may be beneficial for parents with concerns about including their children to observe in inclusive programs, or to speak with parents whose children have had experience in included settings. Furthermore, because program quality varies, parents' concerns may be indicative of poor instructional practices that require interventions, such as teacher training or the reallocation of support services.

Thus, in general, parents hold positive attitudes toward inclusion because they want all children to be accepted (and accepting) and they want all children to have the same learning opportunities. However, parents are mindful of potential threats to their child's psychological well-being and intellectual development. Whereas parents who strongly advocate for their children to be in inclusive settings focus on their child's right to be in general education classes, parents who are less actively involved in the pursuit of inclusion focus on their child's right to an appropriate education. In both cases, parents agree that all children are likely to benefit from participating in inclusive schooling .

Factors Mediating Parents' Attitudes Toward Inclusion

Although both parents who advocate for inclusive education and those who serve as participants in this reform indicate support for inclusion, an understanding of factors that mediate parents' attitudes may help explain why parents assume different roles in this reform. The factors that have been found to mediate parents' attitudes inclusion fall into three categories (i.e., setting characteristics, child characteristics, and family characteristics).

First, parents with children in inclusive settings hold more positive attitudes toward inclusion than do parents of children in segregated settings (Diamond &

LeFurgy, 1994; Green & Stoneman, 1989; Guralnick et al., 1995; Lowenbraun et al., 1990; Miller et al., 1992). This finding is consistent with research that indicates that parents' concerns lessen as soon as an inclusive placement is recommended for their children. Two factors that do not appear to influence parental attitudes are the length of time children participate in mainstream settings (Miller et al., 1992), and whether the parent had requested that their children be placed in an inclusive setting (Lowenbraun et al., 1990). Although research indicates a relation between experience with and attitudes toward inclusion, many questions remain unanswered. First, do parents develop more positive attitudes toward inclusion as a result of their child's experience in inclusion, or are attitudes and experience determined by other factors? Second, are parents' attitudes influenced by their perceptions of the quality of their child's experiences in inclusive education, and if so, would perceptions of negative experiences undermine parents' attitudes toward inclusion? Third, do findings of increased support for inclusion following placement indicate a preference for inclusion, or do the findings indicate that parents tend to be satisfied with the services their children receive at a given time?

In terms of child characteristics, research suggests that the age of the child may underlie differences in parental attitudes. Attitudes toward inclusion appear to be more favorable among parents of younger children than among parents of older students (Green & Stoneman, 1989; York & Tundidor, 1995). Parents may be more reluctant to integrate their children into school-age programs because they recognize that, in the upper grades, there is less attention given to a child's social and emotional development, and a greater emphasis on academic achievement. Furthermore, the reluctance of parents of school-age students to include their children may reflect the specific concerns of parents of children with learning disabilities discussed earlier. These parents seem to be hesitant to give up services they find beneficial to their children and, because children with mild disabilities often receive instruction in the mainstream for part of the school day, parents may be less likely to perceive their children as being isolated from their nondisabled peers as are parents of preschoolers attending specialized programs.

There is little evidence to suggest that the developmental characteristics of the children to be integrated influence parents' attitudes toward inclusion. No relation between the level of developmental functioning of preschool children and parental attitudes toward inclusion was found in the two studies that explored such differences (Guralnick, 1994; Miller et al., 1992). In addition, Guralnick (1994) did not find a relation between the type of disability and parental attitudes, except for mothers of children with behavior disorders. Mothers of preschool children with behavior problems were more concerned about the drawbacks of inclusion than were mothers of other preschoolers. These mothers seem to be particularly concerned that their children will be rejected in mainstream settings, suggesting that the integration of preschool children with behavior problems may pose a challenge for integration, or that parents of these children need to be reassured that efforts will be made to facilitate acceptance.

There are virtually no studies that have directly explored family characteristics as an explanation of differences in attitudes toward inclusion. However, there is an emerging body of research that has investigated the relation between family background and parental participation in special education. Researchers have documented that some parents, particularly those from diverse linguistic and cultural backgrounds, tend not to participate in or challenge educational decisions pertaining to their children because they feel disengaged and powerless when interacting with school personnel. In a study of 24 African-American families whose children were in special education, half of whom were interviewed over 3 years (Harry et al., 1995) revealed the process by which parental involvement and advocacy is diminished. Specifically, the bureaucratic and overly professionalized structure of meetings between school personnel and parents resulted in frustration and passivity on the part of the parents, several of whom were initially advocating for a change in placement for their children. Similar feelings of mistrust and withdrawal were observed in an earlier study that explored the experiences of Puerto Rican families in the special education system (Harry, 1992). One mother in this study noted that "Our opinions are not valued. Many parents do not want their child in a special class or in a school so far away, but they keep quiet. It is very hard to struggle with these Americans. In America, the schools are for Americans" (p. 486). Thus, the suggestion that parents from minority backgrounds tend to be trusting of decisions made by educators and satisfied with the services their children receive may be misleading (Lynch & Stein, 1987).

Research on factors mediating parental attitudes toward inclusion is beginning to shed light on the complex nature of parents thinking about inclusion. In summary, research conducted to date indicates that parents are most favorable following their child's placement, and when young children, and those without behavior problems, are being included. Parents' attitudes seem to be unaffected by the child's developmental functioning, and the length of time the child is in an included setting. Research has not, however, explored whether setting variables, such as program quality, influence parents' judgments. In addition, research has not directly explored how family background, and other personal attributes, interact with setting and child characteristics in mediating parents' attitudes.

CONCLUSIONS AND IMPLICATIONS

Perhaps the most important finding to emerge from research on parents and inclusive education is that, regardless of whether or not parents actively seek to reform special education, all parents want their children to be accepted by others, to develop friendships, and to have an opportunity to learn. Most importantly, the vast majority of parents are confident that these goals are most likely to be met by educating children in general education settings. Parental support for inclusion seems to evolve into advocacy for reform when dissatisfaction, frustration and hope exist simultaneously. However, although these conditions may motivate some parents to fight for change, they may encourage others to withdraw from participation in their children's education. Clearly, for parents, educators, and children, neither extreme is desirable. Therefore, the question that remains to be answered is: "How can parental involvement in inclusive education be fostered so as to benefit students and their families?"

The answer is both simple and complex. First, parents' perspectives on their children's education must be understood, respected, and considered before decisions are made. Second, opportunities for interactions cannot be limited to formal meetings that focus on obtaining consent to important educational decisions. Third, parents should be involved in the development and evaluation of program changes, so that their goals and concerns are addressed prior to implementation. These suggestions, however, represent some of the simpler changes that are needed for effective collaboration in inclusive schools. The more complex changes involve modifications in attitudes and behaviors among both parents and professionals that presently act as obstacles to collaboration.

Based on the data reviewed in this chapter, many parents lack trust in the educational system, believing, for example, that educators underestimate their children or that the services their children receive are provided at the school's discretion. School personnel, on the other hand, often view parents as adversaries (Turnbull & Turnbull, 1997), and tend to attribute a student's learning and behavior problems, that are otherwise unexplained, to conditions within the child's home (Soodak & Podell, 1994). Distrust clearly undermines collaboration. However, to counter feelings of distrust, schools need to create an empowering context for both parents and professionals. Kalyanpur and Rao (1991) defined the attributes of empowerment in this way:

> Empowerment signifies changing the role of a service provider from that of an expert to that of an ally or friend who enables families to articulate what they need. . . [Empowerment] involves caring, which builds supportive relationships; respect, which builds, reciprocity; and the acceptance of differences, which build trust. . . Such empathy involves the acceptance and open acknowledgment of the parents' competence, the willingness to interact with them on equal terms, and the adoption of a nonjudgmental stance. (p. 531)

According to Turnbull and Turnbull (1997), professionals can build reliable alliances that empower parents by understanding their own perceptions; understanding families' characteristics, interactions, functions, and life cycle issues; honoring cultural diversity; building on family strengths; promoting family choices; encouraging high expectations; practicing positive communication skills; and warranting mutual trust and respect.

The possibility for meaningful collaboration is enhanced by the move toward inclusive education. As schools become more inclusive, there may be a change in the continuum of parental involvement, such that a greater number of parents will participate with educators in fostering students' learning and school success. On one end of the continuum, parents who presently advocate for change may be able to assume less adversarial roles. On the other end of the continuum, parents who presently feel disenfranchised may become more engaged in their children's education once their children become members of mainstream classes. The research presented in this chapter suggests that parents are mindful of the opportunities and problems associated with inclusive education. Future research should explore changes in parents' perceptions of their children, their perceptions of inclusion, and their relationship with school personnel as inclusive education continues to develop as an accepted practice in U.S. schools.

REFERENCES

Abramson, M., Willson, V., Yoshida, R. K., & Hagerty, G. (1983). Parents' perceptions of their learning disabled child's educational performance. *Learning Disability Quarterly, 6,* 184–194.

Bailey, D. B., Jr., & Winton, P. J. (1987). Stability and change in parents' expectations about mainstreaming. *Topics in Early Childhood Special Education, 7,* 73–88.

Bennett, T., Deluca, D., & Bruns, D. (1997). Putting inclusion into practice: Perspectives of teachers and parents. *Exceptional Children, 64,* 115–131.

Biklen, D. (1992*). Schooling without labels: Parents, educators, and inclusive education.* Philadelphia: Temple University Press.

Chavkin, N. F. (Ed.). (1993). *Families and schools in a plauralistic society.* Albany: State University of New York Press.

Diamond, K. E., & LeFurgy, W. G. (1994). Attitudes of parents of preschool children toward integration. *Early Education and Development, 5,* 69–77.

Eccles, J. S., & Harold, R. D. (1993). Parent–school involvement during the early adolescent years. *Teachers College Record, 94,* 568–587.

Erwin, E. J., & Soodak, L. C. (1995). I never knew I could stand up to the system: Families' perspectives on pursing inclusive education. *The Journal of the Association for Severe Handicaps, 20,* 136–146.

Green, A. L, & Stoneman, Z. (1989). Attitudes of mothers and fathers of nonhandicapped children. *Journal of Early Intervention, 13,* 292–304.

Green, S. K., & Shinn, M. (1994). Parent attitudes about special education and reintegration: What is the role of student outcomes. *Exceptional Children, 61,* 269–281.

Guralnick, M. J. (1994). Mothers' perceptions of the benefits and drawbacks of early childhood mainstreaming. *Journal of Early Intervention, 18,* 168–183.

Guralnick, M. J., Connor, R. T., & Hammond, M. (1995). Parent perspectives of peer relationships and friendships in integrated and specialized programs. *American Journal on Mental Retardation, 99,* 457–476.

Hanline, M. F., & Halvorsen, A. (1989). Parent perceptions of the integration transition process: Overcoming artificial barriers. *Exceptional Children, 55,* 487–492.

Harry, B. (1992). An ethnographic study of cross-cultural communication with Puerto Rican-American families in the special education system. *American Educational Research Journal, 29,* 471–494.

Harry, B., Allen, N., & McLaughlin, M. (1995). Communication versus compliance: African-American parents' involvement in special education. *Exceptional Children, 61,* 364–377.

Hilton, A., & Henderson, C. J. (1993). Parent involvement : A best practice or forgotten practice? *Education and Training in Mental Retardation, 28,* 199–211.

Hoover-Dempsey, K. V., & Sandler, H. M. (1997). Why do parents become involved in their children education? *Review of Educational Research, 67,* 3–42.

Kalyanpur, M., & Rao, S. S. (1991). Empowering low-income black families of handicapped children. *American Journal of Orthopsychiatry, 61,* 523–532.

Lipsky, D. K., & Gartner, A. (1997). *Inclusion and school reform: Transforming America's classrooms.* Baltimore: Paul H. Brookes.

Lowenbraun, S., Madge, S., & Affleck, J. (1990). Parental satisfaction with integrated class placements of special education and general education students. *Remedial and Special Education, 11,* 37–40.

Lynch, E. W., & Stein, R. C. (1987). Parent participation by ethnicity: A comparison of Hispanic, Black, and Anglo families. *Exceptional Children, 54,* 105–111.

MacMillan, D. L., & Turnbull, A. P. (1983). Parent involvement in special educc :ion: Respecting individual preferences. *Education and Training of the Mentally Retarded, 18*, 4–9.

Meyers, C. E., & Blacher, J. (1987). Parents' perceptions of schooling for severely handicapped children: Home and school variables. *Exceptional Children, 53*, 441–449.

Miller, L. J., Strain, P. S., Boyd, K., Hunsicker, S., McKinley, J., & Wu, A. (1992). Parental attitudes toward integration. *Topics in Early Childhood Special Education, 12*, 230–246.

Mlynek, S., Hannah, M. E., & Hamlin, M. A. (1982). Mainstreaming: Parental perceptions. *Psychology in the Schools, 19*, 354–359.

Peck, C. A., Hayden, L., Wandschneider, M., Peterson, K., & Richarz, S. (1989). Development of integrated preschools: A qualitative inquiry into sources of resistance among parents, administrators, and teachers. *Journal of Early Intervention, 13*, 353–363.

Plunge, M. M., & Kratochwill, T. R. (1995). Parental knowledge, involvement, and satisfaction with their child's special education services. *Special Services in the Schools, 10*, 113–138.

Reichart, D. C., Lynch, E. C., Anderson, B. C., Svobodny, L. A., DiCola, J. M., & Mercury, M. G. (1989). Parental perspectives on integrated preschool opportunities for children with handicaps and children without handicaps. *Journal of Early Intervention, 13*, 6–13.

Ryndak, D. L, Downing, J. E., Jacqueline, L. R., & Morrison, A. P. (1995). Parents's perceptions after inclusion of their children with moderate or severe disabilities. *Journal of the Association for Persons with Severe Handicaps, 20*, 147–157.

Ryndak, D. L., Downing, J. E., Morrison, A. P., & Williams, L. J. (1996). Parents' perceptions of educational settings and services for children with moderate or severe disabilities. *Remedial and Special Education, 17*, 106–118.

Shinn, M. R., Powell-Smith, K. A., Good, R. H., & Baker, S. (1997). The effects of reintegration into general education reading instruction for students with mild disabilities. *Exceptional Children, 64*, 59–79.

Simpson, R. L., & Myles, B. S. (1989). Parents' mainstreaming modification preferences for children with educable mental handicaps, behavior disorders, and learning disabilities. *Psychology in the Schools, 26*, 29–301.

Skrtic, T. M. (1995). The special education knowledge tradition: Crisis and opportunity. In E. L. Meyen & T. M. Skrtic (Eds.), *Special education and student disability: Traditional, emerging, and alternative perspectives* (pp. 609–672). Denver, CO: Love Publishing.

Soodak, L. C. (1997, March). *Parents as advocates for inclusion: A three-year follow-up study.* Paper presented at the annual conference of the American Educational Research Association, Chicago.

Soodak, L. C., & Erwin, E. J. (1995). Parents, professionals, and inclusive education: A call for collaboration. *Journal of Educational and Psychological Consultation, 6*, 257–276.

Soodak, L. C., & Podell, D. M. (1994). Teachers' thinking about difficult to teach students. *Journal of Educational Research, 88*, 44–51.

Stainback, S., & Stainback, W. (Eds.). (1996). *Inclusion: A guide for educators.* Baltimore,: Paul H. Brookes.

Turnbull, A. P., & Turnbull, H. R. (1997). *Families, professionals, and exceptionality: A special partnership* (3rd ed.). Columbus, OH: Merrill.

Turnbull, A. P., Winton, P., Blacher, J., & Salkind, N. (1982). Mainstreaming in the kindergarten classroom: Perspectives of parents of handicapped and nonhandicapped children. *Journal of the Division of Early Childhood, 6*, 14–20.

U.S. Department of Education, (1994). *Strong families, strong schools: Building community partnerships for learning.* Washington, DC: Author.

York, J., & Tundidor, H. (1995). Issues raised in the name of inclusion: Perspectives of educators, parents, and students. *Journal of the Persons with Severe Handicaps, 20, Association for* 31–44.

8

Inclusion Practices In Canada: Social, Political, and Educational Influences

Margret A. Winzer
University of Lethbridge

In recent years, critics have taken schools to task for a multitude of sins. An unrelenting assault on the content, processes, and outcomes of schooling in Canada has elevated school reform to a major movement for all levels and for all populations. In the regular educational arena, a recent analysis of provincial and territorial reports, provided by the Council of Ministers of Education, shows specific educational trends. These include more cooperative efforts at the regional and national levels, more accountability to the public, information technology as an integral part of education, less funding to the administrative side of education to ensure that resources are allocated to classrooms, fewer school districts and boards, a focus on curriculum outcomes and standards to make education more relevant, improved levels of student achievement, more cost-effective ways to deliver programs, the implementation of comprehensive and multi-year assessment programs tied to curriculum standards and outcomes, transition programs, and the evaluation of current development and training programs ("Key trends," 1996).

The present reformist climate is making significant differences to special education in the areas of school responsibility, program delivery, and program implementation. The process of gradual, evolutionary change that has traditionally characterized special education is subject to increasing challenges by a growing legion of critics. Today, law, advocacy, and educational innovation are, together, creating a unique environment supportive of fundamental changes in how students with disabilities are educated (Porter & Richler, 1990).

From many constituencies, the appropriateness of special education as a system, as well as the classification and placement of some students in this system for the majority of their educational experiences, is under attack. The major prescription for the perceived ailments of contemporary special education is a movement variously referred to as *inclusion, inclusive schooling*, or *inclusive education*. Inclusion hosts a range of theoretical positions related to the relation of those targeted for inclusion and the nature of regular educational provision (Slee, 1997). There are many definitions and shades of meaning accompanying the concept and practice, but there is not an interpretation that matches the needs of all stakeholders. Essentially, inclusion in Canada means that students with disabilities will attend the school or classroom that they would attend if they were not disabled. Services are brought to the child rather than the child being removed in order to access services.

As the paradigm shift from segregation to integration becomes increasingly manifest, parents, Ministries of education, and school boards express the desire to follow an inclusive philosophy whereby a child is effectively welcomed into the general classroom (Carney, 1996). However, the move to inclusive schooling has fostered both good and bad practices, and few educational issues have generated the fervor and stimulated the polarization of perspectives in the way that inclusion has since the mid-1990s. A political will is manifest, but the integration of all students who are exceptional into regular milieus remains controversial and relatively precarious. Ideology has not enjoyed an easy transition to educational practice; the movement is balanced over an abyss of tight resources, changing demographics, teacher attitudes, parent expectations, and other social and political variables (Winzer, 1995).

Among educators and allied professionals, the philosophical goals of inclusion are almost universally applauded, but the present form of its implementation has not found universal support. The practical implementation remains the subject of heated debate among special education personnel, psychologists, mental health professionals, teachers and teachers' federations, and parents.

Nor is the issue restricted to educational circles. As a dominant educational discourse social institutions, such as families and government agencies, have been irrevocably drawn in, as have talk shows, government reports, editorial writers, and politicians (Robertson, 1992). The media reports the positions of various interest groups and stakeholders who hold different, often anti-ethical views. The Calgary *Herald* noted, "The debate over how to school special needs children proves vexing and emotional;" the *Globe and Mail* that "Fiscal, social realities prevent student integration" (Galt, 1997, p. 1A).

Much that is exciting and innovative can be seen in Canadian special education and the note should be one of cautious optimism. Special education has shown constant growth in research interests, in the students served, in the age groups included, and in outcomes. Nevertheless, as the paradigm shift occurs, many researchers and observers focus on the lack of a carefully conceptualized blueprint. In its development, Canadian special education has been characterized as "an intricate quilt of political accident, professional ambition, and pedagogical oversight brought together by legislative red tape" (Csapo, 1992, p. 252). Today, and particularly in regard to the practice of inclusion, the enterprise is characterized by ambiguity and inconsistency accented by simplistic and naive declarations of how to achieve the goal. So far, the debate on inclusion has been largely at the philosophical rather than at the practical level, and there is a sense that schools are more prepared to implement the form of inclusion and less prepared to deal with the substance of it. Very often, inclusive schooling is viewed as a discretionary responsibility rather than a core value of the system.

This chapter discusses the current status of the inclusive movement in Canada. It is not one of opposition to inclusion, nor does it promote traditional models of special educational practice anchored in schedules of disablement, compensation, special pedagogues, and institutional arrangements. Rather, it takes a cautionary stance and suggests disappointment as arising, not from individual dysfunction but, from the realities of contemporary Canadian classroom life. The barriers to successful and universal inclusion remain complex, diverse, and numerous. The best intentions are dragged down by large class sizes, inadequate teacher training, lack of outside support for classroom teachers, and concern about the inclusion of certain groups of students (Galt, 1997).

THE CANADIAN SYSTEM

Any discussion of special education in Canada must be prefaced with two characteristics that define the Canadian system. First, the enterprise is particularly open to international influences. Geographically, Canada sprawls across the north of the United States so it is not surprising that, in both historical and contemporary terms, Canadian special education has been directly influenced by events, philosophies, and pedagogy from the United States, and has paralleled or followed U.S. models.

Canadian attitudes, although remarkably similar to those of the United States, are perhaps a little more tentative. We do not have the same population base or the same initiative that leads to reform and innovation. Authors repeatedly contrast the progress made in U.S. special education, particularly with reference to PL 94-142, with the lack of progress in Canada (Carter & Rogers, 1989).

Just as important, perhaps, the literature on Canadian special education is relatively modest, and the research base even more sparse. Our reliance on U.S. models, combined with recent funding cuts to journals and university library acquisitions, translates into research from our neighbors rather than home-grown initiatives. Anecdotal reports of successful inclusion are emerging in the literature (e.g., Horner, 1994; Ruiter, 1997), but there is very little empirical data. Canada does not support an adequate level of funding for essential research into educational issues and there remains a major research gap in the area of inclusive educational practice (Action, 1993).

The second defining characteristic is more encompassing. It revolves around the fact that the Canadian educational system is not one system at all. Canada is a vast country made up of 10 provinces and 2 territories, each with its own separate school laws, acts, policies, regulations, procedures, and legislation. Schools are administered through local school boards, each responsible for a geographical school district. Funding stems from a combination of property taxes and provincial government grants, according to formulas that vary from province to province.

Education as the exclusive right and responsibility of the provinces originated with the confederation of 1867 when the federal government in Ottawa conferred a number of powers on the provinces, among them education. As the 1867 British North America Act (Sec. 93) was chiefly concerned with protecting the rights of linguistic and religious minorities, there is no federal law to outline or guarantee the educational rights of children; that is, the right of every child to education is not entrenched by any constitutional provision.

Different systems operate across the country. Most provinces have tax-supported public, separate (Catholic), and Francophone systems. New Brunswick, a bilingual province, has Anglophone and Francophone schools. Quebec has a Catholic and a Protestant system (although legislation is pending to change to a language-based system). It was not until September 1997, that a referendum in Newfoundland changed the structure of schools operated traditionally by six religious denominations.

In the absence of constitutional provisions, the responsibility for education rests entirely with provincial legislation. Canadian jurisdictions have been slow to enact positive legislation guaranteeing educational rights. Education in Canada is not a single uniform system that is available to every child in the same way, and it cannot be said that the law clearly and unequivocally obliges the publicly supported school system to provide appropriate forms of education for all students, exceptionality notwithstanding. Only two provincial human rights codes (Saskatchewan and Quebec) list education as a right (Mackay, 1987a).

The lack of a federal office of education, combined with the huge geographical distances of Canada, the cultural diversity of the country, and the high urbanization of the population, makes it almost impossible to achieve or maintain policy coherence across the nation, and places any but the broadest statements about education in jeopardy. For special populations (special needs, culturally diverse, linguistically different) the variability seen in the general education area is only compounded. The terrain in special education, for example, is remarkably diverse. Differences in prevalence figures, in etiology, in definitions of exceptionality and labeling, in identification and placement procedures, in eligibility for special education services, in funding formulas, in early intervention programs, and in the legislative underpinnings of special education, are readily observed across the country.

Studies dating from the late 1960s have drawn attention to the shortcomings of Canadian legislation and the provision of special education services (Csapo, 1981; Hall & Dennis, 1968; Poirier & Goguen, 1986; Poirier, Goguen, & Leslie, 1988; Roberts & Lazure, 1970). Although, in recent years, all of the provinces and territories have embraced the concept of equal educational opportunity for all students, the gap in the assumption of universal responsibility is not yet fully closed. Canadian provinces have recognized the right to an education for all children in different ways: Not all the provinces provide equal access to schooling for students with disabilities. Seven of the 10 provinces have mandatory legislation (Newfoundland, Nova Scotia, New Brunswick, Quebec, Ontario, Manitoba, and Saskatchewan), whereas British Columbia, Alberta, and Prince Edward Island have permissive legislation.

All provinces stress an appropriate education that in provincial policies, refers to the provision of additional and possibly specialized services and programs that take into account a child's exceptional needs. It usually involves an Individual Education Plan for the child with a disability that specifies the goals and programs that are tailored to meet the child's needs (Poirier et al.,1988).   In this context, appropriate does not refer to where the education occurs, but to the type of program.

Legislative activity has tended to focus on students with disabilities. Although gifted youngsters are considered to be exceptional in their need for special education, they have not fared as well in the legislative arena. In Canada, both territories and 8 of the 10 provinces include gifted students in some definition of exceptional student, either at the legislative, regulatory, or administrative policy level. The two provinces without a mention are Nova Scotia and Prince Edward Island (Ritchey, 1993).

In Canada, there is no legal mandate on, or consistent definition of, inclusion. Most Canadian legislation speaks to the idea but not to the practice. Only two Ministry of Education policies—those in Saskatchewan and the North West Territories—explicitly refer to inclusion. For example, "Education in Saskatechewan is based on the belief of the innate value and dignity of all people and the understanding that the inclusion of people with exceptional needs into every aspect of community life benefits all. . . in society" (Canadian Council for Exceptional Children, 1992).

More generally, the amount of integration into the general classroom depends on provincial policy and the individual school district. For example, policy in British Columbia speaks in lofty terms to the philosophy underlying inclusion. Inclusion equates with "the value system which holds that all students are entitled to equitable access to learning, achievement and the pursuit of excellence in all aspects of their education. The practice of inclusion transcends the idea of physical location and incorporates basic values that promote participation, friendship, and interaction, (British Columbia Ministry, 1995, p. 7). In British Columbia, space for any remaining special classes must be in areas conducive to interaction with age-appropriate peers (Hampson, 1991).

More pragmatically, Alberta Education, the provincial ministry responsible for providing schooling to Alberta's children, states in its policy manual that "school boards are encouraged, whenever appropriate, to provide programs for exceptional children in regular school environments." The School Act gives local school boards the authority to "determine that a student is . . . in need of a special education program," but school boards are not obliged to enroll a student in a school unless there are "sufficient resources and facilities to accommodate the student" (Butler, Copeland, & Enns, 1996). However, in Alberta not all school boards and schools have policies on inclusion and, even if such a policy exists, it is often not communicated at the school level (Report, 1997).

THE DEVELOPMENT OF SPECIAL EDUCATION IN CANADA

In its early development, Canadian special education paralleled that found in the United States, Great Britain, and most of Europe. Students with deafness were the first to be educated in the first permanent school, opening in Nova Scotia in 1846. Successful results lent a note of optimism that extended opportunities to students who were blind, and then to those labeled as mentally retarded. Large institutions, designed as much to protect disabled persons from the public as to protect the public from the disabled, were the milieu.

By 1910, segregated classes in the public schools were a feature of most urban systems. Day schools, often promoted by parents groups, emerged in the 1940s. Right into the 1960s, institutions, special schools, and segregated classes remained the most important vehicles to serve students with disabilities. Nevertheless, prompted by civil, social, and educational movements in this period, parents, advocates, legislators, and others began to reject the notion that all exceptional students should be educated separately from their peers.

Discontent with special classes continued to mount in the 1970s. Major catalysts for change included the legislative and court systems, as well as parents, often in uneasy alliance with professionals. Parents insisted, with considerable success, that traditional special education systems change, and that their children had the right to education in the regular milieu.

The tempo of legislative activity accelerated during the late 1970s. To the occasional stick wielded by private litigation and parent militancy was added the formidable carrot of PL 94-142, the American landmark special education legislation (Hodder, 1984). Deeply influenced by the American law, a Canadian public policy report on special education was published 5 years after PL 94-142 (Berra, 1989). In 1980, Ontario passed Bill 82, the Education Amendment Act, the first real mandatory special education legislation in Canada (Winzer, 1982).

In the early 1980s, a melding of law, advocacy, and educational innovation created an environment supportive of fundamental change in how students with disabilities were educated. However, the debate on reform in special education was largely away from the grass-roots level of participation by local communities and teachers and, too often, practice was debated at the level of policy, lacking empirical data to anchor discussions.

By the late 1980s, social and budgetary contexts became the catalyst for the reform movement in all of Canadian education. Inclusion was espoused as a cost-cutting measure in some districts where there were drastic cutbacks of special education personnel at the administrative level as the one-system idea took on rapidly. Integration was interpreted by many as a license to close segregated classes without providing the necessary skills and resources to regular classrooms (Csapo, 1992).

In the 1990s, parent and professional agitation continues. Parents have "argued successfully that neither pity nor persuasiveness should be the factors which determined whether schools welcomed our children" (Robertson, 1992, p. 38). Some of the most vocal promoters of inclusion are advocacy groups. For example, when the Canadian Association for Community Living (CACL) established a task force to identify issues facing the advocacy movement for people with mental disabilities in 1987, they identified integrated education as a top priority (CACL, 1987). The Integration Action Group, sponsored by the CACL, today provides sophisticated support to individual families struggling to achieve integration (Porter & Richler, 1990).

LITIGATION

The fundamental rights of Canadians are guaranteed by the Canadian Charter of Rights and Freedoms. As the supreme law of Canada, the Charter guarantees every individual equality before and under the law, the right to equal protection and equal benefits of the law without discrimination, and in particular without discrimination based on race, age, or mental or physical disability. Several sections of the Charter hold implications for policy and practice relevant to the education of students with mental and/or physical disabilities (Mackay, 1987a, 1987b;Vickers & Endicott, 1985).

In Canada, the emphasis on using the power of the courts to settle disputes of an educational nature is less pronounced than in the United States. There is a strong tradition of deferring to the schools' authority in educational disputes, and the courts have embraced a hands-off approach to educational programs (see Mackay, 1987a). Nevertheless, litigation does occur with some regularity and, even if the inclusion movement combined with the Charter has not become a field day for lawyers, there has been a marked increase in activity.

As the Charter provides a legal basis for demands that have not existed previously, many felt that the context in which educational legislation operates would undergo a dramatic shift. Until decisions under the Charter, the dominance of separate provinces in virtually all aspects of education was paramount, and it was hoped that the Charter would influence the federal government in providing for security of educational rights through court decisions that would override provincial jurisdictions (Mackay, 1987a; Manley-Casimir, 1987). In other words, the Charter would allow a constitutional right to education rather than education as a matter to be defined by statute and regulation and delivered as school boards saw fit.

Recent Canadian litigation on special education has addressed the legal rights of children with disabilities as interpreted under the elusive concept of equality enshrined in the Charter. The aspects of educational legislation that are most subject to challenge under the Charter are procedures for student assessment and categorization, placement, the discretion to exclude students from regular classrooms, and the very concept of segregated education (Robertson, 1987).

When the equality rights in the Charter came into force in 1985, the first case heard was from a Nova Scotia couple who, in 1986, obtained a court injunction to keep their son in a regular class in a neighborhood school. Luke Elwood was labeled as mentally handicapped and school officials firmly maintained that he would be better served in a segregated program. The dispute continued until 1987 when, just hours before the case was to open before the Queen's Bench division of the Nova Scotia Supreme Court, the school board initiated discussions that led to a settlement, with the board agreeing to the parents' demands (Mackay, 1987b). The Robichaud case in New Brunswick, filed in December 1988, followed an almost identical pattern.

Neither of these cases were actually heard in the courts. Therefore, the Eaton case in Ontario, Canada's most populous province, is particularly illustrative of current Canadian litigation. Emily Eaton of Burford County, about 100 km southwest of Toronto, an 11-year-old Grade 4 student at the time, uses a wheelchair and a walker, cannot speak, and needs full assistance for personal care. After 3 years in a regular class, the teachers felt that Emily was increasingly isolated both intellectually and socially. The child's parents appealed the decision to place Emily in a special class and, after being frustrated at the board and district level, the case of *Brant County Board of Education vs. Carol Eaton and Clayton Eaton* was heard by the Ontario Court of Appeals. Here, Madame Justice Louise Arbour ruled that, under Section 15 of the Charter, a placement cannot be made without parental consent, as placement without consent is discriminatory (Smith, 1995). In a strongly worded statement, the judge found that Emily Eaton had a constitutional right to attend school with fully able children, despite the insistence of the Brant County Board of Education that she be placed in a segregated setting (Makin, 1997; Smith, 1996).

In October 1996 and February 1997, the Supreme Court of Canada reached a different conclusion. The court decided that an individual child's needs are to be considered to determine the most appropriate placement from a range of options. As well, when an exceptional student has been placed in a general education class with appropriate supports and modifications, and where objective evidence demonstrates that the child's needs are not being met, there is no violation of the Ontario Human Rights Code or the federal Charter of Rights and Freedoms in placing the child in a special class (Makin, 1997). Therefore, excluding some children from mainstream classes is an acceptable form of discrimination, provided that it is done in the best interests of the child. Unanimously, the Court rejected the idea of there being an automatic assumption that children with disabilities should gain entry into general classrooms if that is the wish of the parents. Instead, decisions should be made on a one-to-one basis, using the yardstick of the best interests of an individual child (Makin, 1997).

Although the Supreme Court decision is recent, advocates for children with disabilities are complaining that the decision has triggered a backlash. Some school boards are using the decision as justification for not doing more to integrate students with disabilities (Galt, 1997).

THE DEBATE ABOUT INCLUSION

About 15.5% of all Canadians have a disability. Of the 390,000 children in this number, 89% are mildly disabled, 8% have a moderate disability, and 3%, or about 11,500, have a severe disability ("Prevalence," 1995). According to Statistics Canada and the Canadian Council for Exceptional Children, 23% to 26% of these students are educated in separate settings; the remainder within the general school system (Winzer, 1997).

With about 75% of Canadian children with disabilities integrated to some level, many believe that the movement will continue to grow as more and more jurisdictions break through traditional barriers and forge an even stronger basis, not only for integration, but for the education of all students (Porter & Richler, 1990). Less sanguine observers note that the manner in which more extensive integration can be achieved remains elusive and the argument, debate, and counter debate that surround the issue remain strikingly prevalent (e.g., Robertson, 1992; Winzer, 1995).

In concert with most jurisdictions where inclusion is under debate, widely varied theoretical positions are found in Canada. Some advocate full inclusion in which every child is integrated into the general education classroom. Others support segregated settings for students with intensive educational needs.

Allies of full inclusion challenge the location where supports are being provided to students with disabilities, and pose inclusion as a contrast to providing a continuum of placements. They call for a reconfiguration to unite a balkanized system, stress that inclusion must unify special education and regular education (Barth, 1996), and contend that students with disabilities do not need an array or continuum of programs or placement options (Porter, 1994). According to Pearpoint and Forest (1992), "The inclusion option signifies the end of labeling, special education, and special classes, but not the end of necessary supports and services . . . in the integrated classroom" (p. xvi).

Others contend that a commitment to integrated or inclusive education means that schools, teachers, and the community commit themselves to resolving problems that arise in a way that respects the integrity of the school and its constituents (Porter & Richler, 1990). Schools should make the necessary adjustments for all students. Forshaw (1990) points out that schools should have access to opportunities and supports for stimulating their growth, development and learning within their home school. These opportunities are provided in physically and socially integrated settings, consistent with the principle of using the most enabling environment to meet individual students' needs.

Implicit in inclusive settings is the assumption that learners who are exceptional can be served equally as well in diverse mainstream learning settings as in segregated or pull-out programs, and that regular classroom teachers can duplicate the results of special education and the treatments associated with them. Prominent Canadian writers, such as Donald Little (1988), hold that special education is really nothing more than a thoroughly good ordinary education. Weber (1994) observed that good teaching applies to an integrated class the same way that it applies to any class. Teachers will find that the strategies, techniques, modifications, and inspirations that have always produced effective instruction and management in their classrooms work equally well in integrated settings.

The supposition is that ideology will enjoy an easy transition to educational practice. That is, we can proceed from an ideological and value-laden stance—that inclusion in regular classrooms is the most appropriate form of schooling for all children—to classroom practice; and that we can reduce theorizing to the technical problems of resources, management, social groupings, and instructional design.

When schools reform to accommodate the diverse needs of students, teacher roles change and the circumstances of regular education personnel take on substantial significance.   Theories and ideas in schools and classrooms meld with professional problems; teacher attitudes and expectations; teacher responsibilities; and accountability. Often in Canada, there seems to be more of a tendency to fight the problem than to devise creative attempts to solve it. Among other things, resistance to change arises from the weight of tradition, teachers' attitudes and belief systems, territorial rights, turf defending, and self-preservation (Little, 1985).

A recent national study of 1,492 Canadian teachers found that more than two thirds of teachers believe that inclusion is academically beneficial to special needs children and their peers in regular classrooms, and 90% of teachers cite social benefits (Galt, 1997). Nevertheless, although many teachers express support for the principles of inclusion, they identify critical problems in its implementation.

For example, law and policy in New Brunswick are clearly the most supportive of integration of all the Canadian provinces. However, there has been continuing controversy over the issue, and intense pressure from the province's teachers' unions. In 1986, Bill 85 created a fundamental change in the educational system of New Brunswick (Little, Williams, Word, Fraser, & Churchill, 1991); it brought mandatory special education legislation and directed integration. Union leaders then maintained that integration was placing New Brunswick's already strained education system as risk of collapse (Porter & Richler, 1990). Integration, they said, was "turning classrooms into zoos" and creating conditions in which "teachers can't teach and students can't learn" (Benteau, 1990, p.1). This prompted the education minister to review the integration process in 1989.   However, even in the face of such opposition, the minister's committee reiterated its strong support for integration.

Some of the strongest submissions come from the Alberta Teachers' Association (ATA; 1993; Buski, 1997; "Report", 1997). In general, the submissions support the philosophical underpinnings of inclusion but overwhelmingly express a deep concern on the part of many teachers that, in too many cases, the inclusive process is not working and is, in fact, creating educationally unsound situations. Some feel that there is a failure to meet the needs of either regular or special education students.

When Butler and colleagues (1996) asked 17 practitioners a number of open-ended questions about their experiences with integration, the teachers questioned whether it was a reasonable option, and maintained that not all students can be integrated into regular classrooms. In another study (ATA, 1993), many regular personnel felt unprepared, unsupported, and unable to handle all the challenges at once. One teacher commented that "some integration programs are in fact abandonment or submersion programs" (ATA, 1993, p. 5). Another observed that "Integration of students with special needs in our school means 'dumping' the child in a regular classroom with no aide, no extra time to work with the child, or prepare, and no professional resources to support us" (p. 5).

Criticism is by no means restricted to New Brunswick and Alberta; rather, it is pervasive. When provincewide testing in British Columbia showed a substantial decline in performance since 1989, the Ministry of Education was led to argue that "the large number of immigrants and the integration of special needs children into . . . classrooms is largely responsible for the poor results" (McInnes, 1997, p. 5). In Quebec, reduced professional services, such as psychologists, counselors, and social workers, pad teacher complaints that the system has abandoned them to deal with individual problems (Galt et al., 1997).

The two groups of children who present the greatest challenges to inclusion are those with severe and profound disabilities, and those with serious behavior disorders. Some argue that it is deleterious to the child with behavior disorders, the teacher, and other students to retain children in regular classes who cannot conform to the basic expectations of the classroom. Teachers also remain cautious about welcoming children who are severely and profoundly disabled into regular classrooms.

One of the great fears of teachers is increased behavior problems. The 1993 ATA report contained disturbing testimonials from teachers who said that exceptional students were often highly disruptive in their classes, and failed to learn in any meaningful way. The 1994 follow-up study still found that teachers broadly supported integration but that the fears of regular educators had grown even more acute.

When asked to include students with severe or profound disabilities, teachers feel they have limited resources, are not properly trained, and may not believe that these students really belong in regular classrooms (ATA, 1993; Dahl, 1986; Winzer, 1995). Many special educators echo their regular counterparts. Some believe that children with severe and multiple disabilities may be at odds with a system that has few resources and little inclination to meet their needs. Inclusion, they say, is doing a disservice to these students and they question whether children are gaining academically in the general education classroom, or if they are learning all they need to know.

There is skepticism about whether inclusion is feasible or desirable for secondary students (Fox & Ysseldyke, 1997). What works for older students with disabilities in the areas of functional skill instruction and vocational training in the community confuses placement decisions. Nesbit (1990) pointed out that for senior students with special needs, a case can be made for special programming. He noted that some of the necessary curricular elements are simply not present in the educational mainstream. He also said that it is the special aspects of the senior program that will do much to facilitate long-term normalization.

Although seen as a foundation of educational planning, Individual Education Plans (IEPs) are not prescribed by any laws in Canada. Many question the entire IEP process. They note that "IEPs are an exercise in futility, understood by only a few people, prepared only for a few people, and probably read by fewer still." Parents, they say "want to know in clear, simple terms where their children are, what they can expect and what is the plan of action." Therefore, "The amount of time required to prepare these documents is disproportionate to their value. The time is the teacher's, spent entirely outside of school hours" (ATA, 1993, p. 15).

CURRENT STATUS

Spurred by changing public attitudes, court cases, the work of advocates, and parental pressures, many school district personnel are reanalyzing service delivery options, and debating the merits of whether to serve students with special needs in general or special education settings. The past decade has seen an increasing number of school districts make a commitment to the inclusion of all students with disabilities. But even as inclusion into regular classrooms is becoming more common, and despite some evidence that it is possible, this is still not the norm in the majority of schools across Canada. Change has occurred, but only in selected school districts and in a few provinces (Porter, 1994).

The separate (Roman Catholic) school boards in some provinces have features that have made them more receptive to integration. In many cases, the traditional segregated classes have been linked to the public system and have passed the separate system by. Porter and Richler (1990) observed that the important element for inclusion is the stress that Roman Catholic school systems have placed on the importance of values and the nurturing of family, church, and community throughout the school.

Early childhood special education is a developing enterprise in Canada, with a breadth of early identification and early intervention services in place. Some specialized centers, especially for young deaf children, exist, but an ethic of inclusion is emerging in the early childhood arena. Inclusion at the preschool level is becoming more the norm than the exception (Winzer, 1997).

For school-age students, schools across Canada choreograph different systems. The implementation of inclusionary practices varies widely from province to province, and even among neighboring school boards (Chisholm, 1993). The unevenness across the country seems to reflect a persistent uneasiness about the practice among educators.

Some systems support inclusive schooling and have made fundamental changes. They have matched policy and practice, and adopted policies of full inclusion where all students, regardless of the severity of disabilities, are educated in regular classrooms with their age peers (Flynn & Kowalczyk-McPhee, 1989). New Brunswick and Nova Scotia have adopted integration, as have many boards in large urban centers in British Columbia and Alberta. These include several Catholic school districts in southern Ontario, French-language district schools in Quebec, and some public schools in Manitoba, Saskatchewan, and British Columbia (Chisholm, 1993; Porter & Richler, 1990).

In other cases, educators who follow the inclusive ideology have been at the forefront of developing new approaches and strategies to make inclusion a reality. This often happens at the classroom level where the actions of an individual teacher has established a precedent for colleagues (Porter, 1994). Inclusive settings initiated by individual teachers or administrators may have little or no backing from the administration.

Other districts say that they support inclusive education, but they have not made policy changes to ensure that integrated settings actually occur. In fact, many jurisdictions have adopted the language of inclusion, but continue to rationalize the exceptions to the rule (Porter, 1994). Change represents linguistic manipulation; special education services are not reformed, but simply redistributed or renamed. These districts, chided Porter (1994), treat inclusion programs as simply one more choice on the special education menu.

Some schools and districts follow traditional eligibility criteria and a categorically based delivery system with autonomous special education and regular education. For example, in Ontario, the majority of students with special needs in the public school system are not integrated; in the Catholic system, the majority are integrated. In Quebec, most students with physical disabilities are integrated; those with intellectual disabilities are not (Chisholm, 1993).

Today few want a return to the rigidities of the 1960s, but many do want a range of programs. They argue that education is not a place but a group of services tailored to the needs of an individual child with integration as necessary but not sufficient for quality service. Thus, many educators support inclusionary practices, but also advocate for a full continuum of services, and this is probably the most common model seen across Canada.

A large number of school districts have chosen to maintain a continuum of services that includes segregated options, and they typically approach inclusion on a one-to-one basis. When determining whether to place a student in an inclusive classroom or alternative setting, educators base their decision on student outcomes—in which setting will the child succeed and be prepared to become a productive and active citizen. It is held that case by case decisions are consistent with the essence of special education. Rather than a blanket policy, the special needs of each student must be carefully assessed, and the most appropriate educational placement for that child judged.

CONTINUING BARRIERS

For many Canadian educators, advocacy groups, and parents, inclusion is the clarion call of educational orthodoxy. For others, it is a radical reform to be approached cautiously. The paradigm wars must be referenced to the needs of children with special needs, the requirements of the regular classroom, and the circumstances of regular classroom teachers.

Nor is inclusion a universally accepted movement in Canadian special education. Rather, it is something that is evolving. Philosophical commitment far outstrips practice, and the barriers to inclusion remain high, girded by social and fiscal realities, the ecology of regular classroom teachers, and the changing accountability of the contemporary school system. In many areas, there is little or no advance training for receiving teachers, and no formal support system in place for students or teachers.

Discussions of inclusion have highlighted some of the requirements for success. Inclusive school practice depends on certain key elements; to wit, restructuring to merge special education and regular education to create a unified educational system; appropriate teacher training; positive teacher attitudes with realistic expectations and widened tolerances; resources and supports for teachers; individual supports for students with disabilities, including materials and personnel; developing shared responsibility for students through regular and special education teachers working side by side with heterogeneous groups of students; and teachers sharing their specialties via collaborative teaming.

Even a cursory examination of some of these elements points the continuing barriers to the inclusion of students with disabilities in Canada.

Teacher Training

Changed delivery models necessitate training personnel to adapt to new roles. However, when an ad hoc commission in Alberta ("Report," 1997) identified 19 factors necessary for successful inclusion, one factor seldom present was the training that teachers need to implement inclusion.

Efficient training is absent at both preservice and inservice levels. For example, although good general education programs should prepare teachers to work with all students effectively, explicit efforts to prepare teachers in training to work with students with exceptionalities is a relatively recent phenomena (Maheady, Mallette, & Harper, 1996). Currently, few teacher-training programs at Canadian colleges or universities focus on the educational practices required for inclusive education ("Action," 1993). A recommendation of the national survey (Galt, 1997) was that faculties of education improve their methods for preparing teachers to handle the range of disabilities found in today's classrooms.

In the field, teachers are too often given a 1-day workshop or shown a video and expected to know how to teach in inclusive environments successfully. The Alberta study showed that only 26% of Alberta teachers including students with disabilities had inservice training dealing with integration available (Buski, 1997).

Teacher Attitudes.

As inclusive beliefs are derived from and integrally associated with teachers' value orientations and beliefs, general classroom teachers must be receptive to the principles and demands of inclusion. Canadian teachers philosophically support the ideology, but deep concerns have emerged in the context of regular education, and the issue often expressed is a concern about the boundaries of teacher responsibilities.

Teachers' concerns revolve around a number of areas that are prompted as much by the objectives of special education as they are by the pressures of the school system. The current trend is for ever increasing demands on teachers who are faced with increased student variability, increased student diversity, and new management problems. Today's schools have become intervention sites for numerous learning and social problems affecting students that are growing more profound (McInnes, 1997). And not only are teachers being asked to cater to students displaying a range of social and academic problems, but classes are more heterogeneous than ever before, with varying rates of skills and learning rates. Add time restraints; larger class sizes; widespread debate about standardized achievement testing, and teacher accountability; an explosion of knowledge that must somehow be addressed in the curriculum; limited resources and insecure funding from external sources; and lessening job security. As these factors combine with concerns over lack of training and expertise in special education, and declining support services, it is little wonder that many teachers look askance at the prospect of including students with very special needs.

Resources and Supports for Teachers.

The resource question is a major bone of contention between inclusion supporters and skeptics. At issue—can the ambitiousness of the proposed reforms be accompanied by resources adequate to implement them, and what kinds of resources for inclusion can teachers reasonably expect?

In the recent national study, one respondent wrote that "All students have a right to a regular classroom as long as there is support (personnel and materials), [and] daily time to plan and conference" (Galt, 1997, p. A1). Teachers report that they need 1 hour or more a day to plan for students with disabilities (Scruggs & Mastropieri, 1996). An investigation into the workload of 17,000 Canadian teachers (King & Peart, 1992) found that 77% of teachers felt that they has insufficient time to provide adequate help to students having difficulties and those with special needs. In British Columbia, the Kamloops Teachers' Association found that 83% of primary teachers reported increased stress because of extra workload, partly due to integration (Gloyn, 1991). In Alberta, Buski

(1997) reported that 87% of teachers including students with special needs did not have extra preparation time.

Teachers need additional personnel assistance such as an aide or daily contact with special education teachers (Scruggs & Mastropieri, 1996). In an Alberta study (Buski, 1997), 33% of teachers integrating students with special needs reported the unavailability of professional support such as speech therapists and psychologists; 31% lack of paraprofessional support. There were no special materials or supplies in 64% of cases.

Commitment to quality education for all students in inclusionary settings inevitably leads to consideration of class sizes ("Action," 1993). Both common sense and research suggest that reduced class size is essential. Teachers agree— class sizes should be reduced to fewer than 20 students if those with disabilities are to be included (Scruggs & Mastropieri, 1996). In Alberta, however, a huge 87% reported no reduction in class size (Buski, 1997).

Supports for Students.

Implicitly, inclusion demands that supports be brought to the classroom and to the child and not that the child be removed to the supports. The target of equal education cannot be met by placing students with disabilities in the regular system without these supports needed to accommodate their particular needs (Rioux, 1991). However, maintaining such needed support is an enormous task that requires a degree of commitment, communication, cooperation, collaboration, and funding.

The recent national study found that social realities often thwart effective inclusion (Galt, 1997). In Ontario, for example, the typical cost of an urban elementary child's education is $5000 to $7,000 annually. A child with severe disabilities costs from $14,000 to $33,000 and for secondary level students costs from $28,000 to $39,000 (Nikiforuk, 1996).

Therefore, it may not be the concept of inclusion, per se, that creates the main problems. Rather, it is the failure of official agencies to respond with the needed economic and human resources. A common complaint is that human and financial resources once directed toward educating special students in special schools and classes has not followed the students into regular classrooms (Butler et al., 1996). Cutbacks to the provincial equalization payments from the federal government translate into severe cuts in educational spending. Many provinces use block funding, which means that funding for students with mild disabilities, and for those who are gifted and talented, is part of basic instructional funding. Some boards and some individual schools, when making difficult priority decisions, do not allocate an appropriate portion of the grant for these students ("Report," 1997). Provinces, such as Alberta, that are either unwilling or unable to financially support the integration of exceptional students, have left teachers ill equipped to fulfill their obligations to all of their students (Butler et al., 1996).

In many provinces, confusion and lack of coordination characterize the relation among government departments and agencies that deliver services to students with special needs ("Report," 1997). Speaking to the national study on inclusion, researcher Gary Bunch observed that government services are fragmented, and children would be better served by blending services to create "ministries of the child" (Galt, 1997).

CONCLUSION

In contemporary Canadian special education, the movement variously referred to as *inclusion, inclusive schooling*, or *inclusive education* has been elevated to the dominant educational ideology. Inclusion remains a divisive issue; although most teachers and school administrators agree that the days of total segregation and institutionalization are long over, the manner in which inclusion of students who are exceptional can be most effectively attained has still not been worked out in practice. By-products of the often contentious debate include an increasing polarity of stances, more litigation, strong disagreement from teachers and teachers' unions, and vastly different implementation practices across the country.

As the prevailing philosophical assumptions, theories, and visions that surround the current inclusive movement find their way into real life educational situations, they affect the circumstances of regular classroom teachers. Any change that intends to alter the quality of education for children who are exceptional depends on regular classroom teachers who are often the final arbiters of reform. Although the vast majority of Canadian teachers philosophically support integration, they are increasingly questioning the boundaries of their responsibilities, and contending that they lack adequate training to handle a wide range of disabling conditions.

It is not possible to predict where the inclusion movement in Canada will lead. Educators may propose—but governments dispose, and not always with the requested funding. Our schools are at the intersection of political and social ideals and fiscal realities, and it is economic problems, social realities, and teacher opposition that may thwart efforts. Unless key areas of leadership, governance, funding, and coordination are revised, and supports for teachers and students with special needs increase, it may be that inclusion will become a nonissue or one that falters badly in the face of educational realities.

REFERENCES

Action for integration: A guide to inclusive education. (1993, Summer). *Abilities*, pp. 62–63.Alberta
     Teachers Association. (1993). *Trying to teach*. Edmonton: Author.
Barth, F. (1996). Integration and inclusion: Equal terms? *BC Journal of Special Education, 20*, 36–42,
Benteau, S. (1990, April 28). Wages not only issue. *Saint Johns Telegraph Journal*, p. 1.
Berra, M. (1989). Integration and its implications for teacher preparation. *BC Journal of Special
     Education, 13*, 55–66.
British Columbia Ministry of Education, Special Education Services. (1995). *A manual of policies,
     procedures, and guidelines*. Victoria, BC: Author.
Buski, J. (1997, Winter). Education reform—What you've told us, part 2. *ATA Magazine*, pp. 34–35.
Butler, M., Copland, S., & Enns, E. (1996). Inclusive schooling in Alberta: What teachers are saying.

International Journal of Special Education, 11, 161–164.

Canadian Association for Community Living. (1987). *Community living 2000: A time of change, a time of challenge.* Toronto: Author.

Canadian Council for Exceptional Children. (1992). *Equal educational opportunity for students with disabilities: Legislative action in Canada.* Montreal: Canadian CEC.

Carney, P. J. (1996). Practitioners' views of challenges and issues for school psychologists in the 21st. century. *Canadian Journal of School Psychology, 12,* 98–102.

Carter, D. E. & Rogers, W. T. (1989). Diagnostic and placement practice for mildly educable mentally handicapped students. *Canadian Journal of Special Education, 5,* 15–23.

Chisholm, P. (1993, March 27). Schooling the disabled. *MacLean's,* pp. 52–54.

Csapo, M. (1981). Teachers' federations in the mainstream. *BC Journal of Special Education, 5,* 197–218.

Csapo, M. (1992). Special education in crisis. *BC Journal of Special Education, 16,* 249–258.

Dahl, M. (1986). *The Canadian symposium on special education issues: Proceedings.* Toronto: Canadian Council for Exceptional Children.

Flynn, G., & Kowalczyk-McPhee, B. (1989), A school system in transition. In S. Stainback, W. Stainback, & M. Forest (Eds.), *Educating all students in the mainstream of regular education* (pp. 29–41). Baltimore,: Paul H. Brookes.

Forshaw, K. (1990). *Full service school model.* Victoria, BC: Greater Victoria School District, No. 61.

Fox, N. E. & Ysseldyke, J. E. (1997). Implementing inclusion at the middle school level: Lessons from a negative example. *Exceptional Children, 64,* 81–98.

Galt, V. (1997, August 28). Teachers support disabled in classes: Fiscal, social realities prevent student integration. *Globe and Mail,* pp. A1, A10.

Galt, V., McInnes, C., Lewington, J., Seguin, R., Laghi, B., & Abbate, G. (1997, October 11). Power struggle rocks Canada's schools. *Globe and Mail,* pp. A1, A8.

Gloyn, S. (1991, February) *Results of the primary teachers' survey.* Kamloops District Teachers Association Bulletin.

Hall, M., & Dennis, L. (1968). *Living and learning: The report of the provincial committee on aims and objectives of education in the schools of Ontario.* Toronto: Newton Publishing.

Hampson, E. (1991). The not-so-modest proposal: The fate of special education. *BC Journal of Special Education, 15,* 127–158.

Hodder, C. (1984). The Education Amendment Act (Ontario) 1980: A review. *Interchange, 15,* 44–53.

Horner, B. (1994, Summer). Faith and determination: Inclusive education benefits everyone. *Abilities,* pp. 32–33.

Key trends in Canada. (1996, September). *CEC Today,* p. 7.

King A. & Peart, M. (1992). *Teachers in Canada: Their work and quality of life.* Ottawa: Canadian Teachers Federation Publications.

Little, D. M. (1985). A crime against childhood-uniform curriculum at a uniform rate. Mainstreaming re-examined and refined. *Canadian Journal of Special Education, 2,* 91–107.

Little, D. M. (1988). The redefinition of special education: Special-ordinary education as individualizing in the regular classroom. *Education Canada, 28,* 36–43.

Little, D. M., Williams T. L., Word, L. S., Fraser, B. J., & Churchill M. A. (1991). Two solitudes? To integrate or not to integrate? That is not the question. To mainsteam or not to mainstream? That is the question. A survey and status report of policy and praxis in Canada. *Canadian Journal of Special Education, 7,* 115.

Mackay, A. W. (1987a). The Charter of Rights and special education: Blessing or curse? *Canadian Journal of Exceptional Children, 3,* 118–127.

Mackay, A. W. (1987b). The Elwood case: Vindicating the educational rights of the disabled. *Canadian Journal of Special Education, 3,* 113–116.

Maheady, L., Mallette, B., & Harper, G. F. (1996). The pair tutoring program: An early field-based experience to prepare preservice general educators to work with students with special needs. *Teacher Education and Special Education, 19,* 277–297.

Makin, K. (1997, February). Classroom exclusion acceptable, court days. *Globe and Mail,* p. A 7

Manley-Casimir, M. (1987, February 25). *The new rights reality in Canadian society: The "Chartered" path.* Address presented to the first course in Educational Leadership, St. Bride's College, Littledale.

McInnes, C. (1997, October 11). BC schools slipping badly but warnings ignored, research team says. *Globe and Mail,* p. 5.

Nesbit, W. (1990, March). The efficacy of integrated senior programs. *Keeping in Touch*, pp. 3–4.

Nikiforuk, A. (1996, October 18). Fifth column. *Globe and Mail.*

Pearpoint, J., & Forest, M. (1992). Foreword. In S. Stainback & W. Stainback (Eds.), *Curriculum considerations in inclusive classrooms: Facilitating learning for all students* (pp. xv–xviii) Baltimore,: Brookes.

Poirier, D., & Goguen, L. (1986). The Canadian Charter of Rights and the right to education for exceptional children. *Canadian Journal of Education, 11*, 231–244.

Poirier, D., Goguen, L., & Leslie, P. (1988). *Educational rights of exceptional children in Canada: A national study of multi-level commitments.* Toronto: Carswell.

Porter, G. L. (1994, Summer). Equity and excellence in education: An update. *Abilities*, pp. 33–35.

Porter, G. L. & Richler, D. (1990). Changing special education practice: Law, advocacy, and innovation. *Canadian Journal of Community Mental Health, 9*, 65–78.

Prevalence of disability in Canada rises. (1995, Winter). *Disability Today*, p. 7.

Alberta Teachers Association, (1997), *Report of the Blue Ribbon Panel on Special Education.* Edmonton, Alberta, Canada: Author.

Rioux, M. H. (1991, Fall). Right, justice, power: An agenda for change. *Abilities*, pp. 58–59.

Ritchey, D. (1993, June). Frustration of a parent of gifted children. *Keeping in Touch*, pp. 3–4.

Roberts, C. A., & Lazure, MD. (1970). *One million children: A national study of Canadian children with emotional and learning disorders.* Toronto: Crainford.

Robertson, G. B. (1987). *Mental disability and the law in Canada.* Toronto: Carswell.

Robertson, H. J. (1992, Fall/Winter). Educational reform and children with disabilities. *Abilities*, pp. 37–38.

Ruiter, L. (1997, Summer). Celebrating friendship. *ATA Magazine*, p. 31.

Scruggs, T. E. & Mastropieri, M. A. (1996). Teacher perceptions of mainstreaming/inclusion. A research synthesis. *Exceptional Children, 63*, 59–74.

Slee, R. (1997). Inclusion or assimilation? Sociological explorations of the foundations of theories of special education. *Educational Foundations, 11*, 55–71.

Smith, B. (1995, June). Implications of the Eaton case. *Alberta CEC, 5*, p. 7

Smith, B. (1996, Summer). Implications of the Eaton case. *Keeping in Touch*, p. 9.

Vickers, D., & Endicott, O. (1985). Mental disability and equality rights. In A. F. Bayefosky & M. Eberts (Eds.), *Equality rights and the Canadian Charter of Rights and Freedoms* (pp. 381–409). Toronto: Carswell.

Weber, K. (1994). *Special education in Canadian schools.* Canada: Highland Press.

Winzer, M. A. (1982). Bill 82: Ideal and reality. *BC Journal of Special Education, 6*, 159–169.

Winzer, M. A. (1995, May). *The inclusive movement in Canada: A critical analysis.* Paper presented at the Contemporary Trends Conference, Krakow, Poland.

Winzer, M. A. (1997). *Special education in early childhood: An inclusive approach.* Toronto: Allyn & Bacon.

9

Challenges to Inclusive Education: A European Perspective

Seamus Hegarty
National Foundation for Educational Research, England

Europe is a place of great diversity as manifested in economic, cultural, and educational contrasts. It contains over 40 nation states, with many more languages and ethnic groupings. It has been the source of some of the world's greatest cultural and industrial achievements, but has also provided the arena for bloody wars and barbaric behavior on an almost unimaginable scale.

Education in Europe is even more diverse than the enumeration of its nation states would suggest. Education in some countries is a regional or local responsibility, so that one cannot properly speak of a national education system in these cases. Other countries with more than one distinct education system include Belgium, Spain, and the United Kingdom.

The wide diversity of educational systems is a key backdrop to inclusive education because the general education system provides the context in which inclusive education must be seen. Countries and regions within them attach great importance to their education system, seeing it as integral to cultural identity, and the development of their future citizens. Broader educational movements, such as inclusive education, must as a consequence be conceptualized and implemented within the framework of the general education system, whatever it be. One may note that within the European Union (EU)—which is not the whole of Europe—there is no question of harmonizing education systems. The Treaty of Rome made no mention of education, and the Treaty of Maastricht, which regulates the new EU, strictly limits any supranational involvement in the education at national level. The upshot of this is that general statements about education in Europe are difficult to make, and a definitive account of inclusive education in Europe is simply not available.

Some overview statements can be attempted, however, and this chapter outlines a number of achievements in recent years, and sets out some of the major challenges for the years ahead. Before doing so it draws attention to two particular difficulties that beset any discussion of special education in Europe. A final section considers the challenge of information exchange in Europe in relation to special education, and draws attention to the European Agency for

Development in Special Needs Education, which creates a new context for inclusive education in Europe.

Problems Of Special Education Discourse in Europe

Aside from the problems created by the diversity of educational provision in Europe, there are two further factors that limit discourse on it: the absence of comprehensive information and the diverse ways in which children's learning difficulties are categorized.

The information base that would underpin a comprehensive account of special education within Europe is simply not available. Various efforts by the European Commission, and also by the Centre for Educational Research and Innovation at the Organization for Economic Cooperation and Development (OECD) and by the United Nations Educational, Scientific and Cultural Organization (UNESCO), to assemble comparative information about special educational provision including inclusive education, demonstrate forcibly how difficult it is to obtain good, comparative information.

An OECD study of integration illustrates the difficulties. This sought in part to gather comparative statistical data concerning disability and integration. Although some data were collected and are presented, the task proved extremely problematic and the authors point out that "a substantial number of difficulties exist in terms of classification systems, terminology, operational definitions and methodology" (Evans, Evans & McGovern, 1995, p. 50). The UNESCO reviews (1988, 1995) of the situation of special education constitute further evidence. They sought information on policies, legislation and the provision of special needs education and, although not specific to Europe, they collected information on some 22 European countries. The reviews are a valuable source of basic intelligence on special educational provision worldwide, but the information presented is very uneven across countries and can only sustain a limited comparative discourse. Authors such as Meijer, Pijl, and Hegarty (1994) and O'Hanlon (1995) who address the comparative issue directly are useful sources, but are limited in terms of either coverage or depth. Mention may be made of the *European Journal of Special Needs Education*, now in its 13th year of publication, which provides a forum for research and development in the field of special educational needs with a strong, but not exclusive, European focus.

A second consideration is the extent to which children's learning difficulties are conceptualized in very different ways. An initial shock for U.S. visitors is that children in European schools do not by and large have learning disabilities. This is not to say that they do not have difficulties in learning or, for that matter, in behavior. European children do of course have difficulties but these tend to be described in ways that eschew the term *learning disabilities.* There is not a single, agreed alternative term or set of terms, however. The OECD study referred to here speaks of "a bewildering array of terminology in use" (Evans, Evans, & McGovern, 1995, p. 34). Countries like Italy and the Netherlands have as many as 10 categories of handicap, whereas others, such as the United Kingdom, prefer to speak of special educational needs that are manifested in particular curriculum areas. These differences limit comparative discourse and add to the difficulty of transferring practice from one setting to another.

Achievements

There have been significant achievements in the education of students who have difficulty in school over recent years. Three have been selected for discussion here: the degree to which inclusive education has been accepted, the spread of good practice, and the relation between juridical and professional forces for changes.

Acceptance For Inclusive Education

The location of special education provision has been under active discussion in Europe, as elsewhere, for some 30 years now. Initial stimuli came from the Scandinavian concern for normalizing the life experiences of people with disabilities, and the Italian determination to shut psychiatric institutions and special schools. Other factors came into play, including the emergence of new concepts of handicap and a better understanding of why children have difficulties at school, assessments that focused on individuals' pedagogic requirements as opposed to placing labels on them, the spread of comprehensive schools, the growing concern for human rights and the extent to which minority groups are marginalized in society, and the impact of efficacy studies that failed to show a consistent benefit in favor of segregated special schools over integrated placements (Hegarty, 1993).

The debate has generally been couched in terms of integration; inclusion, or inclusive education, and has only gained widespread currency in relatively recent years. Strictly speaking, the two terms are quite distinct but, in fact, they have a set of meanings that overlap, and it can be difficult to sustain a distinction between them.

The upshot of all this is that the principle of inclusion is no longer in question. It may be understood differently by different people and, as noted below, practice is extremely varied, but the idea that students with disabilities and learning difficulties should be educated alongside their peers in regular schools, wherever possible and appropriate, is no longer seriously questioned in European education discourse. Lest this be disregarded as a trite observation, we should not forget what a dramatic change in attitudes it represents. It was not so long ago that legislation, as well as custom and practice in many of our countries, dictated that the appropriate place of education for many handicapped children and young people was a special school—if indeed they were deemed capable of being educated.

Extent Of Good Practice

There is a tendency in education and social policy debates to problematize issues, to focus on problems and neglect achievements, to highlight the gap between rhetoric and practice, and so on. Inclusive education is not immune from this, and much discourse on it is concerned with how much there is still to be achieved.

A balanced perspective, however, requires some consideration of what has been achieved to date. Reference has just been made to the attitude changes in favor of inclusive education. These are both exemplified and reinforced by legislation and by policy initiatives that seek to further inclusive education. The acid test is whether practice has developed, and schools have become more inclusive in respect of those many students previously excluded or marginalized. The picture is not a uniformly positive one but there is a great deal of good progress to report. The Danish formulation of "one school for all" has been widely accepted, and there are many schools throughout Europe that have reformed themselves so as to become fully inclusive so far as students with special educational needs are concerned. Early approaches to integration tended to entail placing one or more students with special educational needs in a regular school, and making one-off modifications to accommodate them. This can be seen as primitive inclusion at best since the students in question were not seen as central to the school's mission, and required unusual measures to be taken on their behalf. The positive achievement of recent years has been the emergence of schools in which curriculum and pedagogical reform has resulted in a focus on the educational needs of each student. These schools see it as their role to provide high quality education to every student, regardless of their learning difficulties, and deploy their resources as necessary to achieve this end. Statistics on the numbers of such schools are not readily available—and definitional problems would make them extremely difficult to collect—but there are many of them in Italy, Spain, the United Kingdom, and throughout the Scandinavian countries.

Legal Involvement

European observers of U.S. special education are regularly struck by the extent of legal involvements in special education processes. Entitlements are set out in considerable detail, and there are ready measures of legal redress in the event of dispute. Although the clarity of entitlement is highly regarded, its litigious concomitants are not. From a European perspective it would seem that, not only are special educational resources diverted to serve legal processes rather than children, but also partnership and cooperation between parents and providers are put at risk.

European achievement in terms of guaranteeing entitlements may not yet match up to U.S. norms but they have been achieved without undue involvement of the legal system. New legislation in England and Wales that established a quasi-juridical procedure may alter this situation, but the general expectation is that progress should be achieved without having recourse to the law courts. There is a great deal of legislation in European countries designed to secure the inclusion of children and adults with special needs into schools and society. This tends to be permissive rather than prescriptive, and in any case the emphasis is on making structural and attitudinal changes and creating environments where individuals are not marginalized.

Challenges

Despite the achievements, there is still much to do. Five challenges are addressed here: the diversity of practice and the fact that children's access to good provision depends so much on where they live, the role of special schools in inclusive education, the development of an effective teacher workforce, the deployment of resources in line with desired policies, and the place of special education in general school reform.

Diversity of Practice

A first challenge arises from the diversity of practice, from country to country and within countries. As noted earlier, comparative statistics are limited in their coverage, but a set of figures from the OECD study of integration is indicative. Table 9.1 sets out countries' use of special schools and units.

TABLE 9.1
Students in Special Schools or Units

Austria	2.55
Belgium	3.08
Denmark	0.65
Finland	1.85
France	1.26
Germany[1]	3.69
Iceland	0.58
Ireland	1.04
Netherlands	3.63
Norway	0.60
Spain	0.80
Sweden	1.03
Switzerland	4.90
United Kingdom[2]	1.30

Taken from OECD (1995), p. 39.
[1]Former Federal Republic of Germany only
[2]England and Wales only

Intended as an indirect measure of integration, albeit a crude one, what it does show very powerfully is the substantial differences in the use made of special schools and units. In fact, the differences are greater than this table shows because it ignores within-country variation. Thus, in England and Wales, for example, the equivalent figures at local authority level range from 0.6% to 3.1%. Behind the Dutch figure are districts with more than 5% of students in special schools.

These figures are just one example of the enormous diversity that characterizes special educational provision across Europe. This encompasses everything from opportunity to attend regular school and type of support available to assessment practices and funding arrangements. Some of the diversity does relate to integral features of the different education systems, but much of it reflects different levels of commitment to including children in regular schools. Put simply, the opportunities available to children and young people with special educational needs depend, in large measure, on where they happen to live.

The challenge therefore is to address this diversity, and seek to raise all provision up to the level of the best. The fact that significant progress has been made in some locations but not in other broadly similar ones throws down a gauntlet, as it were. Major differences in provision, where they exist, must not be regarded as insuperable, nor used as an excuse for inaction. Progress here depends on collecting and sharing information on key indicators of practice, laying down benchmarks for stimulating and measuring progress, and putting effective implementation strategies in place.

A New Role For Special Schools

A second set of challenges relates to special schools. Certainly, there are far too many special schools in some countries, and a clear policy option is to shut down many of them, as indeed has happened in Italy and some Scandinavian countries. In those countries, with a high usage of special schools, this has to be considered very seriously, but there are additional possibilities. Given that a principal reason for the emergence of special schools was the failure of the regular school to cater for certain students and that a major element in that failure was lack of appropriate expertise and/or commitment on the part of regular school teachers, new landscapes have to be devised before special schools are removed from the map. In many countries special schools represent a major investment in staff and expertise, in buildings and equipment, in software and other materials—the whole range of resources that regular schools lack where students who have difficulties in learning are concerned.

This suggests an alternative way of looking at the challenge posed by special schools. Instead of asking how to shut them down, we could focus rather on how to avoid dissipating the expertise and resources they have accumulated and, more positively, on how special schools can capitalize on these in the task of providing an education of high quality to students with special needs.

The answers will almost certainly have to be found in the emergence of new kinds of special school or other institutions where expertise is concentrated. There is some relevant experience to draw on. In Sweden, for example, the four national resource centers have been an important feature of special educational provision for many years; these centers focus on particular disabilities and act as repositories of information on materials, pedagogical developments, and so on, in relation to that disability. Students are placed in these centers for assessment purposes, but only stay for short periods of time (Pijl, 1994). In the United Kingdom, links between special schools and regular schools are well established with the vast majority of special schools having such a link (Fletcher-Campbell, 1994). These links involve both teachers and students and typically encompass exchange teaching, student support, advice to colleagues, staff development and monitoring. In the Netherlands, clusters of regular schools and special schools have been formed. Each cluster is responsible for about 2,000 students and decides on the deployment of resources across the schools in the cluster (Meijer, 1994).

A recent Green Paper published by the Department for Education and Employment in England (GB, DEE, 1997) pays particular attention to developing the role of special schools. The Green Paper sets out government proposals for action and, subject to consultation, will determine forthcoming policy and legislation. It is proposed that special schools should work more closely with regular schools and support services to meet the needs of all students who have difficulties in learning or behavior. This could entail shared facilities, shared teaching and non-teaching expertise, support for students who move between special and regular schools, special schools becoming part of cluster arrangements with primary and secondary schools, special schools helping regular schools to implement inclusion policies, and special school staff acting as a source of training and advice for their mainstream colleagues. These developments might necessitate the amalgamation of some special schools because many are small. They might also call for a change of designation because the term *special school* will be seen as an inadequate reflection of what they do.

The special school of the future could be a multipurpose institution. Thus, it might

- be a source of information on all matters relating to special educational needs in the locality.
- conduct assessments, particularly in difficult cases.
- provide advice, consultancy and support.
- engage in curriculum and materials development.
- evaluate software, equipment and other materials.
- conduct research and run experimental projects.
- contribute to professional development through joint working, attachments, workshops and formal courses.

·   be a resource for parents.
·   provide counseling and careers advice for older students

This range of functions takes us well beyond the familiar notion of a school, be it special or otherwise. It entails elements of several existing agencies, such as an advisory service, a resource center, a library and information service, a pilot project, a training institution and a careers service. It would involve developing systematically a new kind of institution that would be a powerhouse for special education in its locality. Such an institution might have direct full-time, or near full-time, responsibility for a small number of students but—and this would be its principal raison d'être—it would have a direct responsibility for a wide range of matters relating to special educational provision in its own community.

There are some difficulties with this concept. One difficulty relates to funding and the way in which forms of provision are shaped by the way in which resources are allocated. This is discussed here. A second difficulty relates to the nature of the expertise available to special schools at the moment. Although there is an abundance of expertise related to the assessment and teaching of students who have difficulty in learning, the broad range of functions envisaged here call for a new range of skills that many special schools and staff do not currently have. Third, there is the matter of the locus of responsibility for students with special educational needs. To the extent that special schools remain part of the local map of special educational provision, there is the danger that teachers in regular schools will continue to see students who have difficulties in learning as the responsibility of the special school in whatever guise it continues to exist.

These difficulties can be resolved. What is important is to face the challenge posed by special schools in an imaginative way. The need for expertise will grow, not diminish, in the years ahead. Special schools should at least be considered as a platform for building this expertise.

Teacher Education

In the past, many European countries tended to educate teachers for special education separately from teachers in regular schools, in keeping with the fact that special education was a separate subsystem of the general education system. This was never a satisfactory approach, given the large number of students with learning difficulties there have always been in regular schools. Now that we are moving toward inclusive education, it is becoming less and less appropriate as a model of teacher education. All teachers need some knowledge of disability and learning difficulties, some skills in teaching students with special educational needs, and the ability to contribute to the assessment of students with more pronounced needs. Teachers who work in special education need to be familiar with the mainstream curriculum, and with the learning experiences and achievements of students in the mainstream.

Teacher education arrangements have been changing as a consequence though, as with other topics, the diversity of practice makes generalization difficult.   Arrangements for teacher education vary widely in terms of entry criteria, balance between professional and academic emphasis, location and duration of courses.   The discussion here relates to three topics: the coverage of special needs issues in initial teacher education, arrangements made for teachers specializing in special education, and opportunities for inservice education. More detailed information can be found in Hegarty (1995) and Mittler and Daunt (1995).

A growing number of European countries provide some coverage of special educational needs in initial teacher training. The amount of coverage varies from country to country, depending, for example, on the extent of inclusive education, on induction arrangements and other support for new teachers, and on inservice education opportunities.   Countries where special needs coverage is compulsory in initial teacher education include Austria, France, Italy, Norway, Sweden, and the United Kingdom.   In Austria, teacher education institutions have a general obligation to prepare teachers to teach integrated classes.   In France, initial education courses have a 42–hour module on special-needs issues.   In Italy, there is a mandatory requirement to cover special-needs issues.   In Norway, all those intending to teach in elementary and lower secondary schools must spend a full semester studying special education.   In Sweden, all intending teachers have 10 weeks of special education, of study   and in the United Kingdom, all student teachers in training since 1989 have been expected to acquire a range of strategies and skills suitable for a wide ability range and to be able to identify students with special education needs.   In many other countries, special education is an optional course in initial teacher education, often taken by a large number of students, in countries such as Germany, Spain, and Switzerland there are proposals to make this compulsory.

There are numerous practical difficulties—overload in teacher education programs already, shortage of teacher educators skilled in special education, the existence of different training arrangements for teachers of different age ranges. Despite all this, however, the overall trend is clear. There is a growing recognition of the need to introduce all intending teachers to special needs issues as an essential concomitant of inclusive education, and many countries are taking steps to ensure that this happens.

Inclusive education does not remove the need for some teachers to specialize in special education.   In most European countries, general teacher training is a prerequisite for training to work as a special educator.   Some teaching experience in regular schools is a common additional requirement. Thus, in France, teachers cannot be considered for specialized training until they have taught for 3 years in regular schools.   In Greece, at least 5 years of experience in regular schools is required.

The provision of specialized training is generally on a postgraduate basis. In France, courses are offered at the university institutes for teacher training and at two national centers.   The diploma obtained at the end of a course qualifies teachers to teach students with particular disabling conditions and in particular working contexts. There are six options: hearing impairment, visual impairment; physical handicap, psychological problems, children experiencing difficulties at elementary school, and adolescents with difficulties. Spain has postgraduate courses of 1 to 3 years, concerned mainly with different disabilities, with diagnostic assessment and with therapeutic intervention.

In Norway, a comprehensive study of special education is organized over a four-year period. Although each year builds on the preceding one, students can stop at any point. The first year is a general introduction to special education and is offered by several colleges throughout the country on a full-time or part-time basis. The second year is divided into different types of disability. The third and fourth years cover research methodology, communication, counseling and educational innovation. The Norwegian Postgraduate College of Special Education plays a key role in this provision and also offers doctoral programs.

In Germany, the special education teacher's certificate is acquired after extended post-graduate study. The training requires a study of at least eight semesters in an institution of higher education followed by teaching practice, generally of 2 years, and a state examination. Specialization in two out of nine specialist areas is required. Switzerland has some 10 higher education institutions running full-time courses of 2 to 3 years and part-time courses of 3 to 4 years. Greece and Iceland each have a single institution in which a 2-year full-time course is offered. The Icelandic institution also provides a 4-year part-time variant of its course.

In Ireland, there are various full-time 1-year diploma courses, including the in special education, 1 for teachers of the deaf, and 1 in compensatory and remedial education. Ireland also has 1-year part-time courses for teachers providing special education in regular schools. In the Netherlands, training for teaching in special schools is run by three institutions, with 2-year evening courses organized at various locations throughout the country. The United Kingdom has a large number of courses leading to a diploma or a masters degree in special education. These can be 1-year full-time or part-time lasting 2 or more years, sometimes on a modular basis. These courses tend to combine theoretical and practical elements with course assignments and projects are often based on initiatives at course members' schools. There is also a substantial provision of distance learning courses.

Inservice education necessarily plays an important role in furthering inclusive education because it is the means by which serving teachers develop their skills. There is widespread acknowledgment of its importance in Europe, and opportunities for appropriate inservice education have become much more numerous in recent years. Indeed a number of countries including Finland, Germany, and Greece have specified inservice education for teachers as a precondition for extending inclusive education.

Some examples may illustrate what actually happens. In Spain, the ministry of education has set up a national network of teachers' centers supported by and to some extent coordinated through the National Special Education Resource

Center. The regional centers provide some training of their own, facilitate training offered by other local providers and supplement courses initiated by universities. Similar arrangements exist in France.

In Italy, in addition to national and regional courses, some of which are run by voluntary organizations, there are arrangements whereby individual schools can obtain funds to provide inservice training for all their teachers. In the United Kingdom too, where much inservice education is organized at district level, funds are often devolved to individual schools, where staff are encouraged to define their training needs, and take steps to meet them.

Resourcing

Resources are critical to the development of special education. Both the total amount available for spending, and the way in which it is spent, determine the nature of a country's special educational provision. The former is largely outside the control of special educators, and they routinely complain that there are not enough resources to do everything that is necessary. Certainly, education budgets are under pressure across Europe as the demands on schools continue to grow, but in point of fact special education generally receives a substantial slice of what is available. In England, for instance, one seventh of spending on schools is devoted to special educational provision.

The way in which resources are allocated is a matter for special educators, and a great deal of thought is being given to resource allocation policies, and their impact on quality of provision and on inclusive education. A key development in many countries is the effort to target resources on regular schools so that they can meet the needs of all students effectively and in an inclusive manner. There is the constant dilemma in doing so between earmarking resources so that individual students are guaranteed entitlements but at the risk of being singled out and supplementing school budgets in a general way but at the risk of students missing out on specialist support.

A number of European countries have difficulties in addressing these issues because of historically separate ways of funding special and regular education. These can arise from the involvement of voluntary bodies or ministries other than education in the provision of special schools or from differential allocation of funding between national and regional levels. In Finland, for instance, central government pays 70% of education costs for most students but 86% for students with severe disabilities. Although in most countries the administrative responsibility for all students is now within the education ministry and voluntary bodies, where active, operate within government guidelines, in France more than 40% of students registered as disabled—a total of 132,000—attend schools run by the Ministry of Social, Urban and Health Services.

There is a growing recognition that resource allocation policies can help or hinder inclusion. This has been especially clear in the Dutch system where separate financing for special schools and regular schools has meant substantially more money per head for students in special schools than for similar students in regular schools. A key element of Dutch efforts to promote inclusive education has therefore been to tackle the resource allocation issue directly. Other countries such as Denmark, Italy, and Sweden have resource allocation policies designed to promote inclusion. Thus, in Italy, a class with a handicapped students may not have more than 20 students in total, and no class may have more than two handicapped students.

In the United Kingdom, inclusive education is being bolstered by the development of procedures to provide regular schools with extra resources, both in respect of students with pronounced special needs and in respect of those many students with learning difficulties who are not formally identified. Many different approaches are being tried in order to identify the most appropriate ways of targeting these extra resources. These involve auditing students' special educational needs in terms of defined resource requirements and taking account of the socio-economic characteristics of school catchment areas. The guiding principles include a strong focus on evidence, both by way of requiring schools to state what they are doing with the students already and what they propose to do with any additional resources, greater involvement of schools in deciding how district funds should be spent, and the use of explicit procedures common to all schools and visible for all to see. There is also a new focus on targeting resources at schools rather than individuals. Instead of providing extra funds for individual students, projects which enhance the school's capacity to deal more effectively with a wide range of students are being supported.

Special Education and General School Reform

A final set of challenges relates to general school reform and the fact that schools—regular schools—face unprecedented challenges, some of which may exacerbate the difficulties in meeting students' special educational needs. In Europe as elsewhere there is a growing realization of the importance of schooling. This has resulted in numerous educational reforms that require schools to change in quite significant ways. Raising achievement is the leitmotif against which all educational discourse is measured. Schools face other pressures too: provide better technical and vocational education, develop the use of information and communication technologies, respond to the linguistic and cultural challenges posed by students from ethnic minorities, cope with problems of drug and substance abuse, deal with those children and young people who have been damaged in various ways by those who should have been caring for them. The list goes on and on. Schools are required to solve society's ills, to become more relevant, and generally to prepare young people to live and work in a postindustrial society.

Special educational provision is only one of very many considerations pressing in on school management and has to take its place among them Particularly in countries like the United Kingdom where schools are urged to be competitive and are subject to quasimarket forces, special educational provision is at risk of being sidelined. There is a twofold challenge here. The first is the negative one of refraining from special pleading. When special educational provision is under threat, it can be tempting to revert to presenting children with special needs as objects of charity and deserving of special treatment accordingly. This is of course to forget that their right to education and other social goods is the same as other people's, neither less—as has regrettably been so often the case in the past—nor more.

The second challenge is to reinforce the case for special educational provision by setting it within a broader perspective. If educational achievement and the development of individual potential are important, they are important for all students regardless of disability. If curriculum reform and developments in the use of information technology are beneficial for some students, they are likely to help every student. If education is necessary to prepare young people for life in a rapidly changing world, this is no less necessary for students with special needs than for others. For all these reasons, it is imperative that we locate special educational provision in the mainstream of educational reform.

Information Exchange in Europe

Disability issues at European level have been a concern of the European Community for many years, although the initial focus was not on matters of schooling. The principal thrust has been through action programs running from 1998 to 1995. These entailed a widespread sharing of information and experiences in relation to vocational training, employment, housing, mobility and, in latter years, education. The aims were to promote innovative measures in the integration of people with disabilities, to give them an enhanced value in their communities, and to improve the participation of people with disabilities and their organization at European level.

Education received relatively lower priority to begin with but there has been a communitywide network of 21 projects focused on school integration. These have helped to animate developments at local level and, to a limited extent, promote an exchange of information across countries. Many of the published reports take the form of conference reports, for example, County of Funen (1993) and Rodrigues (1996).

When the European Community programs ended there was a gap in the collection and dissemination of information on special education in Europe. An important step in filling this gap was taken with the establishment of the European Agency for Development in Special Needs Education. This was set up in November 1996 by 17 countries—the 15 EU countries plus Norway and Iceland.

The Agency seeks to provide a framework for European cooperation in the field of special education. Its aims are to

· work for the establishment of an effective system for the collection, processing, and distribution of information regarding new and innovative measures.

- promote European research and development.
- focus on subjects of high priority for the further development of special needs education.
- work for effective change and innovation in the field of special needs education by implementing seminars, conferences and training.
- provide a supplement to programs within other international frameworks such as the EU, the OECD, the Council of Europe, and the Nordic Council.

The secretariat is based in Denmark and is supported by a working partner in each country. All members of the Representative Board have been nominated by ministries of education in the participating countries. The working partners are professionals involved in special education in their own countries, and are responsible for collecting information on topics of common interest, making this available to the Agency in appropriate formats, and responding to inquiries about special educational provision in their country.

The initial focus of the Agency's work has been on three themes:

1. Early intervention. An investigation into issues surrounding early identification and provision of support for children and their families.
2. Teacher support. An examination of strategies, sources and implications of training and support for teachers who work with students with special educational needs.
3. Financing of special needs education. A project identifying funding mechanisms and procedures in all the participating countries plus an analysis to highlight trends.

Reports on these investigations were available in the early part of 1998.

Priority has also been given to setting up national overviews that describe the system of special educational provision in each country. These are intended to facilitate the answering of enquiries but also to enable enquirers to place particular topics in context.

The Agency seeks to build links with existing organizations in the field of special needs education and others with an interest in the area. These include the EU, the OECD, Council of Europe, and the Nordic Council. The Agency has already completed one task for the European Commission—an investigation of the participation of students with special educational needs in its action program in the field of education. There is a particular link with the EURYDICE network, which is the EU agency charged with providing policy information to senior policymakers in European education systems.

The Agency disseminates information in a variety of ways—newsletter, reports, and web site (www.european-agency.com). The website is seen as a key tool, not only for disseminating the Agency's own output, but also for linking into national sites where appropriate.

The Agency is at an early stage of development, but it has considerable potential to generate and distribute information about special education in Europe. It is beginning to be used more widely and, if the participating countries resource it adequately, it could play a significant role in making Europe more intelligible, not only to Europeans, but to the wider world as well.

REFERENCES

Evans, J., Evans, P., & McGovern, M. A. (1995). Statistics. In OECD, *Integrating students with special needs into mainstream schools* (pp. 33–52). Paris: OECD.

The Country of Funen, Department for Special Education. (1993).*Special needs education in Europe for children with mental and physical disabilities.* Proceedings of the European Conference on Special Needs Education for Children with Mental and Physical Disabilities. Odense: The County of Funen, Department for Special Education.

G. B. Department for Education and Employment. (1997). *Excellence for all children: Meeting special educational needs.* London: The Stationery Office.

Fletcher-Campbell, F. (1994*). Still joining forces? A follow-up study of links between ordinary and special schools.* Slough: NFER.

Hegarty, S. (1993). Reviewing the literature on integration. *European Journal of Special Needs Education, 8.3,* 194–200.

Hegarty, S. (1995). Teacher training. In OECD, *Integrating students with special needs into mainstream schools* (pp. 59–67). Paris: OECD.

Meijer, C. J. W. (1994). The Netherlands. In C. J. W. Meijer, S. J. Pijl, & S. Hegarty (Eds.), *New perspectives in special education: A six-country study of integration.* London: Routledge.

Meijer, C. J. W., Pijl, S. J., & Hegarty, S. (Eds.). (1994). *New perspectives in special education: A six-country study of integration.* London: Routledge.

Mittler, P., & Daunt, P. (Eds.). (1995). *Teacher education for special needs in Europe.* London: Cassell.

O'Hanlon, C. (Ed.). (1995). *Inclusive education in Europe.* London: David Fulton.

Pijl, S. J. (1994). Sweden. In C. J. W. Meijer, S. J. Pijl, & S. Hegarty (Eds.), *New perspectives in special education: A six-country study of integration.* London: Routledge.

Rodrigues, D. (Ed.). (1996). *School and integration in Europe - values and practices* (European seminar Helios II). Lisbon: Sociedade Portuguesa de Ciencias da Educacao.

UNESCO. (1988). *Review of the present situation in special needs education.* Paris: UNESCO.

UNESCO. (1995). *Review of the present situation in special needs education.* Paris: UNESCO.

10

Inclusion Implementation and Practices In Scandinavia

Oddvar Vormeland
University of Oslo, Norway

In most countries such as Scandinavia, it is possible to trace the history of education and schooling. Our history reaches back a 1,000 years when the church was established. This event is worth mentioning because its history in many respects has paralleled that of education. We can see this correspondence to this day. Laws for elementary and secondary school still reflect the Christian-humanistic view, especially in the phrasing of educational goals for children and youth. From 1739 to the present, our school laws for compulsory elementary education express the unique worth of every child and student. As human beings, children and youngsters have rights and responsibilities, too. This recognition is consistent with our Constitution which dates back to 1814. Although it must be admitted that such concepts as *individualization* and *equal rights* came to the fore much later, they were still present in the philosophical background that influenced the first special schools for people with visual and hearing impairments established more than 150 years ago.

In the 20th century, fundamental values for education, to an ever increasing extent, have paralleled social and political goals and thinking. More often than not we find our governing ideals in sociopolitical gospels rather than in the divine ones. Values, in the traditional meaning, have fused more and more with our political ideologies to influence debates and decisions on educational goals and means. The central values that steer political decisions in general, and particularly in special education, are reverence for life, taking care of the weak, and social and educational equality of worth and rights of all persons.

These values can also be identified in current social and political ideology that justify the aims of the welfare society. A recent White Paper to the Norwegian Parliament clearly confirms this. Here we also find arguments for new and more comprehensive integration efforts in different societal areas. This is seen as an effective means of raising the level of equity and equality in social and educational settings. Another example worth mentioning is the striving for gender equality. This endeavor paralleled as well as promoted the move toward integration in school.

Attitudes in these matters seem so paramount that few affected are likely to gainsay them, at least openly.

HISTORICAL PRECEDENTS FOR INCLUSION

The idea behind current concepts like positive discrimination and equalization in Norway can be traced from the very first of the royal decrees and laws on compulsory schooling. In a 1739 decree to help the utmost poor, children were also considered for special attention. The first general law on elementary schooling in 1827 identified intellectual faculties and age as factors in predicting educational progress. Sixty years later, in 1889, children with "mental or physical defects" were exempted from school eligibility, perhaps because, at that time, a few special schools had been established while others only were planned. Since then, the policy of positive discrimination has gained support. It gives priority to those with the greatest need when distributing resources, care, service, and thoughtful consideration. The policy is consistent with a renewed Scandinavian social democratic version of the welfare state that is based on humanity and solidarity, and on equal rights and opportunities, irrespective of abilities, gender, social level and background, or residence. More recently, the idea of equality has been applied to productivity and efficiency, which means that results are evaluated more individually than normatively or according to objective criteria.

In time, these progressive values became visible in legal documents, laws, and decrees for education. By 1951, the first and only separate law was passed to establish and support special schools nationwide. Then in 1966, the most comprehensive program for the expansion of special schools was presented in a White Paper to the Norwegian parliament. Educators and the public saw segregation as the best means of meeting the educational needs of gravely disabled youngsters.

The 25 Years of the Special School Law

When the Parliament passed the law on special schools, the public was convinced that a most pertinent, progressive, and lasting method of helping disabled children had been found. But already in 1955, an amendment to elementary school law was passed that required that every local community give special, individualized help for students enrolled in ordinary schools who did not benefit from ordinary instruction. This addition to the 1951 law could be interpreted as a reversal of the special schools authorization that would have fully segregated children with disabilities.

The next 20 years was a period of building positive attitudes for a higher degree of integration of disabled students and of erecting functional bases, legally and practically, to achieve that end. The debate on integration involving teachers, their unions, parents, and other lobbyists, intensified in the late 1960s and early 1970s. At this time, national and international research reports became available regarding the results of special, segregated classes located in ordinary schools. This new information provided strong arguments for a new and more comprehensive integration effort. Additional educational experiments, projects, and research were initiated locally and nationally. Both professionals and politicians felt it was time to move forward with a fairly comprehensive revision of laws for elementary and lower secondary education that were passed by the Parliament in 1975. This confirmed an early commitment for educational integration of all students with disabilities.

School-For-All Policy

The new 1976 law included all school-age children in ordinary schools regardless of their place of residence, race, religion, abilities, performance, or behavior. The law in effect repealed the 1951 special school law. It required that the same curriculum guide be used in all educational settings. It also clearly stated that individual abilities and levels of functioning be considered. The law provided a substantial basis for educational equity and integration in the nation's ordinary schools.

This new framework presented additional, and hitherto, unknown challenges for school systems, individual schools, classrooms, and teachers. As a consequence, quite a number professionals and parents concerned about the content and effectiveness of schools were uncomfortable about possible consequences of this change. Organizations and individuals advocating equal educational rights for students with hearing and visual disabilities, for example, opposed a possible degrading of special schools and classes. This occurred despite the fact that no direct proposals in that direction were suggested. Moreover, the intentions of the decision makers seemed still more on the line of differentiation than of integration.

Teacher trade unions were, not unexpectedly, concerned about the consequences of the change for their members, and for the practical situation in the classroom. Contentions and debates were more theoretical than practical or experienced-based, however. And convincing research results on possible effects were rarely available. Generally, the criticism was that the new law did not distinctly prescribe when and how integration could or should be implemented. One such step toward a clarification was available in the 1987 curriculum guide that stated that "Students with difficulties should have their training and instruction within the framework of the classroom."[1] But this was regarded by many as merely a legend on an educational banner. More earnestly, it was intended to challenge further planning and effort with a specific goal. Later, however, it had to be admitted that a rather long way and a rather cumbersome process would pass before serious aims became reality.

Classmates With Disabilities in Ordinary Schools

A prerequisite for using the concept integration in an educational setting is that students come together in the same school, preferably in the same class or group. By definition the word integrate connotes "to put or bring (parts) together into a whole—and to unify." By using the word in daily life, we should be fully aware of this holistic

---

[1] Monsterplan for grunnskolen, Oslo 1987, p.28

meaning to bring into a whole, to unify. This implies something more than to place students together in same rooms or buildings. It suggests that every student be accepted with his or her unique personalities and to become a constituting, equal part of the group. In practice, then, integration in educational situations must be organized and adapted to meet the individual's abilities and current functioning levels, thereby facilitating knowledge, practical skills, as well as social and ethical competencies.

Lately the word *inclusion*, even in the Scandinavian countries, has come to the fore to displace somewhat the notion of cognate integration. In many instances this seems more to be a play on words than a distinction in content. However, it indicates an active and practical embracing of the concept's holistic meaning. To me, it seems more appropriate, purposeful, and consistent, with current educational, philosophical intentions to use the term inclusion rather than integration, at least in most instances.

IMPLEMENTATION ISSUES AND METHODS

Now I focus more directly on the inclusion implementation and practices in schools, and other educative institutions during the preceding two decades. As indicated earlier, this period coincided with that of the 1976 elementary school law and its 1987 curriculum guide, were the former revised in 1998, the latter the preceding year.

From Special Schools to Resource Centers

Merging the special school law with the general school law did not result in an instant degrading and closing of special schools. Instead, it intensified the debate about segregation and integration. Supporters of special schools pointed to the fact that new institutions had been erected and older buildings renovated recently, and that making good on these investments would not be possible if these schools were closed at this time. On the other side of the debate, there was the argument for equity and social living that is not possible in special schools. These viewpoints gained ground as parents, individually and in groups, pushed for integration. Simultaneously, local school authorities, to a larger degree than earlier, felt empowered to make organizational changes. Several of the more liberal school boards accepted some severely disabled students in ordinary classes. As a result, applications to special schools gradually declined forcing some of them to close. By the mid 1980s, there were still 35 special schools serving approximately 750 students at the elementary level and 5 schools serving approximately 350 students at the upper secondary level.

In a White Paper presented to the Parliament in 1984, the government made a proposal that the remaining special schools be used as resource centers. Quite a number of parliamentary representatives were hesitant to authorize such a reorganization. However in 1991, following the gathering of further information and research data, Parliament made up its mind. It decided that special schools erected and run by the federal state should be converted to competence or resource centers. Consequently, students with disabilities other than blindness or deafness would no longer be accepted as residents for any length of time, at any of the centers. The centers would be used for short-term observations and for various training and rehabilitation services.

As the responsibility for practically all education had already been transferred to the regional and local levels by this time, the foremost challenge facing these new centers would be to give professional service to individual students, and to provide relevant support systems at those administrative levels. Since Norway is so sparsely populated, as is Sweden, its high degree of education decentralization was consistent with the planned use of the centers' external resources.

In addition to the 20 national and regional centers, a special support program was established for the three northernmost counties where the population and schools were more scattered than elsewhere in our long and narrow country. In addition, funds were raised centrally to support a national research and development program for special education over a period of 5 years. In cooperation with the University of Oslo, a specially organized professional study program in special education was established. The intention was to improve the qualifications of the staff of the former special schools now having new professionalized responsibilities. In addition to the national and regional centers, the government established a decentralized counseling service in each of the 19 counties for clients with hearing and visual impairments. The underlying purpose of all these initiatives was to promote and facilitate a decentralized inclusion process by distributing specialized competence, theoretical as well as practical, to where it was most needed. In this way, the municipalities and counties that were responsible for elementary and secondary education could give advice and knowledge to the various schools serving students with disabilities. This would professionalize special education and make inclusion goals attainable.

Resource Centers as Promoters for Inclusion

As the resource centers were destined to play a central role in the reorganization of special education in Norway, it is worth noting how their goals, methods, and functions promoted inclusion. The evaluation of their accomplishments after their first 3 years also confirm the process.

Of the 20 resource centers, 13 were given professional and practical responsibilities in the areas of visual and hearing impairment, language disorders, dyslexia, communication disorders, and behavioral and emotional disturbances. The remaining 7 centers concentrated their activities on service and development for persons with severe learning difficulties, and with mental handicaps, of all ages. This regional focus served different geographical areas of the country.

In addition to detailed surveys, consultations and counseling regarding disabled children and youths, the centers improved the competence of their own personnel and local staff in various relevant fields through locally based courses, projects, and various developmental activities. During the relatively short time of their existence, the centers have provided information and practical advice to various administrative units, teachers, and to those most in need of help in their daily schooling and learning.

Parents and related staff in charge of programs have been more involved in the process of gathering information, providing communication and decisionmaking than ever before. This is consistent with the new policy that requires that parents and guardians be involved when alternative school situations or arrangements are considered. This is especially important when inclusion is one of the options under discussion. Then the school placement must be approved by parents or their substitutes. To an increasing extent, parents are in contact with the service network outside the school, as they are also with the competence centers. In sectors serving individuals with hearing and visual handicaps, parents are invited for short stays in the centers so they can participate in information and courses with their children in preparation for and in the process of inclusion.

To a certain degree, staff members from the centers are also involved in follow-up activities. They visit communities and local schools to give supplementary information and advice to individual students as well as to their teachers. They discuss administrative and education system challenges with principals and other local professionals in charge of relevant programs.

Extended Support Systems as Agents for Inclusion

Thus, resource centers became important parts of an active network that made inclusion of all children regardless of disability in one and the same school system a reality. As such, they never work independently. They function in cooperation with schools and with educational–psychological service units spread throughout the country. This latter service, originally named *school psychology*, developed following World War II. By law every municipality must have such service units. Consequently, when it was decided to include all disabled children in the ordinary schools, it was also determined that educational–psychological services had to be further developed to meet additional challenges associated with their inclusion.

As far as possible, these units are staffed by individuals who have the educational, psychological, social work, and special education skills necessary to assist in the inclusion process. Lately the number of special educators has been increased, and many of them have higher college and university degrees. As municipal employees, these staff persons must also cooperate with teachers and school administrators, and with the local medical, child-care, and social rehabilitation personnel. Also, there is a national education superintendent in each of the 18 county regions responsible for providing a professional follow-up and updating of staff qualifications. Those national administrative units cooperate closely with the educational-psychological service providers on various projects and development work. These efforts usually address the issues related to special education and inclusion. According to the recent evaluation report, these endeavors have been valuable getting the inclusion process started and further developed.

A principal goal for these various operations was to improve relevant learning and training situations for disabled students of different ages during the inclusion effort. Worth mentioning in this connection is the National Center for Teaching Aids, which provides differentiated materials for use in special education settings. In small countries, like Norway, even the various regions are dependent on national initiatives for specialized services like this one. To a great extent, books and other educational materials are produced and distributed by private publishers. Equipment and various types of technical instruments are provided by public regional supply centers.

Single Schools and Classrooms as Inclusion Arenas

In the preceding discussion, I identified the attitudes and resources that were necessary to make the inclusion effort succeed in education settings and activities. The dynamic among the persons involved in the educational process is, of course, decisive as well. At this point it may be worth mentioning that handicaps are not solely associated with individuals because they can be created by demands, expectations and attitudes at micro-and macro-level of policy implementation. What happens during the interactions among individuals and groups in classes and schools will determine how such obstacles are overcome. In this sense, social climate and these organizational and methodical issues are also significant factors in promoting real inclusion. If we accept as a sine qua non that every child, youth, and adult has a unique value that justifies a policy of equal educational privileges for all, then we need to look into inclusion classrooms and small groups to see what is happening in everyday situations. We must consider the following during these assessments.

1. All teaching and practical instruction should be adapted to each student regardless of his or her abilities and level of functioning. This general principle also governs teaching strategies designed to keep up with given subjects and the attainment of goals. Adaptation and individualization must be in the mind of every classroom teacher. In all program planning, organization, and methods, the teacher must adhere to this guiding principle!

2. Even though the curricula guidelines give teachers considerable freedom to chose different paths and methods to reach goals, they also must have professional support and guidance at their disposal. Earlier, I described ways of meeting this challenge. Educators and parents know quite a lot about how to fill the gap between demand for individualized instruction and the resources necessary to accomplish this. Recently, professional deliberations and staff training through internal upgrading of courses at the school level have made those involved aware of such critical factors in the inclusion process.

3. Various models for organizing classroom teaching and instruction also have attracted interest and experimentation since inclusion goals were formulated. With the two-teacher system, for example, a specially trained teacher or aide works with the ordinary classroom teacher. The needs of the students determine the required qualifications of the additional teacher. Resources often set limits for the amount of time allocated for students in need of special help in the classroom. So far there are, at least in Norway, no

extensive or reliable evaluation on the effectiveness of the two-teacher system. Nevertheless, many experienced teachers report positive results when the system includes thorough planning and staff cooperation.

Reduction of class sizes is another way to facilitate instruction for students with disabilities and their classmates. This occurs more frequently at the upper secondary levels where a lower class size may be mandated by law or state regulations. Where needed, special educational teachers often develop individual student curricula and learning programs for various instructional periods. These efforts are usually dependent on the teachers' own initiative so exact estimations of their practical use is not at hand.

In addition to using commercially available instructional materials, special education teachers spend much time and creativity preparing adaptive aids for particular students. Many schools have considerable collections of such material that may stimulate others about what to do. It is regrettable, however, that such "homemade" material is so poorly marketed. However, in some regions, these growing knowledge bases and distribution systems do function as expected toward the inclusion goal.

Supplies and materials to facilitate classroom differentiation during inclusion may also be secured from regionalized centers where technical equipment and computer-based aids are also available. Increasingly, these centers are supplying schools and classrooms with teaching aids as well as with ideas and models of instruction. Nevertheless, the final responsibility for adapting this information and methods to meet the needs of individual students rests with the classroom teachers.

PRESENT AND FUTURE CHALLENGES IN THE SCANDINAVIAN COUNTRIES

After 30 years of various formal inclusion efforts, we might ask "Where do we stand?" This is a pertinent though difficult question to answer for any of the Scandinavian countries. Professionals, politicians, relatives, and public commentators feel that we are still at a crossroads. Consequently, it is difficult to conclude how far we are toward full *integration*, to use this somewhat controversial term. Nor can we present research reports that will render a statement on how far we have yet to go.

Nevertheless, some discernible features about the status of inclusion in the Scandinavian countries stands out. Although the following account is based on, Norway, it is also valid in large measure for the neighboring countries of Denmark and Sweden. I comment briefly and specifically on these two nations after the summary for Norway.

Norway

The 1990s for Norway can be described as the decade of school reform. The new political, social, cultural, and technological climate required changes in education from kindergarten to colleges and universities.

Goals.

It is significant to note that, in Norway, the same school law applies to all levels of general education. It is to create better schools and educational opportunities for all. This stands out as the fundamental official policy and, consequently, it possesses a challenge to the whole education system. The public, politicians, and parents are in full agreement on this goal. At the same time, this law and its regulations emphasize the right of children, adolescents, and adults with disabilities to receive appropriate and meaningful special education, preferably in their home community. In public papers, more than in law, the main principle observed is that students with special needs, at all levels and whenever possible, should be integrated in ordinary groups, classes, and schools. But there is no direct requirement for including *all* disabled in one and the same setting.

Organization and Administration.

The educational system is now being revised. Beginning with the school year 1997/98, school entrance age is lowered 1 year to age 6. This will extend compulsory education to 10 years instead of 9. What challenges and consequences this reform will have for the full integration goal remains to be seen. Consideration of these effects have not been elucidated in the comprehensive planning and preparation documents, either. These problems may be left to professionals in education, psychology, and sociology who will deliberate and investigate the theoretical and practical implications.

   The line of administrative decentralization and delegation will also proceed and in some instances be extended. In relation to educational inclusion this is a factor of increasing importance, as well. Local democratic and professional units and decision makers will be responsible for the practical aspects of implementing educational inclusion at all age levels. Observers and investigators have raised the question of whether this development is compatible with the aim of providing equitable and suitably adapted education for all children and adolescents.

   Then there is the question of economic resources. Because all education in Norway is free, from elementary through the college and university levels, the operating costs must be allocated from national resources by the municipalities and county authorities. This means that it is up to locally and regionally elected boards and committees to construct budgets that are consistent with federal legal and curricula regulations. Complaints are heard from urban and rural practitioners, trade union representatives, parents, and local principals regarding the uneven distribution of inadequate allocations.

   In addition to the inevitable influences of financial resources, there are new resources in the form of advanced technical aids that can make inclusion possible. New products and practices have been developed, tested, and implemented; and recently, even small groups of disabled students have benefited from them through increased learning. Unfortunately, the market for these innovations is small, which makes them high-priced even when subsidized.

The Revised Curriculum.

Across the board, from the general to the more subject-related parts of the curriculum, there are elements of integration and practical suggestions for its implementation. More explicitly than ever the need for individual teaching plans is being emphasized. Various provisions and relevant discretions states that for every student given special education will have elaborated an individual teaching plan. Such plans must point out individual goals—as well as educational contents and procedures. Lately, teachers and educational psychologists have expressed the opinion that individual plans will be of special importance for those with the most severe disabilities. Progressive educators are also recommending that individual teaching programs focus more on students' possibilities and strengths than on their weaknesses and disabilities. That focus on the positives rather than the negatives should motivate the process of positive inclusion.

Denmark

The three Scandinavian countries hold much historical background in common, near as they are to each other geographically. Ethnic and cultural kinship is reflected in their educational history, traditions, and modern development. Making distinctions between these near neighbors is therefore attended with some difficulties. This is also true when comparing policies and practices of including disabled students in ordinary schools. Nevertheless, some characteristic features can be mentioned here.

Over the last 30 years, the Danes have expressed a clear and well-formulated intention to integrate disabled students in ordinary schools. To what degree they have succeeded in these various endeavors is difficult to determine, at least from the outside. Some internal observers describe present attitudes on inclusion as being less enthusiastic than in the 1970s and 1980s. The expression of the "Second-generation inclusion endeavors" reflects current challenges.

Compared to its next-door neighbors historically, Denmark's education has had less centralization and has become more moderate with its regulations. Private and free schools have always enjoyed the freedom to grow and develop on their own. Informal school experimentation occurs frequently. Given this background, it is not surprising that there is more variation in educational options than in many other countries. Consequently, there are many practical variations also in the integrating and inclusion efforts. In harmony with this greater level of decentralization, there are national and regional networks supporting inclusion implementation. These associations are loosely organized. Nevertheless, Danish educational researchers are putting considerable effort into investigating and describing the theory and practice of various inclusion implementation initiatives and their consequences for students, schools, and the educational climate.

In such analyses, effects are identified for individual and group inclusion, and outcomes noted for social as well as academic gains. Social interaction among students with and without disabilities is regarded as indispensable for any successful inclusion implementation outcome.

Susan Tetler, a Danish researcher from the Royal School of Educational Studies in Copenhagen, has conducted some promising pilot studies addressing the theoretical and practical questions of inclusion. In a paper presented at the annual meeting of the American Education Research Association in 1997, Tetler identified four dilemmas posed by inclusive classrooms[2]. These challenges apply equally to Norway and Sweden.

Dilemma 1:   Mastering the heterogeneity of the students. How to manage the single student with special educational needs with the general education needs of the whole class.

Dilemma 2:   Mastering the heterogeneity of the professionals. How to coordinate activities between the special education teacher and the regular education teacher.

Dilemma 3:   Mastering the innovative process of inclusion. How to integrate innovative inclusion practice with traditional teaching practices.

Dilemma 4:   Mastering the development of caring social relations. How to integrate subject-based teaching with student-based caring relationships.

Sweden

Generally, the Swedish school system is based on a set of ideas and ideals similar to those described for Norway and Denmark. A Swedish information pamphlet on special education starts with this manifesto: "Programs for people with disabilities or handicaps ultimately concern solidarity and equality" (Swedish public school system, 1995, p.2). Later it states that the principal challenge is to offer education with quality so that "mainstreaming" does not become "primitive," but, instead, has a "high quality content" (p.10). Inclusion implementation has developed very much parallel to what is described from their neighboring countries. Ideology, goals, methods, and implementation practices mainly bear the same characteristic features.

Again we find that a fairly extensive line of decentralization and delegation practice has been followed. For the special education system, this fact has facilitated the transition from schools for special groups of handicaps to inclusion practices. The remaining special schools now recruit predominantly deaf and hearing-impaired students for a 10-year program.   Students with language disorders or secondary disabilities in combination with a hearing loss and/or visual impairment who are unable to attend a regular school, may be assigned to a state special school.

Sweden has organized its support system somewhat differently from its neighbors. Whereas Norway converted former special schools to "competence centers" with two different steering boards   reporting to the Ministry, Sweden erected the National Agency for Special Education. Consequently, it seems to have better coordination and

---

[2]   Jetler, S: Group Inclusion - as a Stepping Stone to Full inclusion. Paper presented at AERA 1997 Annual Meeting, March 24-28, 1997, p. 5-6.

more efficient contact among different authorities in the central agency as well as in the field nationwide.

The main intention of the Swedish national center is to secure children, youth, and adults with disabilities an education comparable to that received by their nondisabled peers. This goal may be attained by offering municipalities and parents appropriate services and products. Twenty-three locations are erected throughout the country to facilitate contact and communication with those in need of information and support.

No doubt, such a network of professionals, together with available differentiated information, teaching aids, and so on will, in different ways, have a positive effect on serious endeavors for inclusion implementation. Moreover, the often emphasized requirement for a reliable follow-up on objectives and their reforms may be more efficient through a network like this. So even in this respect the Swedes seem to possess an instrument that neighbor researchers and politicians may want at their own disposal. This raises questions regarding how the process of inclusion implementation and its progress might be described and evaluated more accurately and effectively.

REFERENCES

The Swedish Public School System and Disabled Students. (1995, p.2). Harnosand, Sweden: National Agency for Special Education.

Tetler, S. (1997, March). *Group Inclusion—as a Stepping Stone to Full Inclusion.* Paper presented at AERA 1997 annual meeting.

Author Index

Subject Index